PRAISE FOR
HORSE OF A DIFFERENT COLOR

"Squires has written a superb book that provides the ultimate insider's view of big-time racing. His love for the animals he breeds is obvious and easy to share. . . . Squires has managed to capture [the Derby] in a manner which should appeal to true horse people, as well as readers who have exactly two minutes a year to devote to the sport."

—*Rocky Mountain News*

"Reading *Horse of a Different Color*, you might be tempted to quit your day job and try for a toehold in the thoroughbred industry. Don't: First, Squires has a real talent for pony-raising. Second, you can't write as well as he does. Few can."

—*Lexington Herald-Leader*

"The former *Chicago Tribune* editor brings an insider's viewpoint and the skill of a seasoned journalist to his work."

—*Kentucky Monthly*

"[A] wild chronicle of [Squires'] removal to the Bluegrass Country, where he found the humans almost as interesting as the horses."

—*Dallas Morning News*

"Squires writes . . . with clear affection, proving that even a crusty, hard-eyed newspaperman can have a soft heart."

—*Cleveland Plain Dealer*

"Offers insight into the strange world of thoroughbred breeding and racing . . . an entertaining book."

—*Orlando Sentinel*

"Jim Squires is a wonderful horse breeder and a very wily guy. There isn't anyone in bluegrass who's done quite what he has—edit a major newspaper and breed a Kentucky Derby winner. Guess which one was more exciting and fun? I loved this book and laughed all night the night I read it."

—Jane Smiley

"Like so many of the blueblooded beasts he writes about, Squires' new book is a winner."

—*Bookpage*

"Fast paced and fun to read."

—*Library Journal*

"Mixing the pride of a parent with self-deprecating humor, Squires makes Monarchos' dramatic ascent to the pinnacle of his sport a ride we can share, just as he did. It's a ride most racing fans won't want to miss."

—*Booklist*

"Squires' witty prose makes [*Horse of a Different Color*] very difficult to put away as he takes you for a ride and makes you feel the same emotions as he did as it all happened just over a year ago. . . . [A] quick lesson in both the breeding business and Derby Fever in one . . . entertaining package."

—Horse-Races.net, Cindy Pierson-Dulay – 4 out of 5 horseshoes

"A sharply written tale of an autumning media master beating all odds and crafting a classic championship pastiche of a gray bluegrass soul."

—"At the Races" by Jim O'Donnell, *Chicago Sun-Times*

"Squires has the gift for good, toothsome storytelling. . . . A heart pounding finish."

—*Kirkus Reviews*

"A month before the Kentucky Derby I tipped my friends about Jim's little gray colt, Monarchos. Now, I get to do it all over again about his book. This is a savvy, insider's view of the racehorse game told by a man who actually nailed a piece of its most elusive accolade. A genuine page-turner."

—Sam Shepard

HORSE OF A DIFFERENT COLOR

Also by Jim Squires

The Secrets of the Hopewell Box: Stolen Elections, Southern Politics, and a City's Coming of Age

Read All About It! the Corporate Takeover of America's Newspapers

HORSE OF A DIFFERENT COLOR

A Tale of Breeding Geniuses, Dominant Females, and the Fastest Derby Winner Since Secretariat

---

JIM SQUIRES

PublicAffairs *New York*

Published in the United States by PublicAffairs™,
a member of the Perseus Books Group.

Printed in the United States of America.

Book design by Mark McGarry, Texas Type & Book Works, Inc.
Set in Meridien

Library of Congress Cataloging-in-Publication data
Squires, James D., 1943-
Horse of a different color: a tale of breeding geniuses, dominant females, and the fastest Derby winner since Secretariat / Jim Squires.
p. cm.
ISBN 1-58648-180-0 (pbk.)
1. Monarchos (Race horse)
2. Race horses—United States—Biography.
3. Race horses—Breeding—Kentucky.
4. Horsemen and horsewomen—Kentucky.
5. Kentucky Derby, Louisville, Ky. I. Title.
SF355.M65 S68 2002
798.4—dc21
2001059602

2 4 6 8 10 9 7 5 3 1

For M. A.,
standard-bearer of dominant females everywhere

CONTENTS

Be not afraid of greatness: some are born great, some achieve greatness, and some have greatness thrust upon them.

WILLIAM SHAKESPEARE, *Twelfth Night*

PREFACE

I would my horse had the speed of your tongue,
and so good a continuer.

my friend WILLIAM SHAKESPEARE

But now it seems your horse has the speed of your
tongue—which I always did think was pretty damn fast.

my friend PROFESSOR DAVID BADGER

Breeding racehorses for a living is not something a sane, intelligent, mature person experienced in American capitalism would ever attempt to do. Even I knew better. Long experience at formulating business models for a Fortune 500 media company taught me that if there is no way to project making a profit eventually, there is no business—period. But then thirty years in the same business—newspapers—had obviously left me hopelessly addicted to the thrill of labor in a doomed industry. Jettisoned in 1990 with a gold-plated parachute at age forty-seven, after a tumultuous decade as editor of the *Chicago Tribune*, I did what any other shocked and hopeless fool would do. I looked around for new work just as exciting, risky, and unpredictable as my old job had been.

From the outset the similarities between racehorse breeding and being a media corporation executive were striking. For one thing, the beast you're feeding has an insatiable appetite, resulting in excessive amounts of excrement that must be dealt with each day. For another, a lot of time is spent making plans that never get beyond the conception stage. Some projects that do get launched die (literally, in the case of horses) before they can ever succeed. And those that make it to fruition and become a smashing success are inevitably taken over by someone else who gets the credit. When things don't turn out as planned, well then, of course those still belong to you and they were never a good idea in the first place.

One aspect of big corporate life missing in my new business endeavor, however, was second-guessing by big bosses. Having people in suits breathing down your neck when things are going great, yet nowhere to be found when straits are dire, eventually becomes essential to good executive decision-making. Fortunately, this vacuum was ably filled by my wife of twenty years, M. A., shorthand for Mary Anne, perfectionist and born CEO.

Working against the backdrop of a Gregorian chant of skepticism over a new enterprise from such a knowledgeable and conscientious overseer was not only comfortingly familiar, it also underscored the importance of two essential management techniques that in retrospect would have proved invaluable in journalism: (1) the use of drugs, and (2) the availability of a "twitch," which is a loop of rope attached to an ax handle–like stick that when applied around a nerve in a horse's nose tends to have a calming and immobilizing effect.

Horses don't need drugs, unless they're sick. But the people around them do, because horses simply won't do many of the things people ask them to do without being on drugs—specifically tranquilizers. Expecting a three-day-old, 120-pound foal to hold still while stitches are taken in his eyelid is unreasonable. Without sedation and immobilization, the needle would end up in the eyeball of the surgeon, or more likely, the person being asked to hold the foal's head. A combination of skill, twitch and drugs is what makes it possible to clip the hairs from deep inside the ears of a 1,200-pound stallion (racehorses can't go around with fuzzy ears), or to get him safely aboard a jet transport in time to make a race on the West Coast. Had I only known back in my editor days the power of a tiny syringe of Acepromazine, think what miracles I could have wrought on meddling corporate types, publishers, accountants and other irritants who belittled and foiled my precious work. M. A. does not come near me when I am carrying a syringe and a twitch.

However grim the future of print in the world of electronic information delivery, the year I left newspapers everything was hunky-dory. The *Tribune* made about 25 percent operating profit on a billion dollars, my pay was about half a million bucks and the newspaper won two Pulitzer Prizes. Some said I had fallen from the pinnacle of my life's vocation. I thought so, too. Indeed I had lost one of the great jobs in journalism, a post of such prestige and power that I could have never reasonably hoped to attain it in the first place.

My resignation statement, fabricated to spare everyone the humiliation of a firing, said I was leaving to pursue other longtime interests, specifically the commercial breeding of horses in Kentucky. This announcement produced widespread sniggering, especially among my newspaper colleagues who knew the meaning of "canned"—and among horse breeders who knew the definition of "commerce."

A million dollars—the approximate size of my golden parachute—can disappear in the thoroughbred horse industry with the stroke of a gavel or a clap of thunder. Dozens of times each year in Kentucky, Florida and Saratoga auctions, horses worth five and six times that amount sell in the span of thirty seconds. Countless others that might attain such a handsome worth die in their mother's wombs, are struck down by disease or lightning bolts in the pastures, impale themselves on oak board fences or simply break their legs running across a field or down a track and have to be euthanized.

Ten years ago gamblers' odds were more a mystery to me than they are now. But it is safe to say that my chances of becoming a successful racehorse breeder were no better than even with those of me ending up homeless living under the "el" in a cardboard box. That I might eventually breed and raise the winner of the most famous and important horse race in the world—thus climbing to a second pinnacle of sorts—was beyond even an imagination as fertile as my own.

Realistically the most skilled, formidable and experienced horsemen can only dream of breeding a Kentucky Derby winner. More than 30,000 thoroughbred foals are born each year. Only fifteen to twenty make it to the Derby gate and only one can win. In history there have been just 127 winners, while generation after generation of breeders—some fabulously successful otherwise—have devoted their lives to this challenge in vain.

A few days after the steel gray colt, Monarchos, won the 2001 Kentucky Derby, a letter came from my friend Michael Dickinson, the great British-born horse trainer, whose skill at winning big races and developing revolutionary training methods often results in the use of the adjective "genius" in connection with his name. Obviously taken with the word, he used it flatteringly to describe my accomplishment of breeding a Kentucky Derby winner from only my third thoroughbred foal crop.

However, people more familiar with the miraculous nature of my life's journey have other explanations for such a surprising success. I made the mistake of relating Dickinson's compliment to a crusty old pal of thirty years who has been along on a few of my previous stumbles into good fortune. "Breeding genius, hell!" he exclaimed. "All this means is that sunshine will even hit a horse's ass if he stands out in it long enough."

Whatever the source of the streak, six weeks after the Derby Churchill Downs invited the winner's "connections"—owners, breeder and trainers—and their friends back for yet another celebration and the re-awarding of the engraved trophies. For everyone involved, including the track's corporate owners, the Derby is an event to be milked for all it is worth. There can never be too many toasts or reruns.

A dinner hosted by Monarchos's owners, Debby and John Oxley, that weekend in the magnificent Kentucky Derby Museum trackside turned out to be a joy second only to the actual running of the race. It began with the 100 or so guests standing by their tables as the music and color of 127 years of racing tradition whirled around us in a spectacular 360-degree video presentation. It was the equivalent of having a catbird seat in the infield with the ability to see, up close, everything that goes on before, during and after a Kentucky Derby. Waves of emotion began to build, rising off the great performances of previous

Derby heroes—Northern Dancer, Secretariat, Affirmed—finally bursting into an explosion of color and sound from the 2001 Derby that focused on a monster-sized, dirt-stained Monarchos in full flight to glory, nostrils flaring, hooves pounding, eyes glistening, bearing down on you from every direction—as if you were waiting for him at the finish line. Just the recollection returns the shiver to my spine. Relating the thrill of seeing an animal you pulled from his mother's womb rising to such a level of magnificence tests the most fertile imagination and defies adequate description. Even people who'd never seen the horse anywhere but on television were moved to tears. The theater erupted in deafening applause. After everyone else had stopped, I was still standing there, clapping like an exuberant seal, as oblivious to surroundings as I had been on May 5, when I was unable to believe what I was seeing in my binoculars.

Of all the thrills available in life, there is none greater for a horseman than winning the Kentucky Derby. Inside the thoroughbred industry worldwide, particularly for a Kentuckian, the consequences of winning this race are stunning. The level of acclaim among your peers, for example, approaches that associated with winning the Nobel Prize. And the stature and respect it earns among horse enthusiasts is unfathomable, embarrassing and in my case at least—in light of the degree of chance involved—completely undeserved. Many Nobel Prize winners have reported the same feelings of humility, even though the skill, knowledge and effort demanded by their professional achievement cannot be measured against the dice roll involved in breeding and raising an animal. But unlike the Nobel Prize competition, the Kentucky Derby is the most famous and most widely observed contest of excellence in the world. Like the football Super Bowl, the baseball World Series and World Cup soccer, it attracts public attention far beyond that expected from the normal denizens of a particular sport. And because it requires only two minutes of attention each year and occurs within the context of a social event now over a century old, the Derby has attained an extraordinary level of popular significance. Now available worldwide through the miracle of live television, it is the one event with which almost everyone can associate. Simply knowing someone who knows someone who has won the Kentucky Derby endows a degree of coveted exclusivity. On the morning of the 2001 race, my son-in-law, a telecommunications executive in Greenville, South Carolina, casually mentioned to his barber, a transplanted Kentuckian, that his father-in-law had bred a horse slated to start in the Derby. On his next visit to the shop after Monarchos's victory, the barber greeted him with waving scissors, a shouted "Oooweee!" and a celebrity's introduction to fellow patrons as "Mister Monarchos." Simply cutting the hair of a relative of the winning breeder had given the Kentucky native son a rewarding sense of special relationship with the race, literally an "exciting moment."

And for those with a more direct connection, winning the Derby can actually change your life, even against your will and in ways never contemplated. In my case, it expunged from my consciousness a long-felt sense of rootlessness—the unavoidable result of spending most of my adult life as a journalistic and political vagabond. For me being happy where you are meant being rooted in a sense of being rather than place. Solace came from knowing who I was, not where I was. Loving my birthplace of Nashville and all the places I'd called home since—Washington, Orlando, Boston, Chicago, Dallas, Lexington—had made me comfortable virtually anywhere but truly at home nowhere. In the months preceding the Kentucky Derby, M. A. and I had considered selling Two Bucks, our gorgeous old farm west of Lexington where Monarchos was born, and possibly relocating a downsized horse operation elsewhere, perhaps even in Florida or New Mexico—not because Kentucky in any way had failed us but because we are both by nature restless and adventurous spirits.

When compelled by circumstance or wanderlust to move in the past, I had inevitably left behind, attached to cherished people and places, great chunks of my heart and soul—to such an extent that I felt the supply in danger of depletion. Still, leaving Kentucky and starting over yet again had become a viable option. It no longer is. Within forty-eight hours after winning the Kentucky Derby, I had been planted into the fertile loam clay of Woodford County as solidly as if I had died and been inserted beneath the limestone.

On the afternoon of June 16, when the Oxleys, trainer John Ward, Mary Anne and I were again celebrated in the winner's circle at Churchill Downs, we were presented with the "official" trophies. As an award, the breeder's trophy is neither artistically stunning nor extravagantly crafted—a rather small, simply engraved sterling silver statuette of horse and rider.

But the day my name was inscribed on it I claimed a tiny, coveted, precious spot in history for an achievement that, dubious or not, will likely define my life as much as anything else I have ever, or will ever, do—however unfair that might be to the rest of my existence. Where "winning the Derby" ranks in true importance varies with the life of the individual involved. But the handful of owners, jockeys, trainers and breeders fortunate enough to have had the experience must all realize one simple truth—that you owe it all to the horse that brought you there. To the Oxleys, he was the fleet, gunmetal-colored stallion with a bearing as regal as his name. To the trainers and grooms, he was the enigmatic and unpredictable "Sparky" who kept them both entertained and on their toes. And to those of us on the farm who raised him, he was a little, black, bright-eyed bugger with ears that talked and a personality that began telling you the minute he was born about how great he planned to be.

Monarchos fulfilled his promise. He proved to be a helluva ride for everybody, but particularly for the one rider aboard who had spent his entire life watching big stories happen to other people—me. As proof of my newly acclaimed "breeding genius," he became for me one of those signposts in life that delineate where you've been from where you're going, a turning point that altered everything from the nature of my deepest sleep to the shape of the most cursory conversation when awake.

All those years as a journalist had enabled me to recognize an extraordinary tale when I saw one. But I had been thoroughly conditioned to observe significant happenings from the emotional safety net of complete detachment. The impossibility of being at the center of something big and at the same time completely detached from it did not stop me from trying, of course, which made the story even better. When people try to do the impossible, it always does.

In the old days, to unravel such a twisted yarn I would have assigned my best young, energetic, curious and unbiased reporter. But in this case I knew the main character to be so contrary, elusive, conflicted and skilled in the black arts of journalism that few reporters would be a match for him. And I knew his story to be so complex and talismanic that a veteran investigative reporter with grit and expertise would be in order, one who could track mushy ground, one with an eye for the absurd and an ear for code and doublespeak. This particular protagonist demanded a writer with a poison pen and a complete disregard for balance and objectivity. And for the tale to be as unbelievable, entertaining, ridiculous and as much fun in the reading as it was in the happening, a humbling confession would have to be wrung out of the one surly wretch who knew it all—me—which would require someone equally merciless. So having always been a sucker for the challenge of a good story, I willingly became my own target—and with only one glorious benefit assured.

For all of my adult life, when asked by the stranger in the airplane seat next to me what I did for a living, my answer was invariably "newspaperman" or "writer." This was always followed by further inquiry about which big events had been witnessed, which books authored. Thankfully, most of these conversations soon died, owing to the interrogator's lack of familiarity with the answers.

But from this day onward, when asked that question, my reply will be "racehorse breeder," to which the follow-up inquiry will invariably be the same: "Did you ever have a famous horse, like in the Kentucky Derby or something?"

Natural modesty and a soon-to-be obvious aversion to the first-person pronoun will prevent me from owning up to the truth. But at the risk—and delightful prospect—of the conversation going on forever, I will employ a tactic that was taught to me by politicians. I will evade the question thusly: "As a matter of fact, a guy I know particularly well bred a Kentucky Derby winner named Monarchos and it changed his whole life. And he wrote a book about it."

PART 1

BREEDING SUCCESS

1

In the choice of a horse and a wife, a man must please himself, ignoring the opinion and advice of friends.

GEORGE JOHN WHYTE-MELVILLE,
Riding Recollections, 1878

Sometime in the mid-1990s, the Museum of the Horse at the Kentucky Horse Park opened a small art-and-photo display entitled "Women and Their Horses." Among the first to view it was an aging, silver-haired member of both the museum's supporting foundation and controlling board, the Horse Park Commission. Intending only a quick glance at the new exhibit, he ended up enthralled for nearly two hours by the beasts and the beauties who loved them—well past his due time for a long-planned business lunch.

Except for possibly the portrait of an extraordinarily proportioned Lady Godiva impersonator, the exhibit was hardly stunning enough to justify his stiffing a luncheon appointment. Angry for doing so, he fretted in search of an explanation. Finally, it dawned on him why he had been so completely seduced by the photos of women and horses. Of course, why not? He was fifty-five years old and had spent every dime he'd ever made on one or the other.

The dual obsession, he reasoned, had been with him since childhood. There was a mongrel dog named Bob, remembered only as being "big enough to ride," and a four-foot stick of white oak called Silver or Trigger or Diablo or the name of the horse of any other movie cowboy he happened to be imitating at the time. The stick had a length of rawhide through a hole in one end—a "bridle"—and had been sanded smooth and round by his great-grandfather for more comfortable straddling by a five-year-old in short pants. This finishing touch lessened the chance of painful thigh splinters that were always a danger in high-speed gallops though the alley badlands. In foul weather, the perennial gunfights took place indoors, where "horseback" was a chair arm, or even better, the arm of a sofa with cushions that made for soft landings when he was unhorsed. Pillows or thick towels affixed to the furniture with leather belts made the best "saddles." But the indoor rides finally ended just like in the movies—violently—the morning he cinched up a stack of newly folded laundry his mother had ironed the night before.

That was the beginning of the horse part of the love story. The girl part started about the same time when the pursuit of bad guys inadvertently crossed the path of the lovely Kaynell, a six-year-old neighbor girl who went on to dance on *The Lawrence Welk Show*. Kaynell appeared unfazed by the passing one-rider posse, but her later frequent and usually unexpected encounters with his stick-horse opera inevitably sent self-conscious shivers up the little cowboy's spine. Though she once even consented to a dramatic role—a "kiss on the lips" behind the bushes—the romance never flowered. It had been doomed, the backyard hero would eventually conclude, by the ludicrous sight of a kid in short pants running around with a stick between his legs, or Kaynell's embarrassing witness to the spanking he'd endured for saddling up his mother's ironing.

The years since had only validated his adolescent judgment that the two most beautiful and fascinating of God's creatures are women and horses, the order being determined by the period of his life. Whether being beguiled by Kaynell or the steeds of the matinee cowboys, physical attractiveness was long his most important criterion. Trigger, Roy Rogers's gorgeous, well-made Palomino, was a favorite pretend mount, but not Smiley "Frog" Burnette's mare, Black-Eyed-Nellie. The black circle painted around one eye or another for the sake of movie comedy simply made her too ugly. In later years, the word "thoroughbred" became a complimentary term reserved in his lexicon for the classy, sleek, athletic and slim-ankled ladies that always turned his head.

Eventually, it was these beautiful women who taught him the meaning of "skin-deep." And now at the point in life where he felt lucky to wake up on the right side of the grass each morning, he was still as certain as ever that in either world—human or equine—females were the most interesting and the most important inhabitants. Their preeminence was particularly evident when it came to breeding, a subject on which he would come to be credited, although unjustly, with some expertise—but only in the equine world.

By the time he got around to actually shepherding the mating of horses, his definition of a "quality" female had been greatly expanded to include the far more important attributes of intelligence, durability and heart. What he'd been so slow to learn the hard way could have been easily gleaned from books. The male heroes of Louis L'Amour's classic stories of the Old West, for example, were all "men's men"—gentle and thoughtful but still capable of great violence in the cause of justice. And the mates they selected were invariably "women to ride the river with." Riding the river was the most dangerous thing men did in those days, so any companion had to be savvy, dependable and willing to fight somebody. The modern-day equivalent might mean traveling an L.A. freeway or passing through the Miami airport. What we are talking about are women—and mares—that are not only attractive but smart and tough. They make the best companions and the best mothers, though not always the most pleasant.

In twenty years of raising horses, he had been bitten only twice—both times by kind paint mares who normally weren't even aggressive with other horses. These were young mares he'd raised from babies who now had foals by their sides. But they were not mothers simply protecting their young. By this time in the equine-human relationship they knew their owner was no threat to the foals. They were instead exhibiting another decidedly female characteristic—irritation at suddenly being ignored by someone from whom they expected attention. Stallions bite for the hell of it and must be watched constantly, while females bite only when necessary for maintenance of the relationship. And only they know when that is, which makes them far more dangerous. Later, one of the mare's foals, a filly naturally, would put him in the hospital with a kick to the groin.

This incident was not unlike his experience with women. For generations the females had been dominant in his family—smarter, tougher and more aggressive than the men and yes, sometimes, like the mares, even violent. Women whose very presence commanded respect were precisely the kind he'd always found most irresistible. This preference had been key to the long, tempestuous love affair with his wife, who reflected perfectly his attraction to dominant females. They agreed on all the important things in life: the fundamentals of good and evil; the need to protect the environment; the virtues of rural life; the appalling lack of manners in modern society. It was the minor stuff that caused problems, like which direction is north, who last had the car keys, what TV channel to watch and whether it was day or night. The result had been two decades of basic marital bliss obscured on the surface by trivial but incendiary conflict. His never-disclosed admiration of the Lady Godiva look-alike at the Horse Park museum, for instance, would have sparked a fierce challenge on the grounds of artistic merit, and then it would have been quickly dismissed as typical male obsession with female breasts and legs astraddle. Yet she would understand perfectly when in January 1995 he fell in love with and brought home another good-looking, discerning female—the good thoroughbred mare Regal Band. A class act herself, the dominant female at Two Bucks Farm recognized and appreciated peerage when she saw it.

*

First warning had come in a prayer—grace offered before a dinner welcoming newcomer bettors and potential investors to a big day of racing at Churchill Downs: "God willing, may no one lose any more than they can afford to."

And hints to the hazards inherent in the unusual and schizophrenic nature of the horse business were delivered in the form of subsequent assurance: "The people who make their living in thoroughbreds are as honest as their profession allows."

Forewarned is forearmed. Nonetheless there are no more thieves in the thoroughbred business than in any other, maybe fewer. But owing to the nature of the commerce, which is primarily public auctions, they are like bastards at a family reunion—hard to distinguish from legitimate relatives.

The longtime lifeblood of the thoroughbred game has been the infusion of new money, mainly from men made wealthy by other endeavors. They can be characterized generally, if uncharitably, as having more money than they know what to do with. With rare exceptions these are prominent individuals accustomed to attention, attracted to challenge and endowed with a well-developed sense of entitlement to success no matter what they're up to. In the horse business, however, only the first two are guaranteed, and both come easy at the auction sales.

Like everything else, horse-sale crowds are divided by wallet, and in an interesting way. Cheap horses draw only cheap crowds. But expensive horses draw everybody, so the top-end sales resemble industry showcases like the film festival at Cannes or the automobile show at Detroit. Anybody who is anybody plus all the wanna-bes show up. The capability and intention of buying is no requirement. And when new money lands, it attracts immediate attention, like chum cast into the sea.

The thoroughbred establishment—mostly breeders and farm owners rooted in both tradition and old money—are with few exceptions ladies and gentlemen of honor. Some are still actually true "sportsmen" for whom a profitable horse deal is low in life's priorities. They welcome rich new owners as "almost" equals and want them to succeed. In some cases they even attempt to assure it by assuming a kind of dolphin protection role, gently trying to guide newcomers through a sea of bloodstock agents, pedigree specialists, sales consignors, farm and racing managers, veterinarians, mating advisers, agents and consultants of every stripe. These are all reputable vocations vital to the business, populated mostly by honest, ethical, hardworking horse lovers struggling for survival in this tiny, difficult sliver of world commerce. But cleverly disguised among them are the predators and parasites who live off the inevitable proceeds of the game's most common business model: "To become a millionaire in the horse business, you start out with $10 million and wait five years."

Man being as much a herd animal as the horse, the appearance of attendees at thoroughbred horse sales is uniform. Some come from abroad in their own customized 747s, others from the coasts in their Gulfstream executive jets. They alight from Mercedes, BMWs and giant SUVs, and some drive pickup trucks in from Florida and Texas. But regardless of age, shape, size or mode of transport, by the time they reach the sales grounds everybody has on the same jeans, khakis, parkas, comfortable shoes, and cell phones. This common attire makes it impossible to tell a respectable Fortune 500 CEO, there to redistribute his disposable income, from the penniless wretch hoping to wrangle a crumb from the distribution. Some of the so-called bloodstock "experts" tend toward affected accents, distinctive hats and the poor posture that results from incessant staring at horses' knees and ankles, the ancient idea being "no foot—no horse." Still, that old catalog-laden guy in walking shorts of one plaid and a tam of another is as likely to be a bloodstock agent famous for buying a European champion as he is a stoop-shouldered New Jersey accountant in his golf clothes. Either way there is an equal chance he owns neither land nor beast and if asked to feed a horse would not know to which end he should offer the meal.

Whatever their net worth, intentions, motivations or rank in the sale social order, everybody in the thoroughbred world is in dogged pursuit of the same overriding goal. Whether breeding, buying, selling, consulting or snake-oiling, they are all after one thing—"the big horse" that will win the Kentucky Derby, a Breeders' Cup championship, or one of the great classic races in Europe. To the bottom dwellers the financial reward connected with such an animal might mean everything, or simply rent and grocery money for another month. For those at the top, the monetary gain great or small is superfluous to the achievement. But for everyone, simple association with the big horse—whether breeder, owner, trainer or merely a broker of the sale—becomes an identifying industry badge that satisfies the human craving for peer recognition and self-validation. Everybody needs the big horse and there is no more likely place to find it—or a mare that will ultimately produce it—than on the sprawling, perfectly manicured sales grounds of the esteemed Keeneland Association six miles west of Lexington.

Formed on about 150 acres as a nonprofit association of breeders in 1935, Keeneland has grown into a racing and sales complex of nearly 1,000 acres that might well be the heart of the horse business. The thoroughbred industry's most glittering institution, it conducts the world's most important horse sales and has no equal as a conservator of "the finest tradition of the sport of racing." As a business, Keeneland is a hard-nosed, profit-making machine that gives no quarter (except to charity), pays no dividends, and takes no guff from anybody. As a place, it is one of the most beautiful and serene in the world. So even when its emerald brilliance disappears under the snow-mud slush of a Kentucky winter, Keeneland is the place to be, not only for those looking for the big horse but also for potential buyers of any thoroughbred horse, period, who is looking for a new home. And in January 1995, that is where Regal Band found herself—in Barn 12, with the number 586 stuck on each of her ample hips.

The air of haughtiness about the mare and her well-shaped loins were for this particular horse lover a lethal combination. A stuck-up beauty had always been too big a challenge to ignore. Females who declined to return a glance were demanding another look, which he certainly could spare in light of the bloodlines of her pedigree. The story of her life and that of three generations of her ancestors were all right there on a single page of the sales catalog. The study of thoroughbred pedigrees, of keen interest to him for several years now, had been good preparation for moments just like these. Wouldn't the world be better off if people knew this much about each other up front when trying to decide if something is too good to pass up? The question nagged him as he struggled to put a value on Regal Band.

At nine years old she was off to a slow start as a broodmare, but so what? He'd always been attracted to older women. Her being short for a thoroughbred—only an inch over 15 hands—didn't bother him either. That was about the size of her grandsire, the great Northern Dancer, who'd won the Kentucky Derby in 1964 and went on to become the most important influence in the breed in the last half of the century. Besides, the pedigree on her maternal, or dam's, side was populated with giants, like the great broodmare sire Graustark. And long experience breeding stock horses had taught him that a mare's genetic makeup was often more important than her physical appearance. In fact the best producers male and female had often been small physical aberrations—horses that didn't look like the bloodline prototype.

But many thoroughbred buyers simply reason that a small mare means a small baby that will not be impressive at the yearling sales, which can happen. So since they are often buying for clients, they are loath to deliver a mare short of stature, which Regal Band clearly was. And they would be even more discouraged by her rather shady past. Regal Band's first foal had died for reasons unknown, the second was born with a leg so crooked it had to be put in a cast, and her third was aborted during the first trimester. A record like this and being culled from the prestigious broodmare stock of her owner, the renowned Darby Dan farm, was sure to be held against even a well-bred girl at a high-end horse sale like Keeneland's.

None of this bothered the admirer of Regal Band, who had never let common sense or economics regulate his interest in a beautiful, highfalutin female. And Regal Band was both. From one of Darby Dan's best old families, she was nearly black—"dark bay or brown" the thoroughbred people called it—with a lovely white star between highly intelligent eyes. And what a body! Robust but sleek, and with her diminutive stature disguised by a long, slinky walk that only comes from perfectly formed, well-lubricated joints. A model on a fashion show runway. There was no sign of bad knees or even a hint of commonness, both flaws frequently found in the progeny of her young sire, a useful racehorse named Dixieland Band.

Still, the buyer had reason to be cautious. Having raised horses of other breeds for more than twenty years, he had once concluded that it was a mistake to do business with people he didn't know. So up to this point he'd done thoroughbred business only with friends, the experienced horsemen with whom he had served on the Kentucky Racing Commission.

His deal with the charming Texan John T. L. Jones, Jr., called by some "Alphabet" because of the extra initials, had been typical. A former insurance broker and quarter-horse trainer, Jones possessed a personal charisma and a keen eye for horses, which had transformed a fledgling, once-struggling stallion syndication partnership, Walmac International, into one of the few solvent, solely owned stud farms not subsidized or underwritten by a personal fortune.

Walmac's slogan, "Winning the World Over," reflected the secret of its owner's success—an infectious, ingratiating personality and a penchant for doing business on a handshake as trustworthy and ironclad as the best lawyer's contract. It made Jones a perfect horse partner. So they bought a yearling together—a filly, naturally—a big-hipped granddaughter of the great Seattle Slew. The deal would become classic proof of a basic tenet of horse ownership: Whatever can go wrong will, sooner or later.

First the filly had to undergo ankle surgery before she could train. When she finally raced, she broke a bone in her foot that never healed properly and left her lame for life. Inexplicably named Pearlshot by

Jones, she went on to a similarly distinguished broodmare career—four times pregnant and four abortions.

A second partnership with another proven horseman from the racing commission had ended the same way—with an unsuccessful and eventually lame horse and sizable cash loss. Thankfully the horse was a gelding that couldn't be pushed into broodmare service, although it could have done no worse than Pearlshot. A third racing partnership with yet another racing commissioner—a guy who had raised four champions—had been considerably more fun, and therefore an even more "valuable" experience. This time it was a far more expensive but similarly unsuccessful and eventually lame racehorse, and $120,000 plopped into the manure pile.

It was only then that this quick-witted, professionally trained observer finally employed the one enabling skill of his previous journalistic career—deductive reasoning. If so many thoroughbreds were going to go bad, wouldn't it be more profitable to own and sell them before it happened?

So it was with the firm conviction that investment in thoroughbreds might be better done with strangers that the admirer of Regal Band set out in search of the Darby Dan farm manager, Wayne Sweezey, fully aware that having never seen Sweezey without a shotgun he might not recognize him unarmed.

The one living creature Kentuckians have learned to feed as well as horses is the migrating dove, whose arrival in Kentucky in late August also signals the beginning of a critical time for horse breeders, the start of the fall yearling sales. The juxtaposition of these phenomena have important implications.

Of all the stuff doves eat, they love best Kentucky sunflowers, which can be found in abundance in specially designated fields on the back acres of thoroughbred farms. This supply is not coincidence but the result of coordinated cultivation. Market-sensitive farm managers like Sweezey, whose job it is to attract potential buyers to their farms in late August and September to inspect yearlings, love the contrasting color and charm sunflowers bring to bluegrass pastures. They want their special clients and sales guests to see them, too.

But the lovely sunflowers are an even bigger attraction to the doves, who get hungry flying south. So from Labor Day until the middle of October, the sunflower fields erupt in the sound of war. Virtually every afternoon somewhere in central Kentucky, heavily armed horsemen and their guests camouflage themselves in hiding to protect the sunflowers from thousands of the tiny, determined northern invaders which come in gray waves from all directions at blinding speeds in darting, diving, zigzagging attacks. Sometimes the shooters look so much like sunflowers that the doves end up mistaking the barrels of shotguns for a flower stem or tree branch. Avoiding the embarrassment of a live dove roosting on your gun barrel often results in "frantic reloading," a hazardous practice for which Sweezey became celebrated—and well known among newcomers like the prospective buyer of Regal Band. One autumn day the Darby Dan man came to the dove field, late in the attack as usual, accompanied as always by a handsome dog and more shotguns than could be fired at once by a single person, raising the question of whether the dog was even smarter than he looked. A crack shot, Sweezey was also skilled at frantic reloading, when demanded by the ferocity of the dove attacks. One minute Sweezey was picking off speeding doves like they were slow-moving ducks in a carnival gallery. And then—boom! The young farm manager, the blood having drained from his tanned, handsome face, was staring aghast at his antique shotgun, its barrel split and peeled back toward him like a banana. Lucky to be alive, he had loaded and fired the wrong gauge shell, causing his weapon to explode—thus committing what was from then known as "a Sweezey."

Many men would have given up shotguns instantly, perhaps forever. Others would have been too shaken to take a level aim for days. Sweezey just picked up a spare weapon he'd brought along and started knocking down doves again as efficiently as before, reloading as frantically as necessary.

To the admirer of the mare Regal Band, the dove fields and the thoroughbred auctions of Kentucky lay in perfect assimilation. At a time when the land is its most alluring, hungry doves and horse buyers alike flock to an irresistible and dangerous orgy. Flaunting themselves on every vista are enough luscious blossoms and beautiful horseflesh to sate the most voracious of appetites. But cleverly disguised among them lurk the deadly hunters, captive of their own eagerness and perpetually in peril as well, from frantic reloading or other sins of gluttony.

Whether the seller of Regal Band, found standing beneath the Darby Dan sign outside her stall at Keeneland, was a harmless sunflower or a stalker in perfect camouflage was in no way discernible to the prospective buyer, intent on concealing any sign of appetite.

"This is a very good mare, believe me," said Wayne Sweezey, as confident and convincing as he was the day his gun exploded. "She's had some bad luck, that's all. She's a tough luck girl."

It was a hard luck story heard many times before, from the lips of lawyers around police stations and night court. Some of those excuses were credible, too, but not as convincing as Regal Band's, as told by Sweezey. The death of her first foal had been accidental, having nothing to do with her mothering, some poison water or something. The severely malformed limb on the second was not uncommon to thoroughbred babies, whose long legs sometimes get twisted causing them to grow unevenly in the womb. Certainly his crookedness was no genetic gift from Regal Band, whose short, straight cannon bones aligned correctly in the center of her knees. And aborting her third foal, Sweezey suggested, could well have been caused by fretting over the loss of the second, who was taken from his mother and placed with a nurse mare because he was too crippled to grow up in the pasture.

"The family just has more good mares than they need right now," he went on, "and they've had no success breeding her."

By "the family" he meant the heirs of the late John W. Galbreath, the thoroughbred industry aristocrat and real-estate magnate who owned Darby Dan, the Pittsburgh Pirates and Swaps, the 1955 Kentucky Derby winner. When he died in 1988, Galbreath had been a Jockey Club steward for over fifty years and responsible for the success of the influential thoroughbreds Ribot, Graustark and Roberto. Regal Band had been owned and raced by his daughter and son-and-law, Mr. and Mrs. James W. Phillips. Phillips had been a Jockey Club steward as well, and his son, John, would soon become the family's voice in the industry.

"Frankly, I'd like for them to keep her. I like her a lot," Sweezey said. "I guarantee there is nothing wrong with her and she will make you a good mare."

He could have been a defense lawyer. But none of the other horsemen from the dove fields who were solicited for an opinion shared his enthusiasm. Although quick to vouch for Sweezey, nobody viewed Regal Band as much of a prospect, for the same reason that Darby Dan had culled her.

They pointed to the fact that a couple of days earlier Regal Band's crooked-legged yearling colt had sold in a lesser winter sale across town at Fasig-Tipton, a competing sales company, for $4,400, less than half the stud fee of his sire, the Darby Dan stallion Meadowlake. Sending the mare to one sale and her bad foal to another is a common practice when culling. Not many buyers will go searching for the offspring of a mare at a competing sale. The Keeneland computer, which ranks sales horses by pedigree and quality and catalogs them in that order front to back, had put Regal Band in the top half of the sale, but only barely—586 out of 1,312. And when shown her catalog page, one of Sweezey's dove-hunting friends, a veteran of thirty years at the sales, said, "I don't know what she looks like, but I'll guarantee you won't have much trouble buying her today." The smart-ass smile on his face added, "you fool."

But to some fools even the undisputed truth of their own foolishness is no deterrent to its continuance. The four other broodmares already in the would-be breeding genius's band had been selected in accordance with "accepted" industry business principles (there are no sound ones). The mares were all less than ten years old and had unimpeachable pedigrees. But all had been bought the same way—instinctively—without regard to good advice. Dedicated horse lovers know what they like. It's like beauty and art—all in the eye of the beholder. Or, as the used car dealer had once explained when asked how he could possibly ever move an old Plymouth beater on his lot that someone had painted a putrid-looking purple: "Somebody'll like it," he said. "In this world there is an ass for every seat." The axiom would be severely tested when Hip No. 586 went to the sales ring later that day.

Horses in line to be sold at Keeneland wait double file in a wide lane behind and outside the sales pavilion—odd numbers on one side, even on the other. Potential buyers walk up and down the lines scrutinizing the merchandise and asking questions of the consignor representatives that accompany each horse. The level of buyer interest can sometimes be gauged in advance by how many people ask to view the horse at the barn and show up again to see it in the lane. Those who follow the animal into the walking enclosure immediately adjacent to the sales ring are considered potential bidders.

The January sale is decidedly the lesser of two at Keeneland offering babies and broodmares, the premier being a huge November extravaganza. Two months earlier, at the November 1994 sale, 2,488 mares and weanlings had been sold with revenues topping $121 million at an average price of $48,646. The previous January sale had averaged about half that, and January 1995 looked to be a repeat.

Although sale price averages are widely regarded as a barometer of industry health, they are deceiving. The big money is regularly spent on a handful of the highest quality stock, making for a "white meat or feathers" market. As prices rise at the top, the average increases without doing anything for the bottom 70 percent. Long before Regal Band's number came up, twenty-nine horses at the front of the sale had brought $100,000 or more. The Japanese, returning to the U.S. horse market after several years' absence, got most of the white meat, buying eight horses for $1.8 million. The media mogul John Kluge from Virginia bought two horses for $210,000 and $160,000, and Carl

Pollard, a founder of the Humana health care system, had bought a total of three for $580,000, including the highest priced mare for $375,000. The Austrian and Canadian auto parts magnate Frank Stronach, who had been acquiring land and building million-dollar barns around Lexington for the previous four years, bought six horses for $525,000 but was outbid for the number-two mare by a leading Japanese breeder, Dr. Koichiro Hayata, who paid $350,000 for a mare in foal to a Claiborne Farm stallion.

By the time Regal Band's number came up midway through the sale, the market was already feathers. And for her it was the second time around. Three years earlier, fresh off the track after a gritty but not sensational career as a racehorse, she had been bred and offered at the November broodmare auction, pregnant with the Meadowlake foal that later died. Anyone interested enough to check knew that the bidding had reached $27,000—about average for that sale but less than Darby Dan was willing to take. Now back with womb empty and with a worse record than before, no one looked at her in the lineup or followed her to the sales ring.

Hundreds of people were in the sales pavilion and more were jammed around the walking ring in the back where bids are also taken. A neophyte would have surmised that at least a few of them were involved in the auction. But more than 90 percent of the crowd at a horse auction never raise their hands. Half of them are not even paying attention. They are there simply to be around horses and each other, potential witnesses in case something extraordinary happens, which it often does.

Like a dove attack on the sunflower fields, bidding erupts out of the blue and firing can come fast and furious from every direction. Buyers are frequently caught in crossfires, with only the most skilled and veteran observers able to determine who is caught by whose fire and from where. Casualties abound, most often the wounded egos of losers and shot-through bank accounts of winners. There can be frantic reloading and an occasional explosion—a "Sweezey."

This was not one of those times. The sale of Regal Band was far more typical. Despite her blueblood family background, she was regarded by the commercial horse market as being "light on pedigree" because neither she nor her dam had won major races or produced offspring who did. Major races are called "stakes" and those attracting the most competitive fields are graded annually by committees in Europe and North America. Grade 1 designates famous races like the Kentucky Derby and the Arc de Triomphe, while other races are ranked Grade 2 or 3. All stakes winners—graded or not—are signified by the bold, black type in which their names and those of their close relatives appear on the catalog page. Regal's half-sister had earned that precious "black type" with a minor stakes win but otherwise there were no superior stakes runners in the first two generations of her pedigree. The bottom line of this evaluation is that raising a highly profitable foal from the mare would be difficult until one proved itself a runner—a wait of at least three, perhaps four years.

Other than the auctioneer and the green-coated Keeneland handler leading Regal Band around the ring, only two people were involved in her auction.

Unarmed, the seller Sweezey stood unobtrusively behind the sales ring, nonchalantly nodding in Darby Dan's reserve bid—$1,000 at a time. Twenty-five feet away watching him was the other half of the minimum required to conduct commerce—the buyer. Every time the farm manager answered the auctioneer's call, so did the former Chicago newspaper guy turned horseman—all the way to $14,000. When Sweezey bid $15,000, the other guy quit, leaving Darby Dan still the not-so-happy owner of its own horse.

Unlike respected Darby Dan, which was simply bidding against a reserve amount previously submitted to the auctioneer, some sellers submit no written reserve and have no intention of taking their horses home. Sometimes they plant a "shill" in the crowd to lure up the price. When the shill's bid is the final one, they have been "caught speeding." The shill then quickly disappears to avoid signing the sales ticket. Even at staid old Keeneland, bidders have been seen to run from the pavilion and disappear into the parking lot, forcing a resale of the animal later in the day. One local horseman became infamous for the tactic, ceasing only upon the startling realization that his last escapade had been captured by newly installed surveillance cameras.

In Sweezey's case, he'd simply made one bid too many. He signed the ticket "RNA"—Reserve Bid Not Attained—and took the mare back to the barn. When he got there the under-bidder was waiting with an offer that would not be refused—to take her off Darby Dan's hands for the amount of his last bid—$14,000. It would turn out to be the best money he ever spent on a beautiful female.

Like all new residents arriving at Two Bucks Farm, Regal Band had to stand a cursory inspection by the farm's dominant female, an obvious imposition to them both.

Surveying her husband's acquisition with a sharp eye honed from ten years of raising, riding and showing world-class stock horses, she walked around the mare like a judge in a halter class, examining every aspect of her conformation. Regal, suspicious of interaction with any stranger, signaled her resentment with flattened ears.

Two titans of independence meeting in bone-hurting cold.

Back when the dominant female was still a teenager, some idiot—a male no doubt trying to be helpful—had published in *Housekeeping Monthly* "The Good Wife's Guide." A bible of chauvinism, it laid down rules on how to greet your husband upon his return from a hard day's work: with "a warm smile," "a delicious meal," and "a ribbon in your hair so you will look refreshed." It also suggested that women "over the cooler months . . . light a fire for him to unwind by" and to never "ask him questions about his actions or question his judgment."

These were the kinds of things taught the dominant female by her Czech mother but that had never crossed her mind since.

She gave Regal an evil eye.

"Not bad." This was as effusive as she got with compliments, the breeder's ego being too big already. "How much?"

"Fourteen thousand. Stole her."

"How'd you do that?"

"Hell, nobody else bid. I was the only bidder."

"What's wrong with her then?"

"Nothing."

"That you know about?"

"Right."

"So why weren't they bidding?"

"I don't have a clue. Spotty record, I guess."

"What's spotty?"

"Dead foal. Crooked foal."

"Pretty spotty. You must just know more already than they do, right?"

"Look at her. This is a great-looking mare."

But the buyer's remorse to which he was prone had been ignited. "Well, we can always get her in foal and sell her in November. She'll bring a lot more in foal."

"She's not in foal now?"

"No. Barren. Aborted a Meadowlake."

"Oh, well. That's nice. Good luck then." She shook her head and gave Regal another once-over. "Good-looking mare, though."

His attention having been properly refocused, without either a bite or groin kick, the dominant female left the barn and returned to the house. But not, he was certain, to light the fire.

2

O! for a horse with wings.

WILLIAM SHAKESPEARE, *Cymbeline*

A horse that flies has been a wish of man since the first meeting of the two species. The Greeks so loved the idea they came up with the winged horse of the gods, Pegasus, whose name men usurped for parades and a constellation. In New Zealand the great sire Sir Tristram is buried standing up, just in case the opportunity to fly away ever presents itself. But if a horse ever does sprout wings and leave the earth it will likely do so from the proven launching pad to glory, a limestone mound in central Kentucky.

Two Bucks Farm, where Regal Band moved to begin her new life, would be perfect for takeoff. Only ten minutes west of Keeneland by horse van, it drapes over one of the knolls closest to the sky in Woodford County, which will surely be the last political jurisdiction east of the Mississippi to be paved over. Woodford County is home to some of the greatest thoroughbred horses in the world, such as Triple Crown winner Seattle Slew, leading sires A. P. Indy and Deputy Minister, and

Kentucky Derby winners Thunder Gulch and Fusaichi Pegasus. They live on showcase stud farms around the towns of Versailles and Midway, with famous names like Lane's End, Three Chimneys and Ashford that resemble square miles of manicured parkland. Two Bucks is not one of them, not legendary or even storied for that matter. But its worth as a perfect equine habitat is nonetheless typical. Its 132 acres rest atop some of the deepest deposits of rich topsoil in the region. Flowing beneath are clear springs that bubble up from deep stone caverns and into creeks that snake through lush bluegrass, orchard grass, alfalfa and clover, creating a natural smorgasbord that nourishes horses to an impeccable condition unsurpassed in the world. On the farm's highest point, beneath the ancient shad bark hickory and the box elders, is a big old house with 20-inch-thick walls that dates back to 1789. The remains of some of the residents from that era rest under old marble squares in the backyard near the stone smokehouse, and sometimes up on the second-floor gallery prowls at least one ghost. But being a woman, she steers clear of the dominant female, who doubts her existence.

Anyone passing the big iron gates fronting Two Bucks or surveying its miles of black fence might conclude that the owner is just another "rich guy trying to buy the game." They would be wrong. Once known as Prospect Hill, Two Bucks was a victim of one of the thoroughbred industry's worst crashes, the late 1980s when foal production outstripped demand and greed drove horse prices first through the roof and then down to oblivion. Dilapidated and grown over, it was rescued from the repossession rubble of a bankrupt Kentucky insurance company for half its advertised value by the eye of the dominant female, who had made a living for years selling real estate around Chicago. Named after the rival whitetails that had staked it out, Two Bucks was a reclamation project to be spiffed up and sold when the real-estate market came back. Only it didn't, at least not right away and not before the dominant female's husband began buying castoff racehorse mares, for what good reason only God knew. Certainly the buyer didn't.

One thing about him, he could read. And everything he'd read said that thoroughbreds were a numbers game. History held that success came from breeding the best to the best, and some of the wealthiest, most driven people in the world had long been hard at it. The model for success had been established by historic Calumet Farm, only a few miles away, which had raised eight Kentucky Derby winners and two Triple Crown champions. Its modern counterpart was Stone Farm in nearby Paris, from which Arthur Hancock, grandson of the legendary founder of Claiborne Farm, had produced two Kentucky Derby winners in the 1980s, and later would send out a third. Although mined from some of the best breeding stock in the land, the achievements of both Calumet and Stone still had to be justly celebrated as extraordinary.

In recent years wealthy Japanese, Arab and European investors had spent millions accumulating the best Kentucky bloodstock, literally taking hundreds of top mares and their offspring out of circulation. The Arabs and Europeans, particularly, had done the same to the land, gobbling up huge chunks of the best farms. And all were breeding the best to the best. This was not a game for a guy in short pants who rode stick horses. The new owners of Two Bucks realized that simply raising a profitable horse of any breed was difficult challenge enough. Horse breeding is more an art than a business. Success is to be measured one stroke at a time, the way artists do a painting. So he and the dominant female laughed together at his silly justification for suggesting they live on their newly fixed-up acquisition and try raising a few thoroughbreds.

"Who knows?" he said, "As lucky as we've been with horses, we might raise a Kentucky Derby winner."

Right. And then ascend directly into heaven and sit at the right hand of the Lord, which he knew there was about as much chance of him doing. Or fly off to Santa Fe on wings of your own—which was the goal of the dominant female. First her pilot's license and then a new house in the mountains of New Mexico—as soon as the farm sold.

"Well, you can never tell where runners will come from," he insisted. Then he dredged up the stories he'd heard from his racing commission friends. The 1977 Triple Crown winner Seattle Slew being an ugly $17,000 yearling out of a modestly bred mare and a $5,000-stud-fee first-year sire. Winning Colors, the 1988 Kentucky Derby winner, bred on a 33-acre farm in Scott County by a man with one good mare.

"It could happen again," he assured her.

But even he was neither daft nor desperate enough to believe it. No longer a dreamer, he knew his prospects in the thoroughbred business were as lousy as the next guy's. But years of making a living at work he loved had spoiled him. Who ever wants a fairy tale to end? Like the job he'd held for a decade as the editor of a great newspaper, he saw the imposing Two Bucks, with its tree-lined roads and antebellum countenance, as a place too grand for its occupant. And he embraced it the same way—tentatively—as something surely to pass on to a more appropriate owner.

At least thoroughbreds might generate a little revenue until the farm could be sold. His first one, Lichi, had proven that. A top South American–graded stakes winner, Lichi had once sold for $100,000. But he had bought her at the bottom of the Keeneland sale in 1992 for $8,000—and for the same reason he would later buy Regal Band. She was a classy athlete.

A big, proud bay with doe eyes and perfectly balanced front and hind quarters, Lichi set the pattern he would follow. Blessed with blazing speed, she had been raced successfully until she was seven years old by some wealthy Texans who then bred her a few times and sold her before any of the offspring had a chance to succeed or fail at the racetrack.

Lichi was a beautiful speedball, had earned more than $200,000 against the toughest competition, and had half her life ahead of her as a broodmare. She was carrying the foal of a young sire whose 65 foals of racing age included 54 runners, 44 winners—11 as two-year-olds—and 8 stakes winners. Yet the mare had been a cull, available at a bargain price because she was the commodity of a trendy, impatient trade that could see in her no quick profit. She was already ten years old, her first two-year-old runner had not won, and her South American pedigree was considered unfashionable and therefore not commercial.

But the following year Lichi's first foal, a quick filly named Ocean Bay, won two stakes races in Arizona, raising the value of her other offspring. Her third foal, a full sibling to the first, then brought $21,000 at the Keeneland yearling sale—two and a half times her mother's purchase price. It was this profit that yielded both the cash to buy Regal Band and the parameters of the tiny niche in which Two Bucks might operate—the ruts left by money in a hurry. Even in its doldrums, the racehorse business was clearly one addicted to speed from top to bottom. Babies had to run fast early in their lives, broodmares had only three years to produce stakes winners and stallions better have big runners in their first two foal crops—or else. Despite its reputation as a decaying relic from another age, the old "Sport of Kings" certainly had not been immune to the "give-it-to-me-quick" virus that had infected the rest of the modern world.

The culture looked a lot like Wall Street, which did not fit him. Every time he had reached quickly for something in life he had come up empty-handed. But when finally immunized against the headlong rush, it was to horses that he was indebted for the vaccination. They had taught him the danger of shortcuts and the virtue of patience and provided him experience in a technique vital to all habitual moon-reachers like himself—how to buffer inevitable disappointment with lowered expectations. Besides, horses came with intangible benefits.

One of his predecessors as editor of the *Chicago Tribune* once said that as he got older he came "to prefer the company of dogs to men and books to dogs." And having spent a decade in that same job, the Two Bucks owner had developed a decided preference for the company of horses to almost everything else.

The addition of Regal Band increased the Two Bucks broodmare band to five. Two weeks after her arrival a veterinarian stopped by one morning to give her a prebreeding exam. Barren mares need a clean bill of health and must be cultured for infection before admitted to the breeding sheds, which open in mid-February.

While the vet was there, the most expensive mare on the place, a young maiden stakes winner named For Dixie, decided to give birth. A nice guy and friend of several years, he volunteered to assist the foaling. Having a doctor around for new arrivals is common on some of the large farms but not on small ones like Two Bucks. Only once in fourteen years, out of more than 150 births, had a veterinarian been needed to assist in the foaling of the owner's paint and quarter horses. The vet in the barn that morning was the one who had once responded at midnight to help deliver a cutting horse whose mother refused to lie down. Together they had accomplished the near impossible—pulling and catching a thick, slick 80-pounder before it hit the floor and broke something. Once shed of her burden the mare then collapsed to the stall floor with severe contractions and began to thrash around violently, threatening to roll over the foal. The owner had held the mare down while the vet dragged the foal to safety in the barn aisle. So naturally the offer to help with For Dixie was gratefully accepted.

Although properly presented—front feet and head first—the foal was unusually large, and it quickly became apparent the maiden needed some help. The one good position behind the mare for an assistant was properly conceded to the vet, who promptly pulled the foal at an angle that resulted in a serious rectal-vaginal tear. The foal was fine but the mare went into shock, which inhibited her milk supply. Because it was on the weekend and a nurse mare was not immediately available, the foal had to be bottle-fed until one arrived two days later. As the substitute mom was being unloaded from the van, the real mother's milk arrived in streams, a heroic last-minute rescue from adoption. Mother and son lived happily ever after, but the mare required expensive surgery—twice—and was unable to be bred again until the following year.

An additional $1,000 expense and the unexpected loss for a year of 20 percent of income-producing capacity is tough for any small business. But in horse breeding it is typical for a quarter of the broodmares to be unprofitable in any given year. For those who invest their money to produce racehorses and those who eventually wager on their nose, the risk is about equal. At the end of each day, the horse player knows what he has lost, but the breeder may not.

There was no way to know how much the loss of For Dixie's production year would cost until the following November, when her nearly orphaned foal was offered at the Keeneland auction. What was a For Dixie foal worth in the marketplace? The size and caliber of the crowd gathered around him in the lineup behind the sales pavilion would tell the story.

The betting odds for horseplayers are set by professional handicappers who study racing performance statistics. For horse breeders they are established by a group of professionals known as "pinhookers," speculators who buy baby horses at one age in hopes they can be sold a year or two later at a profit. Some buy "weanlings" less than a year old and sell them as yearlings. Some buy yearlings, start them under saddle and sell them at "training sales" in the spring of their third year. Some trade in both. Among these pinhookers are some of the best bloodstock evaluators and horse trainers in the world. They also include some of the boldest gamblers, most colorful characters and sharpest operators who would be equally at home on Wall Street or the Chicago commodity markets. As a group they have the attention span of a flashbulb, the predictability of a drunk driver and the consistency of a can of worms. And they find nothing more exciting or profitable than betting on a new thoroughbred sire fresh off a hot racing career—before he's had a chance to fail.

In the fall of 1995, the hottest new sire was a horse named Gilded Time, who had won the two-year-old championship with a brilliant victory in the 1992 Breeders' Cup Juvenile. Chronic lameness, a common problem with the modern thoroughbred, had kept him out of the Triple Crown competition the following year, but he had gone to stud with all the assets pinhookers love. He was big, good-looking, copper-colored and had the look of an eagle in his eyes.

Breeders liked him, too, for their own reasons. A grandson of 1967 Horse of the Year and three-year-old champion Damascus, he was a good outcross for the broodmare population because he carried no blood of the two most popular sires of the previous twenty years—Mr. Prospector and Northern Dancer. More important, industry titans W. T. Young and John R. Gaines had purchased syndicate shares in Gilded Time and would send good mares to his first book. Best of all, the stud fee of $10,000 was relatively inexpensive—and the pinhookers loved the "early speed" he had exhibited as a two-year-old.

The first Gilded Time foal to show up in the sales ring was offered by Gaines himself and bought by Young, which had the not-too-thinly-veiled appearance of an effort to get the stallion quick out of the gate as a sire. The founder of the Gainesway stud farm and the Breeders' Cup, Gaines had established himself as a "maker of stallions" and industry visionary, as well as a general pain in the ass for the thoroughbred establishment. Having sold Gainesway to a wealthy South African, his latest innovation had been a heretical move away from the sale of yearlings to the offering of expensive, world-class weanlings at the November breeding-stock sales. In 1995, he sold the sale's highest priced weanling for $650,000, and would also again in 1996, at $1.4 million. Among the consequences of his strategy was a dramatic increase in the number of pinhookers who returned to the select yearling sales the following year as top-end sellers instead of middle- and low-market buyers, squeezing the breeders on both ends. Gaines's Gilded Time colt, a robust chestnut replica of his father, brought $160,000, despite being discounted for having only one testicle descended.

The second Gilded Time colt to sell was the even more robust, charismatic and nearly orphaned foal of Two Bucks Farm's most commercial and now out-of-commission broodmare, For Dixie. He had been strategically positioned by the sales consignor, Johnny "Alphabet" Jones's Walmac, to sell in a coveted spot on the fourth day.

From the minute the colt arrived on the grounds he created a sensation. His mother, also a daughter of Dixieland Band, was a younger, bigger version of Regal Band, and her ten-month-old son looked more like a yearling than a weanling. A striking bay, he was heavily muscled, shined and combed to perfection. Cool and professional, he strutted around in a big, loose striding display of confidence. Fearless from birth, the colt had once taken out a four-board oak fence trying to get to another horse and had emerged without losing a hair. Walmac regarded him as the "complete package" and pushed him to everyone.

The pinhookers were all over him—taking radiographs of his joints, which were perfect; scoping his wind passage, which they found large and symmetrical; and even employing ultrasound to measure his heart capacity, which one of them confided to be "exciting." All were indicators of a promising sale.

Then came the ultimate tipoff—two quietly conveyed offers to buy the colt before he entered the ring. This practice is not uncommon at thoroughbred auctions, although it is seldom discussed openly or written about in industry publications. While not patently unethical—everybody still has an equal chance to buy the horse in the ring—it leaves an impression of chicanery that the long-besmirched racing business does not need. Worse, it is a practice easily distorted to fraud that can result in naive, unwary buyers paying more and sellers getting less than they should for a particular horse. All that is needed is an unsavory buyer's agent, one phony bidder and a seller greedy enough to keep his mouth shut—a combination not difficult to assemble.

Usually such presale finagling is just another form of bet hedging, a bird-in-the-hand decision by an owner. Never knowing precisely what the horse will bring in the ring, an owner can through oral or written agreement sell the horse in advance for a set price. This arrangement only guarantees that the buyer bid up to at least the preset amount. Once bidding in the ring reaches that point, the horse in effect has a new owner who can keep raising the stakes until he has won the bidding, or let the horse go to a higher bidder. Either way, the original owner, to whom the sale company will deliver the proceeds, gets to keep only the prearranged amount. Meanwhile, the presale buyer gets either the horse at the preset price, or the difference between what he had guaranteed and the final sale price.

Often these deals are conveyed to the owner at the last minute by an intermediary who has a trustworthy relationship with both sides, which was the case with For Dixie's Gilded Time colt. In the minutes preceding the sale, as he watched the crowd gather around his horse, the anxious Two Bucks man was twice pulled aside by friends bearing gifts of sales-ring guarantees of $100,000. This was fifteen times the stud fee and $25,000 more than he had paid for the mare carrying the foal a year earlier. Even an ex-journalist could figure out that these were both good deals.

One was actually better—and more deceptive—than the other. In the event the colt brought more than $100,000 in the ring and was bought by a third party, one presale buyer was willing to split his profits fifty-fifty with Two Bucks. This prospect caused the seller to sweat profusely in wonderment over whether the dominant female could be counted on to honor their agreement, which banned her from the sales grounds during sales of Two Bucks horses. If she was there, she was a threat to queer any deal, and the place was teeming.

A lot of the big spenders were gathered around the Gilded Time colt. At horse auctions they travel in clumps that include veterinarians, accountants, and equine conformation experts, some of whom double as coat and catalog holders. Sheikh Mohammed bin Rashid Al Maktoum, for example, leader of the brothers who rule the oil-rich Arab state of Dubai in the Persian Gulf, often moves in an entourage so large he completely disappears in the middle of it. As lore has it, once the entourage was moving past a television monitor showing the hammer falling on the sale of a horse for $675,000.

"Who bought that?" he inquired.

"Why, you did, your highness," one of his men replied.

"Ah," smiled the sheikh. "Very good."

Sheikh Mohammed was not among those looking at For Dixie's

baby but his men were. So were the Maktoums' longtime rivals as connoisseurs and collectors of expensive horseflesh—the Irishmen of Coolmore. Slightly fewer in number, they compensated by wearing huge, down-filled parkas and distinctive hats that made them resemble a single metallic giant amoeba moving through the barns. Whatever their appearance the expertise of the Maktoums and the Irish and their willingness to pay for quality thoroughbreds are unquestioned. A lot of other good horsemen also were swarming the Gilded Time colt, among them the cigar-chomping bloodstock agent Buzz Chace, who bought horses for a big new player named Ernie Paragallo, a liberal spender and the owner of a then-fabled two-year-old named Unbridled's Song.

The sight of all this was enough to make a horse owner wish for a soulmate with whom to celebrate and anticipate. Unfortunately for the Two Bucks man the exact whereabouts of his soulmate—the dominant female—was still unknown, which made him nervous. The colt was to sell in ten minutes.

The reason she wasn't at his side offering moral support and running commentary had to do with the business arrangement they'd made upon moving into Two Bucks. A woman of superior judgment, she had decided against a thoroughbred partnership in favor of the travel business—an agency and a tour company. This was a good idea because she believed horses are to keep, not to sell. Ever. No matter the price. To her they were all pets and family members impossible to part with. This viewpoint had been driven home to him painfully and dramatically in the summer of 1991, when she sabotaged his great Eastern Summit Paint Horse Sale.

Having an excess of young paint stock, he had organized and put on the sale at the Kentucky Horse Park as a preliminary to the American Paint Horse Association's national show. A well-known auctioneer from Mississippi was hired and consignors brought offerings from all over the country. Among the sixty or so entries were five horses of his own from whom he desperately needed to part company. Except for a world champion reining mare that drew an early hip number, the others were bunched together late in the sale, their numbers drawn almost back to back.

The reining mare sold in a routine manner, but for less than she was worth, which turned out to be his best luck of the day. Though the crowd was sparse and the number of serious buyers few, each time one of his own horses entered the sales ring, bidders appeared out of nowhere and vigorously supported them, driving up their prices. At first he was thrilled, but when the first one sold for more than it was worth he recognized the ticket signer as the dominant female's close friend, a woman who didn't know a horse from a cow. Was this animal going home to her apartment? When his next horse sold, there she was bidding again. This time she lost but to a bidder he knew couldn't afford a horse—one of his wife's travel agency employees. What the hell was going on?

Before he could find out, the third horse was in the ring and there was the dominant female herself bidding against the farm's accountant. A partner in the travel agency ended up signing the ticket, and a neighbor with no farm bought the last of his entries at an outrageous price. The dominant female had salted the crowd with her pals, all "shills" and all armed with no idea when to stop bidding. The "buyers" didn't even know enough to mark the sale slips "Reserve Bid Not Attained." So the sales looked real, which meant commission had to be paid to his sales company in which there were partners. And the auctioneer's cut was based on horses sold. These were all added costs and there were no sales proceeds with which to feed these "buybacks" when they returned home.

Despite all that big money now gathered around For Dixie's Gilded Time colt at Keeneland, he could end up a buyback, too—if the dominant female was out there in the crowd somewhere, ready to raise her hand. Still owing responses to the hedge-bet offers, and with these things weighing on his mind, he began to search the pavilion crowd for his wife or any of her known accomplices. An employee who answered the phone at the travel agency had said, "The owner is out." And during the telephone conversation he noticed a young partner in the tour company, Scott Goodlett, enter the sales pavilion. But Scott vowed he was there on his own merely out of curiosity and had not been dispatched by the dominant female. "She said she couldn't bear to watch you sell the colt," Scott insisted. "I don't think she's coming."

The Two Bucks man knew his wife better, but there was no time to look further. The emissaries of the presale buyers had to be found and their offers declined—not because of objections to the practice, but because there was now no difference between the two offers. Both sides were now willing to split with him any excess over $100,000. He couldn't turn down one guy and make the same deal with the other. The two were best friends. There was no more time to negotiate. The colt was coming toward the sales ring. A gray-haired man was literally running ahead of him, in a hurry to get inside the pavilion. It was Frank Stronach, the auto-parts magnate who five years later would become the nation's leading thoroughbred owner and leading breeder in the same year as well as the proprietor of two of America's premier racetracks, Gulfstream Park and Santa Anita. But that day he was just another big timer literally running to bid on the first colt that the tiny Two Bucks Farm had ever offered for sale at Keeneland. He never got the chance.

On the fourth day of a November sale, when some of the horses are still near the top of the market, the bidding on a colt of the quality of For Dixie's Gilded Time weanling would normally begin at $10,000 and proceed steadily in increments of $5,000. But the auctioneers always start out asking for considerably more and then working their way back down to reality, rhetorically, like "Who'll give a hundred fifty thousand?" And when no one does, he lowers it, as auctioneer Tom Caldwell did that day, saying, "How about a hundred twenty five?" Still no one. But when Caldwell said, "Okay, one hundred thousand . . . ," Ernie Paragallo shot his hand in the air for the benefit of the bid spotter behind the sales ring. Out front in the pavilion Frank Stronach frowned and shrugged his shoulders. Everyone was stunned, including Caldwell himself, who was already on his way down to $75,000. The only reason to start the bidding on a colt at the top is to try to run everyone else out. That was Paragallo's style. He'd done it before, and it almost worked this time. Most of the bidders folded immediately. Finally, somebody bid $110,000 and the bidding began to inch upward, eventually stopping at $150,000.

The seller silently congratulated himself. In his mind the indecision about whether to take the bird in the hand had turned into a bold gamble on the one in the bush. He thought Paragallo, then enjoying a reputation for buying future stars, had bought the colt. When told it was "a pretty, dark-haired woman inside the pavilion," he thought first of killing himself, then of strangling the dominant female. No, not again. In the past, not knowing the name of a "pretty, dark-haired woman" might have sparked within him a twinge of regret. But this time he collapsed in glee when she turned out to be a total stranger, Brenda Jones of Silver Oaks Farm in Florida, a former quarter-horse trainer and a pinhooker who had not been intimidated by Paragallo's opening gambit. Fortunately the bidding had moved so fast that the dominant female—who was there as suspected—had never gotten her hand out of her pocket. Even her hands become slower and heavier when they are lifting six figures. For Dixie's colt was the highest priced weanling sold that day at Keeneland and the second–highest priced weanling of Gilded Time's first crop. At the yearling sale the following September, he would sell for $175,000 to a rich guy in search of "the big horse"—Sheikh Mohammed's older and considerably lower profile brother, Sheikh Hamdan, owner of Shadwell Farm.

Picking the big horse out of a sale or arranging the right mating to produce one is a gamble akin to a dice roll or selecting the right color at a casino table. Sheikh Hamdan was betting that Gilded Time's speed and prowess on American dirt tracks and the endurance suggested by his mother's conformation and pedigree would be the perfect combination—not for the grass classics of Europe, where the Maktoum runners were already dominant, but for the American Triple Crown races where they wanted to be.

In the hands of the best trainers in Europe, the For Dixie colt, now named Misbah, turned out to be a useful runner, winning at two and three years old before being returned to the United States to defeat good allowance competition at Belmont Park and Saratoga. He was a periodic "bleeder," a term used for what amounts to a wreck in a horse's respiratory system at the peak of strenuous exercise. For reasons still a mystery, sometimes the lungs of a racehorse will bleed excessively during a race or hard workout, impeding oxygen intake and thus performance. Never a stakes winner, Misbah was nonetheless eventually purchased from the Arabs as a stallion prospect and now stands at stud on a small farm in Kentucky. Wealthy owners like the Maktoums breed or purchase hundreds of colts like Misbah every year in hopes of winning the big American dirt track classics. Even if they don't turn out to be a big horse, at least they get the chance to be.

Breeders not wealthy enough to race their own babies must depend on getting them into the hands of owners with such commitment and resources, a tough proposition on a small budget. The horses must be, like Misbah, a "complete package" of bloodlines and physical attributes. Some horses look like athletes but aren't, and some of the best equine athletes don't look the part. The key to winning racehorses—a competitive spirit—is a quality that can't be seen at all, at least not in a sales walking ring or parade around the barn on a shank. One youngster's will to win might not become apparent until he "hooks" another while galloping together on a training track, or until the adrenaline surge hits when the first starting gate pops open. Others sometimes show heart the night they are born, or the first time they are turned loose with a playmate. Some breeders can detect it. Some can't.

Big horse or not, For Dixie's first baby had amounted to a home run for Two Bucks. The colt had sold for twice what the mare in foal had cost a year earlier. A couple of more like that and the thoroughbred game might look like a business after all. The euphoria that accompanies such a triumph is what made Keeneland the gushing revenue stream it had become. Success inevitably stimulates the appetite for more. With the $150,000 from For Dixie's foal sitting in his

Keeneland account, the seller began doing what most sellers at horse sales do—looking for a good reason not to take the profit home. What Two Bucks needed was a couple more mares bred to hot, young sires. For Dixie wouldn't send another foal to market for two more years. No inventory, no sale, no euphoria.

The 1995 November sale was probably the last of the decade at Keeneland where bargain broodmares were plentiful. It went down in history as "the sale that soared" and ignited a remarkable industry recovery over the next five years. Over eleven days Keeneland sold 2,900 horses for more than $140 million, a $19 million increase over 1994. The trend of more horses being sold for more money would continue through the end of the century. Over the course of the year 2000, a total of 8,074 horses sold at Keeneland's five auctions for $754 million, earning the sales company nearly $38 million in commissions alone.

More significantly, the 1994 and 1995 sales marked the return of the big-spending foreigners in search of more U.S. breeding stock. The Japanese alone spent $18 million in 1994 for 81 mares and 16 weanlings and nearly $23 million the following year, buying 82 mares and 11 weanlings and accounting for nearly 31 percent of the sales revenue in the first two days. At the 1995 sale the Maktoum family dropped $4.7 million, Coolmore bought 3 horses at better than $500,000 each, including $1.3 million for the dam of 1990 Kentucky Derby winner Unbridled. Hungarian-born Count Zichy Thysson bought 5 horses costing a half million or more, including a $1.4 million mare. And a mare in foal to the industry's most popular but aging sire, Mr. Prospector, topped the sale at $2.5 million.

The mad scramble for the big horse was raging again. And nestled snugly in his down-market niche, the peacock-proud proprietor of Two Bucks made his own little lurch, purchasing two more discarded mares for a piddling $42,000 each, thus returning all his profit from the Gilded Time colt, plus more, to the Keeneland sales company. At the "numbers" game there was no question who played it best.

3

My purpose is, indeed, a horse of that color.

WILLIAM SHAKESPEARE, *Twelfth Night*

Snake was black as coal, quick as a cat and named for the way he could strike with his front feet and bite a handler at the same time, his little muzzle darting cobra-like back toward the thigh. Errant child though he was, Regal Band could not have been prouder of him. She must have known he was the key to her future.

"You've got to do something with Snake," complained the little red-haired farm manager. She was jerking on a rope shank attached to Snake, who was walking on his hind legs. "I'm not handling him any-more until you put a chain in his mouth or something."

Fear and anger are natural reactions when confronted with a 650-pound animal who can move 35 miles an hour, kill you with his head or all four limbs, and has been trying to drag you a mile to the main road. But they are the absolutely wrong emotions to display to a horse. Horses have a remarkable "sense of your sense" and take their own behavioral cues from what is going on around them.

Sensing fear only makes them more fearful, which most often is what is causing the problem in the first place. Self-preservation being their overriding instinct, eating and running away is what they naturally do best.

Snake running away with the 110-pound female farm manager attached was the problem now confronting the Two Bucks owner, long experienced with both horses and executive decision-making.

"Give him to Bruce," was his solution. Bruce was the farm manager's considerably younger, bigger and stronger first-rate assistant, who'd been taught all the right horse handling techniques.

"He's gotten meaner'n hell lately," Bruce declared.

"It's that damn eye," offered the farm manager.

The sclerotic membrane of a horse's eye, the area around the cornea and pupil, is usually dark. But Snake's right eye was white like a human's. Seattle Slew has an eye like that. Snake got his from his mother, Regal Band, along with the little white star in the middle of his forehead.

"He needs some more of that Dorrance stuff," Bruce suggested.

That's what the farm help called the horse-handling techniques they'd all been taught—that is, except the red-haired farm manager, who had declined to learn. She knew everything already.

The Dorrance stuff is a simple system of patience, reward and restraint named after the old Oregon cowboy brothers Bill and Tom, who fostered it among the stock-horse people. It had been around for centuries. The plains Indians were experts at it. So must have been trainer Tom (Lone Plainsman) Smith, who used the horsemanship he'd learned from Native Americans to miraculously turn a taciturn thoroughbred named Seabiscuit into a superstar. Nothing more than considering things from the horse's point of view, it is a system of "willing" communication that is the secret of all great horsemen and animal trainers. Once mastered, conflict between man and beast ends forever.

Snake, however, was a frequent truant from the school of Dorrance and often inattentive during lessons, which always take place free of restraint in a round pen about 50 feet in diameter, preferably one that is enclosed and secluded from noise and other distractions. The Dorrance stuff doesn't work unless the horse's attention can be focused on his human companion. Snake always put his white eye on you, like the wolf showing his teeth to Little Red Riding Hood: "The better to eat you with, my dear."

The Dorrance teacher is in the center of the pen with a cowboy lariat or a lunge line, which he swings around above his head and toward the horse until it moves away. It is the motion they find threatening. The underlying premise here is that the horse is by nature—like all other animals with eyes on the side of the head—a "game" animal, the natural prey of "hunter" animals whose eyes are set in the front of the head. A few minutes of staring into a horse's eyes and making threatening gestures above his natural line of sight will very soon have him trying to leave the hunter's company—which of course he won't if the enclosure is the right kind and the "hunter" has a deft touch. Flinging a loose rope, even a gray-haired old breeder can soon have a terror like Snake under control. The idea is not to terrify the horse, only to establish who is in charge of the territory, and ultimately the relationship. Properly executed, the horse will soon tire and begin exhibiting body language that says it is a peace-loving, grass-eating animal who'd really rather be friends than paw your head off.

Some horses have been so irreparably damaged psychologically by human stupidity, it can take months to gain their confidence. But most young stock will soon be standing as close as possible to their new friend, actually seeking security from human companionship—two happy herd animals. Then it is only a matter of keeping a horse's attention. Eventually it can be led, ridden, bathed and loaded into trailers, airplanes, and starting gates—all based on a relationship of mutual trust.

Both Snake and Bruce had picked up the idea very quickly. Snake just dropped it every now and then.

When Bruce took the shank from the farm manager, Snake went straight up and struck out with both feet, one narrowly missing Bruce's chin on the way down and scraping against his jacket.

"See, I told you, He's gotten meaner'n hell," declared Bruce once more for emphasis.

The breeder was no longer afraid of horses, though he once had been—deathly afraid when he rode the white oak stick and loved the real thing only from a distance. Their sheer size terrified him, but their attraction proved stronger than his fear. His mother was afraid of horses, too, but she didn't want a son afraid of anything. So she kept putting him up on ponies until he got over it. The summer he was four years old little black Tony, the carnival pony, bit him so many times on the legs he looked like a victim of child abuse. When the preacher came to visit she'd put the kid in long pants, to hide both the bruises and the evidence of where she'd been contributing her quarters.

Now, fifty years later, Regal Band's rearing and striking black colt was among the least of his fears. "Give me that silly boy for a while, then," he said, taking the shank from Bruce and heading Snake for another Dorrance lesson.

That night the episode was relived vividly in his dreams, with his unruly student circling him in the round pen, kicking out threateningly and menacing him with his white eye until, tired from fleeing the rope, he had run himself out. And then Snake had come puppy-like to the center and nuzzled his friend's shoulder in search of attention. In the morning the teacher awoke peacefully for a change, roused by Snake's soft muzzle instead of the disturbing climax of his recurring and mystifying nightmare.

Ultimately named Morava—after the Moravian homeland of the dominant female's immigrant father—Snake answered the question of whether Regal Band could produce an offspring with the right stuff to be a "big horse." His sire was Secret Hello, a gritty, taller version of Regal Band selected as her mate because he came from the wonderful broodmare Ciao. That was the central idea—breed the descendants of great mothers to the descendants of great mothers—a middle-class version of "best to the best." That Secret Hello stood for a paltry

$5,000 at Walmac International—where Johnny Jones would not hold Regal Band's sorry record against her—played no little role in the selection. Matching up an average mare with a stallion whose get will be considered fashionable by the flighty trendchasers two years later is at best a crapshoot. Stallion managers want the date books of hot young first-year sires, like the champion Gilded Time, filled with proven producers or young stakes-winning mares such as For Dixie. So the opportunity to visit newly minted racetrack heroes is seldom available to blue-collar girls like Regal Band. With her history, no mating could be planned with the Maktoums or the Japanese in mind anyway. An American pinhooker willing to risk $20,000 on a Regal Band foal would be a reach. So what she needed was a good-looking, live, properly conformed foal on the ground with the look of a runner. Snake fit the bill.

Foaled in February 1996, Snake grew up with three other colts in a rolling, 20-acre field with plenty of steep inclines. In Kentucky, where there are steep inclines there are rocks that grow out of the ground overnight and new holes that weren't there the day before—a marvelous if treacherous fitness course. Once thoroughbred colts are weaned and turned out together, their lives become a constant "tough man" competition, a kind of Marine boot camp. Every morning the recruits come into the barn to be inspected and patched up. Then they go back out where for the next 22 hours they do their damnedest to kill themselves—or at least to acquire permanent blemishes that will diminish their sale value.

Because horses aren't usually named until they race, youngsters usually go by the names of their fathers. Snake's buddies included a stout, red Marquetry colt, who was the biggest and best-looking of the four, and a handsome bay Mt. Livermore son, who though the youngest was a speedburner. The runt and doormat to all three was a little feminine-looking colt by Beau Genius, who, like Snake, had earned himself a nickname—Whacko—because he was afraid of anything that moved, including his own shadow.

All of them could run and would later make racehorses, but Snake could give them a 50-yard head start and motor past them in three heartbeats. He took delight in doing it. Given a choice of passing on the outside or darting by them through a narrowing opening on the fence, he invariably chose the hole. If he had to knock them over or the fence down to get through, that was even better.

One afternoon in the fall of 1996, the Two Bucks colts were honing their racing skills for the benefit of the breeding genius and the dominant female, who were propped up on the fence. Six months earlier Regal Band had been bred back to a slightly more expensive, commercial sire named Black Tie Affair who was popular with the Japanese, the idea being that with broodmare prices rising she could be resold at Keeneland that November at a slight profit—maybe. Broodmares are a depreciable expense for tax purposes. But Regal Band's future was so tenuous that she was still being carried on the farm as "inventory" that had been purchased for resale.

The owners watched Snake wreaking havoc in the pasture, repeatedly running down one companion and then the other until all three were standing heads down, sides heaving in the center of the field. The black colt still had not had enough. For the next ten minutes he raced alone from one end of the pasture to the other, blasting through the middle of his friends—teeth bared and ears pinned, taunting them to take after him again.

The dominant female must have seen this as admirable behavior.

"Maybe you shouldn't sell Regal Band," she observed.

"You don't ever want me to sell anything."

"That's a heckuva colt."

"I know. If he's not a racehorse I'll never raise one. He's very cool—no temper—but he's so competitive he tries to stomp the pigeons on the way to the paddock."

"No kidding?"

"Yeah, the cats, too, if they're around."

"What are you going to do with him?"

"Sell him as a yearling."

"I think you should keep him and the mare, too."

"We can't afford to do both," he insisted.

"Well, I sure wouldn't sell her until after that guy goes to the races."

Waiting to sell Regal Band until Snake had a chance to make it on the racetrack meant keeping her until she was twelve or thirteen years old, a point where many breeders write mares off as failures if they haven't produced a stakes winner.

"That's a gamble. If she hasn't produced a good runner by then, she'll be worthless."

"So you're telling me you've gotten yourself in a business that discriminates against old ladies?"

"I guess so."

"Wasn't Secretariat's mother old when he was born?"

"Yeah, eighteen to twenty I think."

"They must have forgotten Secretariat already. How much is Regal Band going to bring in November?"

"Not much. Probably what we paid for her, plus the $15,000 stud fee. Depends on how popular Black Tie Affair is at the moment. You know how that is."

"So why not keep her? You don't have all that much invested."

As usual the dominant female had a good point. But saying so would have been unnecessary encouragement, her confidence being already overdeveloped. At the time nothing was at stake but his horse-trader's ego. But deciding to keep Regal Band until Snake made it to the races turned out to be a milestone on the road to "genius."

As Two Bucks pipe-dreamed of a big horse, one was about to take up stallion duty about ten miles away at Pin Oak Stud, part of a wondrous stretch of real estate along Highway 60 that suggests Kentucky might be all bluegrass and black fences. But hardly anyone in the horse business was paying attention. That's because even winning the American two-year-old championship is not "big" enough when your social credentials aren't up to snuff.

For a business that draws its lifeblood from the small wagers and hard labor of the proletariat, the thoroughbred world is remarkably patrician from top to bottom. And nowhere is the caste system more rigid or discriminating than in the breeding shed.

By every measure Maria's Mon had been a dynamite racehorse, just what the pinhookers ordered in terms of early speed and achievement. At two he had met and defeated the best horses of his generation, and not just barely. He smoked them, winning three graded stakes races between July and October 1995. First there was the Grade 3 Sanford, a traditional coming-out party for precocious two-year-olds at Saratoga, the mecca of racing's elite. Among those vanquished that day by Maria's Mon was the vaunted Editor's Note, who the following spring would win the Belmont Stakes and finish third at the Preakness. Next, the big gray streak virtually assured himself of the Eclipse Award as champion two-year-old by winning two important Grade 1 stakes at Belmont Park, the Futurity Stakes in September and in October the prestigious Champagne, the race that had validated Secretariat, Seattle Slew and Affirmed as legitimate Triple Crown threats.

But two things were wrong with Maria's Mon. Less than two weeks after winning the Champagne and just hours before he was to be entered in the Breeders' Cup Juvenile, he'd suffered a condylar fracture above his left front ankle, thus missing the race that is the traditional reputation-maker for Kentucky Derby prospects. As a racehorse he was never the same again. After a brief comeback as a three-year-old he was retired, while the ballyhoo that accompanies the Triple Crown chase went to horses like Ernie Paragallo's colt, Unbridled's Song, who won the Juvenile, and Hennessy, son of the awesome Storm Cat, both of whom Maria's Mon had whipped in the Champagne.

But that was only half his problem. Maria's Mon was basically a "Florida horse" with a suspect pedigree, another blue-collar "freak" who on the basis of his lineage could not be expected to pass on his excellence to the next generation. Florida was infamous for producing thinly pedigreed speedsters who could run the legs off many of the Kentucky bluebloods. The 1990s were no exception. Holy Bull had just been named Horse of the Year and three-year-old champion. Skip

Away and Silver Charm would soon repeat the honors. All three were sired by Florida-based stallions. Although the sire of Maria's Mon, Wavering Monarch, stood in Lexington at Glencrest Farm, his fee was only $5,000 and his book was routinely filled with middle- and low-level mares, including some from out of state who then returned home to foal. Such foals would not be "Kentucky-bred," and if and when they ran on to glory—as Holy Bull had just done—it would not reflect positively on the world capital of horse breeding.

Every now and then, a very good mare would be shipped in from New York or Florida by a wily breeder with a sharp eye for quality and value. That's what Dr. E. C. "Pug" Hart and his wife, Susan, were looking for when they bred Wavering Monarch to Carlotta Maria, the undistinguished gray daughter of the distance-loving Caro. Young, unproven and in need of a mate with size and substance, she was a failed racehorse owned by the Harts' clients, Mr. and Mrs. Morton Rosenthal, who bred to race, not necessarily to sell. And Caro had a reputation as a sire of good broodmares.

Wavering Monarch was a big, good-looking horse who could run. And that was precisely what Carlotta Maria put on the ground when she foaled Maria's Mon—a perfectly balanced animal with a striking head, a giant stride, a long-sloping shoulder and powerful hindquarters that rippled with strength and definition.

He was just the kind of colt Pin Oak Stud owner Josephine Abercrombie and her farm manager Clifford Barry had eyes for. They'd first seen him as a "grand-looking" yearling in a pasture at the Harts' Florida farm, where they had gone to acquire another stallion. While Maria's Mon was steamrolling the other two-year-olds, the Rosenthals had rejected a passel of offers from potential buyers. Only after the injury did they agree to sell half their colt to Abercrombie.

To understand why Maria's Mon had beaten the tar out of so many good colts, all a good horseman had to do was watch him walk across the barn floor. He looked like a great athlete and moved like one. But hardly anyone—who was anyone—came to see him.

Normally, breeders want to be in the top third of a stallion's book—which means they want their mares regarded near the top in quality among all mares being bred to a particular stud that season. But the owners of average mares looking for a big return on their stud fee flock to where they think the action will be on first-year sires. Being at the bottom of a hot freshman sire's book was preferable to being in the top echelon of one who is getting no attention, or in the middle of the book of an older horse standing for a comparable fee. What is fresh and new is always better.

A lot of really good mares were headed to first-crop stallions in the spring of 1997. But they would be going elsewhere. Both Editor's Note and the Kentucky Derby winner, Grindstone, were going home to Overbrook, where the world's most successful commercial sire, Storm Cat, attracted more good mares than there were seasons available. Some of the overflow would be steered toward Grindstone, who would open at $20,000, and Editor's Note at $10,000. Most important, each horse would get a share of Overbrook owner W. T. Young's sterling broodmare band, the way Gilded Time had.

Unbridled's Song, meanwhile, was opening for $30,000 at Taylor Made Farm, where oodles of good mares were boarded and would find their way to his book. The Irish owners of Coolmore, the world's greatest stallion maker, had paid a reported $8 million for Hennessy and would breed him to 150 or more mares at $40,000 a pop. Well into their drive to alter forever the basic economic model of the stallion business, the Irish had also bought the Preakness winner Louis Quatorze and the sprinter Honour and Glory, both of whom had lost to Maria's Mon in the Futurity Stakes. Coolmore's worldwide marketing prowess and global stallion roster comprised a mare magnet unmatched in the history of thoroughbreds. If Coolmore's principal owner John Magnier had bought Maria's Mon, the mere fact that he had done so would have assured a first-year book of 100 at a stud fee of $15,000. A lot of mare owners never even go see a stallion before booking a mare. They depend on cursory pedigree compatibility and stud farm reputation. Their thinking was, if Maria's Mon was all that good, he would have been snapped up by Coolmore and wouldn't be standing for $7,500 at Pin Oak.

Though superbly maintained and operated, Abercrombie's farm was new to the stallion business and had no record to suggest it could put a stallion on the leading sire list in his first two years. The thoroughbred game keeps everybody guessing. Everybody wants what everybody else thinks everybody else will want when the first foal crop runs three years hence. And as the 1997 breeding season opened, that was not Maria's Mon.

As discouraging as this might have been to Pin Oak, it was irrelevant at Two Bucks, where there was never any indecision when matching mares to stallions—only substantial suspicion that no one, including the ever-confident Two Bucks decisionmaker, had the slightest clue to what they were doing anyway.

The mating of thoroughbreds at the leading Kentucky stud farms is a long-practiced art that combines the beauty of a ballet with the culture of a surgical procedure. More elaborate in some sheds than in others, a common element is a cadre of attendants who prepare the mare like a hospital patient bound for the operating room. First she is scrubbed with disinfectant and wrapped in all manner of garb from gauze wrap on her tail to little padded bootlets on her hind feet that would lessen the impact of a kick.

Then the mare is exposed to a "teaser," most often a quarter horse or a pony, who tests her willingness to stand quietly for "cover"—the term of art for the act itself. Once the shed manager is satisfied the mare is not dangerously hostile, the stallion is brought out, usually in a high state of anticipation. Most thoroughbred studs show up in the breeding shed like they are going to war. They prance in under chain restraint, pawing and squealing, with necks bowed, eyes flashing, tails flailing in all directions. Of course their only interest is the mare, who by this time has a protective cape across her shoulders, a twitch on her nose and a strap holding one front foot off the ground to insure against kicking her suitor. No other animal in the world gets so much help in accomplishing what nature intended as individual achievement. Depending on the farm, there can be as many as four handlers, a "shank man," a "twitch man," a "leg strap man" and even a "tail man" in latex gloves who will move the mare's tail aside and assist entry by the stallion if necessary.

There are a few female stallion managers, and women veterinarians are quite common, but women are seldom members of the breeding shed crews, presumably because they would not like being called "leg-strap women" or "tail girls." Although they would be quite comfortable among the Irish contingent at Pin Oak, where the breeding is a model of decorum, some women might be put off by the bullfight atmosphere of the all-Hispanic crews at some of the farms. "Amigos" have more fun than "the Micks"—at work anyway—and are more prone to laugh lasciviously and shout profane encouragement to the equine lovers.

Maria's Mon needed no encouragement. He danced into the Pin Oak breeding shed, secure in a bridle and bit in the hands of Clifford Barry, but looking as if he would demolish the place if freed. Regal Band, however, an ice maiden if ever there was one, was decidedly unfazed by his theatrics. Now in the eleventh day of her foal heat cycle and only hours before ovulation, her demeanor was what you'd expect from a dominant female of superior lineage: Quit showing off, buster, and get this over with.

Years of experience visualizing the size and shape of the products of potential matings had imbued Regal Band's owner with supreme confidence in the physical cross aspect of horse breeding, often called equine biomechanics. He knew the art better than pedigree analysis and so naturally weighted it more heavily in planning matings even though fully aware it often goes haywire. Crooked-legged horses bred to each other often produce perfectly correct foals. Two giants can produce a midget.

Framed together during the cover, it was apparent that Regal Band and Maria's Mon constituted as perfect a physical match as a breeder could arrange. Once again the sire was simply a larger, more powerful version of the beautifully balanced, smooth-striding dam.

As for the market's skepticism about the sire's pedigree, well, the owner of Two Bucks was in no position to hold that against anyone—even a horse. To the contrary, he saw in the pedigree exactly the kind of K-Mart version of "best to the best" that he loved as a breeder. The sire of Maria's Mon, Wavering Monarch, was from the branch of the Raise a Native line known for producing great broodmares and was already establishing himself in that arena. Raise a Native was best known as the sire of "the sire of sires"—Mr. Prospector. But he had also been responsible for two of the greatest American racehorses of the century, Affirmed and Alydar, both of whom became great broodmare sires. What's more, Wavering Monarch's mother was a daughter of Buckpasser, another distinguished broodmare sire and the main modern conduit for the blood of the great mare La Troienne, one of the most reliable sources of racing prowess ever.

A mating of Maria's Mon and Regal Band blended those two leading female bloodlines with that of another famous "blue hen" broodmare, Darby Dan's On the Trail, whose daughters had produced graded stakes winners galore.

Perhaps it was because his own mother had been such a dominant figure in the home that the preponderance of his faith lay in the female influence. The more he delved into the history of horses—particularly the thoroughbreds—the more he became convinced that great stallions most often came from great mothers. And he had been delighted when his notion had been buttressed by new scientific conclusions that male offspring actually inherit their "hearts" from their mother—both the size of the physical muscle and the nature of emotional intelligence.

As Maria's Mon dismounted and was led away, the hopeful mare owner envisioned the prospective offspring as a grand-looking replica of the father, a deep-chested, beautifully necked horse that stands over a lot of ground; powerful enough behind to have the precocious early speed of his father, but lithe and narrow enough to run on the turns and with the long-shouldered endurance of his mother; overall, just a bigger, more awesome, gray version of Snake, hopefully with the same love of running.

This was only a dream, of course. That's all it ever is. The reality was that however blue the blood in their veins from generations back, both Regal Band and Maria's Mon had fallen a good ways from the tree of thoroughbred aristocracy. The breeder saw them as two castoff descendants of royalty hooking up in a quest for restored respectability. He knew the brutal market would award neither sire nor dam credit beyond that they could bring on themselves. And as with all other living beings, only the offspring would ultimately determine the worth of the parents and the wisdom of their union.

The following September Two Bucks went to the Keeneland yearling sale with favorably low hip numbers and uncharacteristically high hopes. A shrewd Florida pinhooker named Becky Thomas had inspected the four Two Bucks colts at the farm earlier in the year and cherry-picked the big, impressive son of Marquetry. She paid a handsome price of $125,000—more than eighteen times the stud fee of $7,500—another "home run." The yearling was the foal carried by one of the mares the owner had bought in November 1995 for $42,000, and now one of Thomas's clients planned to send the Marquetry colt to a highly regarded young trainer to launch him on his racing career.

This presale purchase left three colts to be "prepped" at Two Bucks for the September event. Prepping, a process of daily exercise and grooming, takes about an hour per day per horse and is best accomplished by two grooms working together.

By this time the female farm manager who didn't like Snake had departed. Better her than him. "Bigger farm, better mares and more money" were her reasons for leaving with little notice the week of the Kentucky Derby. Her successor lasted only two days.

This series of events left a two-man crew struggling at Two Bucks—Bruce and the breeding genius. They quickly decided to ship Snake and Whacko, both now walking the straight and narrow, to their sale consignor for the final sixty days of conditioning—at a cost of $30 per day each. This expense added another $3,600 in sales costs to the 10 percent commission Keeneland and Walmac together would clip off the top of their sale price.

The Mt. Livermore colt, meanwhile, would continue to be prepared at Two Bucks, where he was considered a top sale prospect. Mature and well-built, he was the foal being carried by the other $42,000 discard bought during the Misbah euphoria of 1995. Since her purchase, the covering sire, Mt. Livermore, suddenly had become very fashionable. His stud fee had rapidly doubled to $30,000 and landed his handsome son in the "select" first two sale days—Hip No. 602 out of 3,668.

The consignor, Lane's End Farm, which specializes in top-of-the-market stock, thought he might bring $175,000—yet another home run. But that was before the X rays.

In the preceding year, Keeneland had come up with a new sales innovation that in addition to being a revenue enhancement program for veterinarians eventually changed the nature and economics of all future sales of young stock.

Previously, buyers selectively chose to take radiographs of the bone joints of prospective racehorses. This procedure was usually done on only the most expensive horses, or to clarify some suspected flaw. But frequent postsale disputes over potential but undisclosed infirmities drove Keeneland and other sales companies to establish a sale "repository" where buyers can view a set of thirty-two radiographs on each young horse.

Although supplying radiographs is not officially mandatory, it might as well be. A horse without a set of X rays in the repository is automatically thought to be one with something to hide and discounted accordingly as a risky proposition. Sellers must hire vets to take the radiographs, which cost from $425 to $600, depending on the number of views and the prominence of the cameraman. And buyers must hire vets to read them. But the cost of not having them is even greater. Because of its efficiency as a means of dislodging money from the seller, the X-ray viewing facility came to be known derisively as the "suppository." And it worked like one on Two Bucks. The magnificently fit Mt. Livermore colt who was pulled repeatedly from his stall for viewing by interested buyers and whose throat was examined and found acceptable by numerous veterinarians had his sale killed by the "suppository." He was found to have a small bone chip floating near his left rear ankle joint. Although unlikely ever to inhibit his racing ability and easily removed by arthroscopic surgery, the chip dramatically discounted the colt in the sales ring. Live bidding reached only $65,000, a price $100,000 less than his reserve, and he went unsold.

The Mt. Livermore colt was Two Bucks' "commercial horse" in the September sale, the one being counted on to generate cash flow for the farm the way Misbah had done two years before. The two left to sell—Snake and Whacko—were both low-dollar items. If each brought twice their stud fees—a reasonable expectation—the total would be less than $30,000.

Few horses have a set of perfect X rays but both of these did. They were irrelevant, however, as nobody bothered to examine them. The one vet who had scoped Snake's throat to write the required repository report had been astounded by its unusually large size and perfect symmetry. But no one asked to see the report.

Not many thoroughbred colts have all their leg joints properly aligned, either. But both of these did. Yet virtually no one went to the sales barns to see them before they entered the ring a few hip numbers apart early in the sale—way too early, in fact.

As strategically well-placed as Misbah had been when he topped the sale, Snake and Whacko had been just as strategically misplaced. Well-intentioned Walmac had put the two colts as far forward in the sale as possible. As with Misbah they were on the first Wednesday. But this time the big money had gone home and the little money had not yet arrived.

Not only did no friends approach the owner with presale deals, they fled from his entreaties even to look at his colts. When they stood in the presale line behind the sales pavilion, no one was there to inspect them.

The Mexican handler for Walmac assigned to Hip No. 1128 had

obviously never heard of the gringo "Dorrance." And had he even tried to look Snake in his evil white eye it would have been impossible. His time in and around the walking lanes was spent on his hind legs, trying in earnest to drag the amigo to Lexington, or Tijuana maybe. Snake was from Secret Hello's third foal crop, which is known as the "bubble year," a risky time to breed to a young horse. Secret Hello's owner, former *Washington Star* publisher Joe Albritton, would not allow the stallion to cover more than forty mares a year—presumably to keep his progeny in short supply and therefore more valuable. While this was a traditional philosophy, a foal crop of forty was only about half the number needed to get a good representation at the track and enough winners to make the list of leading sires. A horse who doesn't make the leading sire lists in his first two years is not usually long on the bluegrass, and Secret Hello would be gone the following year. He had thirty named foals in his first foal crop, twenty-three of whom ultimately won races, nine of them when they were two years old in 1995. But the day Snake passed through Keeneland, Secret Hello was still a secret to the yearling market buyer and remains one to this day. His yearling average that year was $7,700. The only way Secret Hello could have been any colder as a sire would be if he had died.

Snake attracted only one bidder other than his owner, who had the last word at $9,000 and bought him back. Where was the dominant female and her phony bidders when they were needed?

Whacko—Hip No. 1113—behaved like a well-mannered little mannequin but drew only two bids and sold for $5,000—half his stud fee. Never again to be chased or bitten by Snake, he went to Puerto Rico where he would win frequently but where even winning frequently gains no respect.

Fortunately the dominant female was still honoring her voluntary "ban" from the sales. Not only would she have bought back the unwanted runt Whacko, she would have been saddened by the disappointment evident in the face of her crestfallen husband. The September sale, normally the income producer for Kentucky breeders, had generated a total of $5,000 for Two Bucks. But sales costs and commissions—due even on horses not sold—totaled nearly twice that. The abject failure had been as devastating as the Misbah sale had been exhilarating. The peaks and valleys of this business were as distant as heaven and hell. Even the turtle-shell hide developed in the roller-coaster newspaper business had not sufficiently hardened him. For this kind of sale result it was the Two Bucks owner who had not been properly "prepped."

Once again a perfect gentleman, Snake kept all four feet on the ground and loaded nicely into the van for the trip back to Two Bucks, where along with his blemished Mt. Livermore running mate he would add considerably to the overhead for least another six months. When thoroughbreds don't sell as yearlings, another year's upkeep of at least $15,000 each must be expended before they can be sold as two-year-olds in training.

During the eight-mile drive back to the farm, the chastened farm owner wondered about the prescience of a closing paragraph of a magazine profile done on him a few years earlier in Florida, where he had once edited a newspaper. Had he that day at Keeneland finally reached the destination the magazine had foreseen in his future?

Written by a former associate with whom he'd had difficulties, the article had first taken him to task for abandoning journalism in favor of adventures in politics and horse breeding—and then reached this conclusion: "As long as there is a village without an idiot, this guy will have work."

Hey, this could be the village.

PART 2

SAVING MONARCHOS

4

Up staggered the foal,
its hooves were jelly-knots of foam.
Then day sniffed with its blue nose
through the open stable window, and found them—
the foal nuzzling its mother,
velvet fumbling for her milk.

FERENC JUHASZ, Hungarian poet

She had never heard of the Dorrance cowboys and her English wasn't perfect, but the little pony-tailed immigrant had the best possible qualification to work at Two Bucks. She spoke "Horse" like it was her first language.

She had spent most of her young life with horses, encouraging them, smiling at them, trading the constant cheerfulness in her eyes for the natural kindness in theirs. They could read each other like books, of course only in Lithuanian.

Sigita had found the Two Bucks horses grand-looking and happy, but she was not so sure about the owner, who might be a kook—asking her to get up on the fiery black colt with the wild eye who'd seen his first saddle only the day before. But when the colt walked off like a carnival pony and never turned a hair, she reverted to the wait-and-see optimism that was her attitude toward any new job.

The entire "breaking" process—he insisted on calling it "starting"—

had taken perhaps six hours. In four days together they had started two yearling colts under saddle and had them loping circles like circus horses. This kind of progress had always taken her a couple of weeks, so maybe the owner knew something. Then he came up with the goofiest thing she had ever heard of: Instead of having a night watchman to shepherd the foaling mares, they were going to sew into the mare's vaginas tiny little transmitters that would "call you on the phone when the mare was ready to foal." This guy might be a fruitcake after all.

He showed her a little blue rectangle the size of a matchbox, only narrower. In a shelf on the side rested a small magnet—about a third of a matchstick—with surgical thread attached. A veterinarian came and stitched the box to one side of the mare's vulva, the magnet to the other. When the mare's water broke or the foal's feet began to pressure the area, the magnet was supposed to dislodge, sending an electronic signal that activated a dialing machine which called everyone who lived on the farm and delivered a recorded message: "This is the Two Bucks Foal-Alert System. Please come to Barn 2."

She'd believe in this contraption when she saw it work. And shortly after 11 P.M. on a mild Monday night in early February, it did. Still awake and dressed when the call came, she took less than three minutes to get from the manager's house to the foaling barn. When she got there the kook, whose house was a minute or so closer, was already kneeling in the stall beside a squirming black blob, whose head was already poking through his sticky traveling clothes.

"This one got here in no time," he said. "Regal just lays down and spits them right out. She's the only mare on the place that will get them on the ground before you can get here."

Actually he'd been at the barn when the alarm sounded, nightwatching anyway because Regal Band had tipped him off with a peculiar behavior pattern detected during two previous Two Bucks pregnancies.

"She is surly as hell the last week," he explained, "bites the stall bars when you walk past. Then in the last few hours before the foal arrives she gets all lovey-dovey and wants to be petted. When I gave her water at 10, she was all over me. I knew she was about to deliver, so I just stayed down here."

Her pattern was remarkably true to form. All three foals had arrived 342 days after conception between 11 P.M. and midnight. However irregular her past, in her new life Regal Band had worked like a clock. Pregnant on one cover, normal gestation period, and textbook delivery.

"Looks like a little bugger," he said.

Regal Band's previous two colts also had been small at birth, 75 to 80 pounds, which allowed them to slip easily into the world without trauma. Like this one, both had been jet black, and they'd been healthy from the start with noticeably thick bones and correctly aligned joints.

This foal indeed looked small, but Sigita couldn't tell much more about it, even the gender, because the rascal was still snug in the bag he came in, umbilical cord apparently still attached.

Barring complication, mares and foals are best left to their own devices for a while after delivery. The kooky owner seemed intent on this approach and backed out of the stall to watch from the aisle. Regal Band rested still as a statue, her head cocked to see the product of her labor at her haunches. But the foal began to stir, arching his wet black neck up from the yellow straw, his head turning this way and that, eyes like glistening ebony quarters—a cobra rising from a basket, only with sharply pricked ears.

The foal appeared to be watching a black and white barn cat, who was slinking along the edge of the hay storage area high in the barn rafters. A fat and reliable greeter of all new arrivals, Mr. Nonesuch never missed a foaling. But at the sound of a barn door sliding he darted back into the hay. It was the dominant female, who had also gotten a foal-alert call at the main house. Having retired after years of service as a foal night-watcher, she now frequently showed up tardy at the big events, bringing both curiosity and hot coffee.

The alertness of the foal caught her attention immediately.

"Oh, my," she said. "Look at that one. Boy or girl?"

"We don't know yet," said Sigita, who was standing ready with her trusty vial of iodine solution to disinfect the foal's navel. The umbilical cord is often severed during delivery, or shortly thereafter by the foal thrashing around. Sometimes it stays attached until the mother gets to her feet, after which the foal's navel stump needs to be disinfected.

Because Sigita viewed stump dipping and gender-determination inspection as a single event, she was doubly anxious. The kooky owner, however, apparently wanted everyone to guess the foal's gender by the look on its face—some kind of competition.

"So what do you two think it is?"

"It's a colt," Sigita speculated.

"Looks like a colt," said the dominant female. "Even prettier than the last one, better eye."

"No doubt about it then," said the kook, undoubtedly disappointed that there was no disagreement to foster discussion. "If his legs look as good as his head does, we'll be in business."

Regal Band's Black Tie Affair colt had been a gray model of Snake, only better looking. He had been sold as a weanling for $38,000 in the November 1997 Keeneland sale, which of course had displeased the dominant female and which she remembered while evaluating the new foal.

"At least wait until morning before you sell this one," she said, now as regally high-headed as the new foal.

The pronouncement, delivered as she moved toward the door, was correctly interpreted as a "good night." Among the many fruits of their years together was a certain persistence and efficiency of argument.

At the sound of her leaving, Mr. Nonesuch sprinted across a barn rafter again and Regal Band decided to get up.

Thoroughbred horses are born with spindly legs almost as long as they will ever get. It is the density of the bones and their proportion to the rest of the body that changes most significantly with growth. As a result thoroughbred foals seem to have more difficulty standing for the first time than other horses and hoofed animals. Those born in box stalls sometimes get steadying support from helpful humans to prevent injury from crashes into walls or hard barn floors. Those left to get up on their own almost always fall several times. Almost never are they as quick to their feet after birth as their mothers.

But when Regal Band extended her front legs to raise herself, her newborn was somehow in a position to do the same. As she rose, so did the foal; the mother in the slowly leveraged way of a practiced horse, the baby in one quick jump. Snap! Pop! There it was on its feet, trembling from one end to the other, in a perfect four-square brace.

"Well, I'll be damned," said the owner. "I've been foaling horses for fifteen years and I never saw a baby get up with his mother before in my life."

Sigita smiled. "Athlete," she said, lifting the tail for a gender check.

Indeed that's what he turned out to be. The next morning it was 47 degrees and sunny in Lexington, a nice day in February. He went outside with his mother and tried out his new legs.

The only thing that energizes a horse farm like the arrival of a new foal is the departure of an old one for a whole lot of money.

While Regal Band's new baby taught himself to lope perfect circles around his mother, the Mt. Livermore colt that had failed to sell as a yearling the September before was learning to run in a straight line with a human being on his back. The colt was headed where his Two Bucks breeder never intended for his horses to go and where this one in particular had no business going—to the industry's crash course school of horse racing.

Most thoroughbred horses are sold as "late" yearlings—in the fall of their second year of life—primarily because they have reached the point in their physical and mental development when they can be most efficiently started under saddle and taught to be a racehorse. Like high school athletes, they've reached 90 percent physical maturity and can be assessed for their potential in athletic competition. Other types of horses expected to perform, like hunter-jumpers and cutting horses, are culled for athletes about the same time. But their training regimen is considerably slower and actual competition comes much later in their lives.

For decades literally thousands of young thoroughbred colts have been picked out at yearling sales and purchased each year with one race in mind—the Kentucky Derby, the first jewel of the Triple Crown, which takes place on the first Saturday in May each year, four months after a horse's third calendar birthday.

Even trainers not interested in the Triple Crown want to get their hands on their future charges before they turn two years old, so their training regimen can be coordinated with their physical and emotional maturity. Like people, horses do not all mature at the same age. Some are physically and mentally further along than others. But horses have an added problem in that for marketing and competition purposes they all are considered to have the same birthday—January l. So a colt born in January is almost twenty-four months old when he turns "two," but a horse born in May or June has had 25 percent less growth time. To complicate matters further, equine skeletal and muscular development often is incomplete until horses are four.

So when most horses begin enduring the stress of athletic training, at between eighteen and twenty-four months old, neither their brains nor their bones have fully developed. Some can race when they are two years old. Some, like the Mt. Livermore colt, should not be asked to do so.

It is usually only the precocious, early maturing babies who can be pushed along fast enough to race at age two—a traditional prerequisite for contesting the Derby and the other classic three-year-old races from which most of the valuable stallions emerge. It was the urgent quest for these animals during the booming, hurry-up decade of the 1990s that caused a third source of potential Derby horses—the sale of two-year-olds in training—to become all the rage. Even staid old Keeneland, which had always regarded this type of sale as a down market of last resort unworthy of its esteemed name, jumped in headlong. And so did tiny Two Bucks, with neither name nor esteem to risk. But at both ends of the thoroughbred spectrum, the attraction was the same—Japanese money.

No buyers were better heeled or in a bigger hurry than investors from Japan, where racing had caught on as public entertainment in a way American enthusiasts could only envy. The Japanese go to the races in far greater numbers and bet far more than Americans do. A Japanese track will often handle more wagering in a single day than an average American racetrack does in an entire meet. Almost overnight Japanese buyers began making their presence felt at sales of American two-year-olds in training the same way they had previously spurred the yearling and broodmare markets.

By the mid-1990s, the dream of every pinhooker in America was to sell the Japanese a two-year-old racehorse like Unbridled's Song, the son of 1990 Kentucky Derby winner Unbridled that Ernie Paragallo had bought for $200,000 at Saratoga in July 1994. Eight months later, at the Barretts select sale for two-year-olds near Los Angeles, Paragallo spectacularly sold Unbridled's Song to Japanese import-export tycoon Hiroshi Fujita for a record $1.4 million. The two-day sale set every kind of record imaginable for two-year-olds, including gross revenue—$22.5 million—and average price—$140,000. Stunningly, thirty-nine horses sold for $200,000 or more, nine for more than $400,000 and the overall average was higher than that at both the Saratoga select yearling sale and the September Keeneland yearling sale the previous year. The Japanese alone spent nearly $15 million, 67 percent of the sale's gross revenue and twice as much as they'd spent at Keeneland's top-of-the-market July yearling sale.

If the sale itself wasn't spectacular enough, Paragallo later returned Fujita's $1.4 million—the highest price paid for a thoroughbred of any age since 1992—and took Unbridled's Song back when he was discovered to have a bone chip in his right front ankle. But it was only the huge price and the relatively minimal significance of the ankle flake that made news. Bone chips—and other skeletal destruction—are common occupational hazards for both the two-year-olds in training and the people who buy and sell them.

Two-year-old thoroughbreds are 800- to 1,000-pound animals supported by legs with bones the size of broom handles. More significantly, these are bones not yet hard enough to withstand the stress and trauma of daily racetrack training, a regimen that basically calls for an hour or so of strenuous exercise and 23 hours of standing in a stall. This routine can result in uneven or incomplete bone growth and lesions known as osteochondritis dessicans, or OCDs.

Since the advent of the radiograph repository, they have become better known as "goddam OCDs" and the bane of the existence of all owners of young thoroughbreds, especially the pinhookers. For sale horses, the "goddam OCDs" have but one implication—weak bones. They are basically soft spots in the bone surface that can either fill in and harden like normal cartilage or become an insidious cyst that eats away at the bone until it cracks or negatively implicates a joint, ligament or tendon. The negative possibility raises in the mind of every prospective buyer what it did to Mr. Fujita—that someday when his horse was flying down the track in a Triple Crown race, the joint would jam or the bone would snap, causing the horse not only to lose, but likely to break down and have to be euthanized on the track, probably before a worldwide television audience. And then everyone would suspect that the owner and trainer knew their horse had OCDs and recklessly ran it anyway.

Fearing both financial loss and global embarrassment, buyers therefore flee from "goddam OCDs" as if they were the devil incarnate, even though the horse might never be bothered and could go on to win $1.3 million and become a sire worth many times that, as did Unbridled's Song.

Some horses do break down while racing because of bones weakened by OCDs. Equally as many or more do so because their leg bones and joints are malformed to begin with, or because they take a bad step while favoring something sore or painful elsewhere in their bodies. A horse favoring one foot, for example, can ruin another by shifting to it an inordinate burden of weight. Most injuries and breakdowns can be traced in some way to the repetitive stress placed on bones, joints, ligaments and tendons by horses during exercise. It can happen in the pasture when they are babies, or on the track when they are nine years old. But it happens most frequently to young horses while they are two-year-olds in training or immediately thereafter, before their bones have had a chance to mature and harden. Eventually the stress of racing sends all horses to the sidelines for one reason or another.

The chip in his ankle never bothered the famous Unbridled's Song, but bad feet did, which is another thing he had in common with the Mt. Livermore colt. When growing up at Two Bucks, he was often fleet enough to keep up with his pasture pacesetter, Snake. But he frequently came back to the barn from these encounters with his feet in tatters, a problem not uncommon among offspring of his sire. Not only were his feet a bit small for his big body, they were not hard and tough enough to deal with the rocks that Snake skipped over as if they didn't exist. Many were the days when the Mt. Livermore colt went to the front pasture at Two Bucks with his feet padded and gaily wrapped in red tape against bruising.

Familiar with the sight and its cause, the dominant female was both stunned and unhappy to find out that he was headed for a training sale. Not only did he have terrible feet, he was a "late" colt, born in early May, up to four months behind older and tougher horses like his traveling companion Snake.

With her unerring moral compass dead on the right direction, she chastised her husband and regretted not having partnered with him in the horse business, which would have given her an equal say in the decision, and thus a veto. "I can't believe that you of all people would do this," she scolded him. "You take such good care of him, and then you send him off to be wrecked."

Even the pinhookers, many of whom had fallen for the Mt. Livermore colt while inspecting the Two Bucks yearlings, had passed on him for the reason of his May birth. Pinhookers like colts born in January and February, for they know better than anyone the nature of the travails ahead.

However, the good caretaker of horses, whose moral compass had been permanently adjusted for pragmatism by his years as a corporate media executive, was adamant.

"Oh, he's pretty mature for his age. Besides, living with Snake has toughened him up a lot."

But the nature of his response was also a legacy of previous experience in another field of endeavor—politics. This was "doublespeak." And if forced by later events to "clarify" it, a press secretary would have explained that what he really meant to say was: "He's gotta go. He's our only hope for revenue before the fall sales."

He'd known revenue shortages in the newspaper business. But the reality of it in the new life he had chosen had been driven home to him one day by a visitor, a stranger brought to his farm by a fellow racing commissioner. The guy was loaded and shopping for a hobby farm, and the racing commission buddy knew that Two Bucks had been purchased originally as a real-estate investment and might still be for sale. During his visit, the out-of-towner had asked how many thoroughbred mares the farm owned. When told eight, he had just nodded and said nothing. But later, thinking he was out of the owner's earshot, the visitor was overheard laughing with the intermediary who brought him, also an extremely wealthy individual. "How in the hell would you like to try to run your life on the income from eight mares?" he asked.

The belittling and condescending nature of the comment reminded the Two Bucks man not only of why he'd disliked so many corporate high-rollers, but also how brutally honest and accurate their assessments so often were.

Except for the sale of Regal Band's Black Tie Affair weanling, Two Bucks had realized no revenue to speak of from the 1997 November breeding-stock sale, which had established a high-water mark for the industry. Nearly $200 million had been spent in the first seven days of the twelve-day sale—more money than ever spent at a thoroughbred auction anywhere anytime in history. But while the industry was celebrating its complete revival, Two Bucks had gotten virtually nothing for its yearlings in September and a barely profitable price for its best weanling.

The farm needed a sale in the worst way. And indeed, sending to two-year-old-training a seventeen-month-old colt with bad feet, who had already had a chip removed from his ankle, was in fact the worst way.

Remorse over his own callousness and fear of reprisal—in the form of moralistic carping forever by the dominant female—did result in his adding to the wretched decision a humane caveat. Instead of sending the colt directly to a trainer that pinhooks for a living, the owner shipped him along with Snake to a South Carolina conditioner known specifically for gentle handling of two-year-olds, Mitchell C. (Mickey) Preger, who had trained the champion mare of 1983. Maybe his champion's name—Ambassador of Luck—would be an omen. Preger accepted the colt with the provision that training would be halted and the sale forgone if the colt exhibited any signs of stress or injury. Miraculously he did not. Training barefoot in the soft sand of the Camden training center, he flowered in the hands of Preger's son, Mickey, Jr., and was turned over, sound of foot and mind, to Kirkwood Stables, a leading consignor of two-year-olds, which put him on a plane to California. Having learned as a reporter that by the time a bandwagon is recognizable, it is already moving too fast to board, the owner of Two Bucks was running after it anyway.

The tidal wave of Japanese money in the mid-1990s had made Barretts Select the premier marketplace for two-year-olds headed abroad. But by the time Two Bucks and the Mt. Livermore colt got there it was a sale on the road to decline, soon to be overshadowed as a two-year-old market by mighty Keeneland.

Sales in Florida the preceding month had been spotty, the number of horses up and the number of buyers down. But in California it was the nature of the missing that was most discouraging. After noticeably slacking off in both 1996 and 1997, the Japanese didn't bother to show up at all in 1998.

But the Mt. Livermore colt could run very fast—which was still really all that mattered.

*

Watching horses run is without question the best way to evaluate their potential for any athletic competition. The practiced eye will catch the efficiency of their "action"—how one part moves in relation to another—the length of their stride, how they carry their head and neck, their general demeanor or attitude toward running. From all this an expert can determine what kind of surface best suits the horse, whether it is built to be a sprinter on dirt or a longer distance "route" horse on grass—and, most important, whether it can run at all.

Like so much in the thoroughbred world, sales of two-year-olds in training have their origin in a social event—a coming-out party of sorts on that special afternoon when the racing elite, already gathered at the Saratoga spa for the annual August meet, would walk over to watch the juveniles "gallop" on the grass.

Galloping is what horses do for fun in the pasture, so watching them gallop under saddle and rider was how they were evaluated. What they do at training sales, however, is "breeze" or "work." The terms have been synonymous in the lexicon since the day in 1963 when *Daily Racing Form* columnist Charles Hatton reported on the training of a brilliantly fast son of the legendary Native Dancer.

"Raise a Native worked five furlongs along the backstretch at Belmont Park this morning," wrote Hatton. "The trees swayed." Raise a Native was not galloping. He was running all out.

Horse trainers in Raise a Native's era and every other agree wholeheartedly that how fast a two-year-old can cover one-eighth of a mile is virtually meaningless in evaluating his future as a racehorse. Yet in the 1990s both the best and the worst of them allowed this measure to become the standard of worth and purchase of young runners at all the nation's thoroughbred sales.

The disgraceful nature of this reasoning is inescapable. It became the simplest and most effective way of justifying for naive owners the outrageous prices they were having to pay for horses whose quality and pedigree would never justify them at a yearling sale. The combination of the booming world economy and booming interest in quick profit on a "big horse" had seduced them just as it had seduced sellers and sales companies. Everybody knew that the faster the horses "breezed," the more the Japanese would pay for them.

How fast a horse can actually travel an eighth of a mile depends largely on four factors—natural fleetness of foot, the weather that day, the nature of the surface and how tired the horse already might be from running. Unlike human athletes, horses have not gotten bigger, stronger and faster over the years. But two factors have changed—the surfaces they run on and the medications they might be given to enable performance.

While some horses move more efficiently on soft ground, which is more forgiving and therefore less stressful to hooves and bones, most of them move faster across hard surfaces, which over time are more likely to cause stress-related injury.

While two-year-olds used to be assessed late in the summer or early fall before they were to turn three, the important juvenile sales take place in winter, when many of them are still short of twenty-four months old. Because the sales take place in warm-weather spots like California and Florida, they inspire images of young horses running barefoot across soft sandy beaches, like the gallops at the Camden Training Center in South Carolina. But the opposite is true. In both states the combination of sun and the scarcity of rain keeps racetracks the texture of concrete. The top can be maintained loose and sandy but the base is effectively interstate highway. The result is that whether on grass or dirt, the times recorded by horses running in California or Florida—in training or in actual races—are generally "faster" than those in the rest of the country.

In North America, horse races are measured in furlongs—eighths of a mile—and timed in fifths or tenths of a second. Until Secretariat came along in 1973, the fastest the Kentucky Derby had ever been run was 2 minutes flat by the mighty Northern Dancer—which is one of the reasons the race became known as "the fastest 2 minutes in sports." The Dancer covered the one and a quarter miles—10 furlongs—in 120 seconds, an average of 12 seconds a furlong, or about 38 miles per hour.

Races at shorter distances can be run considerably quicker, especially on surfaces consistently harder and "faster" than the Churchill Downs strip. The *average* time for a three-quarter-mile (six-furlong) race by top stakes-quality horses at Santa Anita, a track not far from the Barretts sales complex and one of the nation's fastest, is 1 minute, $8^{2}/_{5}$ seconds. It is commonly expressed as 1:08.2 or 1:08.40. A horse traveling three-quarters of a mile in 68.40 seconds is averaging about 11.40 seconds a furlong—or between 40 and 41 miles per hour.

When two-year-olds eventually compete in six-furlong races at Santa Anita in the autumn before their third birthday, the average time is a full 2 seconds slower—1 minute, $10^{2}/_{5}$ seconds. This means they are averaging 11.73 seconds a furlong, slightly faster than Northern Dancer in the Kentucky Derby, which is half a mile longer, and considerably slower than a good older stakes-horse going three-quarters of a mile at Santa Anita.

But during the 1990s any thoroughbred traveling that slow at a juvenile sale fit Walter Matthau's definition of Jack Lemmon's linguine when he threw it against the wall during their famous scene from *The Odd Couple*—"ga'bage."

In inciting his spectacular 1995 sale at Barretts, Unbridled's Song sped one-eighth of a mile on two different occasions in $10^{1}/_{5}$ seconds. Times such as these were by the end of the decade both commonplace and mandatory for the top-selling horses. Carried over two furlongs this speed produces frequent quarter-mile times of "21 and change," meaning that horses sustained a speed of slightly less than 45 miles an hour for a quarter of a mile, a relative sound barrier for a horse.

Kirkwood Stables, the South Carolina consignor that took the Mt. Livermore colt to the sale, was not known for sending out the fastest horses. The reputation of the proprietor, Kip Elser, was for producing a horse fast enough but that would also "stay together" after the sale—meaning one that was less likely to have been permanently damaged by the ordeal. Kirkwood horses had a history of going on to win stakes races.

Still, in order to compete successfully then and now, Kirkwood's horses have to fly, which is exactly what the colt from Two Bucks did—an eighth of a mile in 10.60 seconds. This made him a big hit.

Not only was he a bullet going over the grounds, his radiographs in the "suppository" were perfect. The chip was gone from his ankle. His throat was clean, symmetrical and performing perfectly. Despite being younger than most of the others, he was big, handsome and shined to perfection. He had attracted the attention of exactly the kind of owners Two Bucks was looking for—the one group of Japanese buyers on the grounds and Michael King Racing, a high-powered stable, owned by and named after a principal in the noted television producing company, King World, which syndicated *The Oprah Winfrey Show.*

So impressive was Hip No. 196 that the sight of him being led into the sales ring made the Two Bucks owner's own throat clog up with anticipation. Wearing the horseman's uniform of boots and khakis and baseball hat, a cell phone stuck to his ear, he positioned himself just outside the rear of the pavilion. Just another bloodstock agent consulting a client concerning the lot about to be sold, or preparing to place a discreet bid by phone.

Meanwhile, the colt strolled into the sales ring on the end of a shank and confidently surveyed the crowd from prancing toes as if it were a pasture with Snake in it somewhere.

Outside the arena, watching through the glass, his owner conveyed the image through his cell phone to the dominant female back in Woodford County and repeated the bids as they began to flash by on a giant monitor above him: $10,000 . . . $20,000 . . . $30,000 . . . $50,000.

"Moving pretty good," he said. Then "$70,000 . . . $80,000 . . . $90,000 . . . $100,000. . . . That's double what we paid for his mother."

He could feel the tension flowing out of his face, weeks of worry crevices in his forehead flooding with liquid ease: "$150,000 . . . 160 . . . 170 . . . $175,000."

"That's more than you expected at Keeneland," she said.

"It's still going . . . 180 . . . 190 . . . $200,000 . . . still going."

This was home-run territory, as exciting as the day he saw Frank Stronach scrambling to bid on Misbah at Keeneland and as stunning as the pinhooker Paragallo opening the bidding at $100,000.

But the Mt. Livermore colt was not done: "210 . . . 220 . . . 230 . . . 240. This is all live money," he said. "Our bids stopped at 174."

He wished he could see the dominant female's face, to see if she could hide this elation, too, the way she always did. Like the mare Regal Band, she preferred to show only disdain or indifference, keeping secret all the good stuff. You didn't want to play poker with the dominant female. But her usual mask was not needed now. The cell phone and silence were doing their work nicely.

"Still going," he said: "250 . . . 260 . . . 265."

He loved repeating the numbers, so relieved and into it he was playing with her a little bit now, trying to taunt her into a display of excitement. She wouldn't bite.

He repeated the auctioneer some more, word for word: "$270,000, . . . Do I hear $275,000? 275? . . . Anyone?"

That was it. The gavel came down. "Sold. $270,000." But he didn't inform her right away. He went silent, too, like he might have suffered a rapture-induced heart attack or stroke of some kind. He knew that in the dark safety behind her cell-phone mask she would be doing an anxiety dance to know, up on her toes like the colt himself. Was the sale over? How much? Or, more likely for her, did the horse even sell at all? Had something gone wrong? What was going on?

She could not hold out for long, he knew. Her own weapons, the cell phone and the silence, had been turned on her now. With him she would always pay a price for being an ice maiden.

"Well?" she said finally, the exasperation in her voice. "What's going on? What's going on?"

He smiled in dual victory: "270. We got 270."

Silence. She was composing herself.

"Congratulations," she said, professionally, like she was closing a real-estate deal with a stranger. Like it was his horse and his money, not theirs, and that she had no personal interest in what had just happened.

There on opposite ends of a cellular connection, they both knew better. No doubt in his mind she was as thrilled as he. But ever the worrywart, she looked upon enjoying the moment as feckless frivolity. Enticing her into feckless frivolity had long been among his missions impossible, one of those female "irresistibles" he couldn't let alone.

Back in Woodford County, the dominant female knew that he knew she was glowing with satisfaction. Happy that he had not dumped the colt for $65,000 the previous September, which would have been considerably more prudent and still profitable. That sum would have covered both the original cost of the mare and the stud fee on her second pregnancy. Buying the yearling back, paying the grand for the ankle surgery and trying the treacherous two-year-old in training route of which she had been skeptical had been a major risk she admired him for taking. But showing the Two Bucks man exuberance over the success of his gamble—not only with their money but with the health of a nice young horse—would only encourage him up more beanstalks to be chopped down. And he'd climbed enough of those already on his own. This was a man who thinks he knows everything and takes neither direction nor discouragement. No feckless frivolity for him. No, sir. She'd sooner strip off her underwear in public.

Outside the sales pavilion in California, the Kentucky home-run hitter was crossing the plate to high-fives, back pats and way-to-goes. The professionals who had liked the colt but had missed the profit opportunity were especially congratulatory. Mindless betting at high odds is what they appreciated most.

But as far as the hitter himself was concerned, they could have it. He reveled in the moment—but only for a moment. The party going on in his mind took place under a huge banner which read "Luck—Not Genius."

That the young Mt. Livermore colt, soon to be named Roger the Dodger by his new owner Michael King after his partner and brother, had survived training and run sound and drug-free at Barretts was a miracle. That he would be bought by a trainer as good as Steve Young for an owner as potent as the King racing stable gave it a gilded edge.

That it could ever happen again was highly unlikely.

Though not a religious man, he knew what had just happened had biblical roots—the thoroughbred industry's version of passing through the valley of the shadow of death. Some omnipotent power beyond his understanding must have been responsible for his safe passage, and if at all possible he would never pass this way again.

If this view needed validation, it was not long in coming. Roger the Dodger had to be rested for months before returning to training. And when he did, his bad feet prevented him from becoming a racehorse. Despite Young's valiant and expert efforts, Roger the Dodger, who was among the fastest thirty horses at Barretts, never started a race. Neither did the fastest and most expensive colt in the Barretts sale that year, Public Figure, who was bought for $1 million by an important new player in the game, Prince Ahmed Salman of Saudi Arabia.

Both animals constituted beautiful, brilliantly fast but glaring evidence of why the Two Bucks breeder never wanted another creative masterpiece from his breeding program to end up at a juvenile training sale, and why he was about to climb another beanstalk trying to prevent it.

5

Ride a cockhorse to Banbury Cross,
To see a fine lady upon a white horse,
Rings on her fingers and bells on her toes,
She shall have music wherever she goes.

RIDE A COCKHORSE, Anonymous

If Murray Smith were an automobile instead of a lovely young Florida pinhooker, she would be a red Corvette convertible—sleek, fast and expensive. Besides being blond and glorious-looking, she also has a keen eye for a young horse that will make money. So it was not surprising that when she came to Kentucky shopping for yearlings in March 1999, she hooked up with the veteran British-born bloodstock agent Richard Galpin, whose keenness of eye in the same regard is legendary. Nor was it coincidence that Galpin would take her shopping at Two Bucks in Woodford County. A frequent visitor to the farm, he had previewed the previous year's foal crop many times and knew of at least one colt there likely to catch her eye. Equally important, having long ago sized up the Two Bucks owner, Galpin realized that escorting a buyer who was such an eye-catcher herself might be of some benefit. In light of recent history, to close this particular sale he would need a diversion or a perk of some kind.

The Two Bucks guy was different from many breeders in that he was willing to sell privately to pinhookers off the farm. Some farm owners simply do not want to take the time to shine up baby horses for bargain-hunting tire-kickers whose goal is to "cherry-pick" the foal crop. Others cannot stand the ego deflation that occurs when the pinhookers, who often know horses and the market better than the breeders, score big at public auction after owning the baby only a few weeks. The Two Bucks guy didn't seem to care how much cash he left on the table for the pinhooker, as long as the original deal was deemed profitable enough to him. He subscribed to the mantra of Nelson Bunker Hunt, the legendary Texas billionaire who rose and fell along with everyone else in the "sport of kings" in the 1980s: "The more everyone makes the better." That and a periodic weight problem were all he and Bunker Hunt had ever had in common.

But with the finicky breeders, there was always something. And the hurdle the bloodstock broker Galpin faced that day was, like the breeder himself, considerably more complicated than price.

On the day that Galpin was to escort the vaunted cherry-picker Murray Smith, the Two Bucks owner still had a bad taste in his mouth from his last sale to a female Florida pinhooker, Becky Thomas. The previous summer, when Galpin had scouted the Two Bucks babies, he had fingered two as standout possibilities for his pinhooking clients—the early gray colt by first-year sire Maria's Mon and a robust bay, born April 30 and sired by the red hot second-year sire Tabasco Cat, whose first foal crop had sold like gangbusters at the November 1997 Keeneland sale. In July 1998, Becky Thomas had gone to Two Bucks, fallen in love with the Tabasco Cat colt, and begun trying to buy him. The price—a whopping $137,500—and the deal were not finalized until late August, following a meeting with Thomas at Saratoga. Because the colt was actually sold long after the August 1 deadline for the Keeneland November 1998 breeding-stock sale and didn't even change hands until September, the Two Bucks owner had assumed—erroneously—that the colt could not show up at public auction until the yearling sales the following year. Certainly he didn't expect to see the colt cataloged in the premier weanling sale that November—which is exactly where he showed up.

Either Becky Thomas had entered the horse before she actually owned him, or she had somehow managed to get around the entry deadline, which was not all that uncommon. The pique of the Two Bucks man should have been aimed not at Thomas, who was just conducting her own business, but at his own ignorance. By then he should have known that in the thoroughbred business rules come in dual sets—one for the "ins" and one for the rest. Whether being interpreted by sales company inspection teams, racing secretaries or "suppository" veterinarians, rules for the right horses with the right connections are quite flexible, while those for the rest can be quite rigid.

No matter how the Tabasco Cat colt got into the November weanling sale, he should not have been there. Late spring foals often do not make good November sale weanlings for the simple reason that weaning is a traumatic event that temporarily sets back growth and development. The rush to strike at the sales while Tabasco Cat was still a hot-market sire had pushed the six-month-old colt through weaning and two changes of environment in eight weeks. The big strapping baby who left Two Bucks in September looked gaunt, depressed and awkward in the sales ring in November—not a good representative of either the sire Tabasco Cat or the dam Lichi, who had been one of Two Bucks' most profitable producers. Although hammered down as "sold" for over $100,000, he did not actually change hands. Worst of all Thomas obviously had to be disappointed with her purchase, which was not good for the breeder who liked her and respected her taste in horses.

Like Becky Thomas, the pinhooker beside Galpin in his Jeep Cherokee as he drove to Two Bucks was looking for, in her own words, "a quick profit." Although Murray Smith had built her reputation buying yearlings and selling them as two-year-olds in training, she had no such intention that day. Whatever she bought would be put into the summer or fall yearling sales. Galpin's problem was twofold. First he had to convince the Two Bucks guy that his buyer was sincere—that a sale did not mean the colt's certain destiny was the big Calder speed contest the following year. And then he had to have a special horse, one that could make a profit for the breeder in March and for Murray a few months later. By March, yearlings are so far along in their development that breeders have a good idea what they will be worth in the sales ring three months later. To leave a lot of profit on the table at this point, the breeder would have to be pretty strapped for cash. But Galpin's long tenure in the horse business had seen him in many deals in which his position was more pinched and the participants far more outrageous. Though from vastly different backgrounds, he and the Two Bucks owner had much in common, including age, paunch and a history of controversy. If no sale resulted, at least they would both have a good time admiring Murray Smith at work.

Waiting for Galpin in the yearling barn, the Two Bucks owner had the distinct feeling of going through the motions. Even if the persistent old Brit kept his appointment—which he often didn't—or showed up late—which he often did—the preparation for Murray Smith was all futile.

"Galpin's client has a great eye," he told Sigita. "She won't jump on anything but the gray colt and he's not going to a pinhooker."

Sigita had become accustomed to these emphatic declarations, all uttered with the authority of a death sentence. She had seen them also reversed with equal finality overnight, almost always with an elaborate explanation. But she believed he meant it when he said he wouldn't sell the gray colt, who within a few days after his birth had been proclaimed "the best horse on the farm ever."

Regal Band's babies were invariably his favorites. And his special relationship with the Maria's Mon colt had been established early. He would be forever at the fence watching the colt move—which Regal's suckling did constantly, running perfect concentric circles around his mother, each one larger than before; then he would reduce them again, each one smaller as he returned to his mother—rings that could have been illustrations in a geometry book. Then the colt would nurse, nap and start over. Each day he would venture farther away until all the mares and babies were encircled. Once satisfied with his bravery, he would screech to a halt, wheel and run an obstacle course back through them toward his mother, kicking up a heel at each as he passed. "Just like Snake," the Two Bucks man declared. "He can run all day."

Sigita had seen tears in her boss's eyes the night he sold the Black Tie Affair weanling out of Regal Band at Keeneland; had seen the desolation on his face when a year later Snake came home from the racetrack with a stress fracture above his ankle before he ever had a chance to start. Most people would have given up on a cheap Secret Hello gelding as a racehorse, but not him. Snake had screws surgically implanted in his ankle and was back running again, strong as ever. At Two Bucks, Regal Band's babies were such treasures that Sigita had even been reluctant to disclose that it was the Maria's Mon colt she had discovered buried in the sand and trapped under a fence.

Each afternoon during the summer, Regal and the three other mares in her pasture were brought into the shade of the spacious, airy training barn and allowed to spend the hottest part of the day cooled by huge electric fans. The pens were made of 12-foot metal corral panels with a bottom rung about a foot off the ground. Underneath one panel late one afternoon, she and Bruce had found the Maria's Mon colt wedged to his ribcage, a half-foot deep in the sand, his head and forefeet on one side, his hindquarters on the other. There was no way to pull him to safety.

Horses that discover themselves "cast" usually panic and struggle, sometimes breaking their own limbs with violent flailing. A world champion reining horse belonging to the dominant female broke a stifle joint and had been lost that way while on loan to the Kentucky Horse Park.

In these episodes, rescue is often the most difficult and dangerous part. But the Maria's Mon colt remained cool and lay undisturbed and motionless while the corral gate was disassembled and removed. Only when completely free did he repeat his now familiar deer-like leap to his feet and return to his mother, his only souvenirs slight abrasions on his leg—and his ego. If his pride had been damaged, no one could tell by looking.

At first Sigita had told the owner only that "one of the babies hurt his leg on the gates" and suggested that the metal pens no longer be used for afternoon naps. He'd brushed off the recommendation until told that the cast colt had been Regal Band's. Afterwards, the metal corrals were never again used for foals or weanlings.

In light of all the grousing she had heard from her boss over the outcome of the sale of Lichi's Tabasco Cat colt, Sigita could not envision the Maria's Mon colt being sold that day. They were all counting on him to be the successful runner Regal Band needed to become a profitable broodmare. And already consignors had been around to inspect the remaining star of the foal crop for marketing at the yearling sales. So if Mr. Galpin's client had interest only in the gray colt and the Two Bucks owner wasn't going to sell him to a pinhooker, all the brushing and shining she was doing in preparation for the visit was for nothing—not unusual in her line of work.

As women go, Murray Smith does not depend on charm as a business tool. Her Sphinx-like demeanor might well have been copied from another pinhooker of equally renowned eye, the Irishman Bobby Barry, also a regular shopper at Two Bucks. Both see everything when they look at a horse but do so as if any sign of life on their part would somehow double the price they ultimately would have to pay. Bobby Barry's silence has an instinctively friendly feel to it, but Murray Smith's smacks of feline aloofness, an untouchable encasement of rarefied air. Watching her walk around the farm as if she feared smelling something foul was reminiscent of Bobby Barry, and it occurred to the farm proprietor that if either ever came again he should recruit the dominant female as hostess, so as to equalize the elevation.

Still, if forced to choose between having a horse purloined by Bobby Barry or Murray Smith, there was no contest. Besides having a wonderful eye for the horse, Murray Smith owns the world's most impressive pair of blue jeans, which she frequently wears on shopping trips and into which she had been poured that March day. The jeans have a way of dominating any barn, sales pavilion or pasture in which they appear. So neither the bloodstock agent nor the owner of the gray colt noticed how high Murray Smith's nose was being carried that day, or caught a single glance of indifference.

The visit was brief, the inspection cursory. And when the visitors had gone, they left behind not a single sign of interest. Their Two Bucks hosts were doubly relieved. Not only had there been no offer on the colt, he had accepted the inspection of his feet by strangers without trying to kick them into oblivion.

Prior to weaning, the Maria's Mon colt had been a model of good conduct. From the minute babies are born at Two Bucks, they are led and handled daily. And each day during the first three weeks they are "asked for their feet"—which means to allow a human being to lift each foot off the ground so the hoof can be cleaned. They soon do this willingly, a lesson learned for life, which prepares them for what they must do every day when they become racehorses.

But what a foal learns while still in his mother's care often must be repeated after weaning. And so, when his mother moved to the other side of the farm without him, the Maria's Mon colt became a prime candidate for "Dorrance school." Although the farrier had trimmed his hooves four times previously, the colt would not allow trimming the first time it was tried after weaning. When the blacksmith reached for a front foot, the colt reared and struck. When he moved toward a hind leg, the sharp little feet shot out repeatedly with bone-breaking force. Suddenly the model of deportment became a model of Snake. Methods of behavior modification can be best learned from the mares themselves, who begin disciplining their babies from birth. A foal who nurses too aggressively the first time is bitten sharply on the rump right away. The owner of Two Bucks once saw a quarter-horse mother cure a kick-happy newborn by simply lifting a rear hock (knee) into his midsection and sending him flying across the stall. The colt never kicked at anything again the rest of his life.

At the ensuing Dorrance class, the Maria's Mon colt was simply moved in a circle in his stall on the end of a lead rope until he was tired. Every time he stopped, an effort was made to lift a rear foot. When the colt kicked out, he received an instant, loud, open-handed smack on the kicking leg and was forced to move in a circle some more. A half-dozen slaps later he had learned that if he didn't kick out, he wouldn't be scared by the noise or chased again.

By the time Murray Smith and Richard Galpin came around picking up the colt's feet and running their fingers along the tendons of his legs, the whole process had become acceptable between his ears.

Still, the experience had been an important test. Regal Band offspring were smart little kids. They often refused to accept from strangers what they eagerly received from people they knew. Perhaps the Maria's Mon colt had sensed what Sigita and the others had not—exactly how hard Murray Smith had fallen for him.

The visitors had scarcely left the neighborhood when the bloodstock agent called back on his cell phone asking for a price. The proprietor was ready. He figured the colt, nice as he was, was worth only about $40,000, which was better than five times the $7,500 stud fee. Pinhookers like Barry and Smith never liked paying over $50,000 or $60,000, especially for the offspring of unheralded first-time sires like Maria's Mon. So Galpin was given a number designed to put an end to the matter once and for all—"$105,000 to me"—which meant that Galpin's customary 5 percent finder's fee would be added on top. Galpin blanched and hung up, but he called back momentarily.

"She's willing to go $100,000. And you and I can work something out on the commission," he reported.

This response was totally unexpected. Murray Smith could not possibly be willing to pay so much for a colt with so little on his catalog page. Becky Thomas hadn't even looked seriously at him the previous July. Several other shoppers had bypassed him, too.

The breeder didn't want to sell the colt to a pinhooker, but the offer was too good to pass up. How the hell could he not?

Stalling, he asked Galpin to give him a little while to think it over. A mess was developing. Murray Smith had put the proprietor of Two

Bucks precisely where he had been too many times before in his life—caught between two attractive women. This time it was worse. Both had money.

He didn't want his gray colt to be owned by the good-looking, pinhooking Murray Smith. He wanted him to have the same owner as his sire Maria's Mon—the good-looking, horse-racing Josephine Abercrombie. And the colt had already been more or less promised to her—and for a lot less money.

Josephine Abercrombie is not a red Corvette convertible. She is a Mercedes, vintage at that and in remarkable condition to boot. A multimillionaire oil, gas and real-estate heiress, she owns blue jeans older than Murray Smith and they still fit quite nicely, thank you. Long before Murray came along, Josephine had worn her jeans to Two Bucks, too, to see the same baby horse and thought him fabulous. And unlike Murray, Josephine did not turn up her nose at the owner. She was friendly, vivacious and full of compliments. She'd charmed him right out of his socks. Four times married, she knew how to look at men and the possessions they prized. Even men fired by her were left admirers.

When she pulled a good horse from the trainer Sir Mark Prescott in 1997, the British press descended on him for reaction. "Ms. Abercrombie sent me wonderful horses and I will miss them," said the witty trainer. "But a woman who has dispatched so many husbands certainly has the right to dispatch her trainer."

Following her visit to Two Bucks, Josephine had sent a photographer back to take pictures of the Regal Band foal, along with the comment that he was a dead ringer for Maria's Mon and might well be the best baby in his first crop. This gesture was followed by a not-so-well-disguised feeler from a friendly veterinarian concerning at what price the colt could be bought by Ms. Abercrombie. The Two Bucks man sent back the message that "she can have him for $45,000." A few days later her farm manager, Clifford Barry, sent another message that the price was fine but Pin Oak had decided against purchasing any of Maria's Mon babies privately, opting instead to wait until public auction when they were yearlings. Wherever Regal Band's colt was to be sold, Barry said, Ms. Abercrombie would be there looking to buy him.

This is a common practice. Sometimes stallion owners deliberately pay excessive prices at sales for first-crop babies to attract public attention to the sire and drive up the early sale averages. Now and then they even quietly buy all or a portion of an exceptional baby in advance, leave them in the sales under the names of their breeders and then run up the price astronomically. The cost in sales commissions is probably eventually deducted as an "advertising expense," which indeed it is.

Either of these scenarios would have made the Two Bucks owner happy as a pig in sunshine, because it would have meant that Regal Band's colt might go to the races in the blue and gray colors of Josephine Abercrombie. The only daughter of the founder of Abercrombie Minerals and Cameron Ironworks, Josephine was accustomed to winning. Her farm, Pin Oak, was named after the building company of her fourth husband, E. Barry Ryan, a third-generation horseman whose family had long held membership in the thoroughbred elite. After his death in 1993, she had followed him as a steward of the Jockey Club, racing's most exclusive and prestigious organization. She quickly established a quality racing stable that competed successfully at the top tracks in Europe and North America, winning an Eclipse Award and racing the 1995 Canadian Horse of the Year and three-year-old champion Peaks and Valleys. Her horses were prepared in the classic European style at Pin Oak's own training track before being sent to the best trainers in the world. For a Two Bucks horse, especially a first crop son of Maria's Mon, there would be no better chance in life than being purchased by Josephine Abercrombie.

As far as the Two Bucks man was concerned, the Maria's Mon colt's future had been set. But now, what about Murray Smith and her $100,000, which represented better than a third of the Two Bucks yearly operating budget?

There was still no answer to the question when Galpin called back. In the bloodstock agent's mind, the hard part was over. The sale price had been agreed upon. His commission, he was certain, could be "worked out amicably."

But the Two Bucks owner was still looking for a way to collect the $100,000 and still not risk this particular colt in a sale of two-year-olds in training. If Murray Smith didn't turn her "quick profit"—which would be difficult at the price she was paying—the horse would end up in the Fasig-Tipton Select sale at Calder Race Course in Miami the following March, which was a speed contest. In spite of all the good trainers who took part, like Kip Elser at Kirkwood, the breeder still viewed this end of the horse market a last resort—something akin to selling your children into the hands of slave traders.

So he began asking the hard questions that would at least put Galpin on the defensive. "What is she going to do with the colt? Two-year-old in training, I guess."

Galpin did not share the concern over the training sales. Neither did he understand why the seller of a horse wanted to somehow claim a right to influence what happened to it afterward. He thought the concern overdone and inappropriate. How do you deal with this guy? There was no proper response, so he spit out the bad truth quickly, nonchalantly, as if it were irrelevant.

"No, one of the yearling sales," Galpin said. "She wants to turn him over quickly. Keeneland in September I'd assume."

The profane response Galpin expected from the other end of the phone was not forthcoming. The money must have gotten the best of the Two Bucks man. At least he knew what his horse was really worth—that $100,000 today was a whale of a price, one he absolutely could not count on topping in August or September. It was the buyer who was at risk here.

But at the other end of the line a "perfect" but highly implausible scenario was taking place in a cluttered mind, one that would keep the colt out of a sale of two-year-olds and put him directly into the hands of a racing owner.

Other than the Keeneland July yearling sale, which is primarily a showcase for million-dollar yearlings, the highest-profile public auction for thoroughbred yearlings is the nation's oldest, which takes place in August at Saratoga Springs, New York, during one of the most prestigious race meets. Dating back to the 1890s, Saratoga August has always been a boutique where over the course of four days fewer than 300 horses are put under the microscope of the most demanding buyers and the most fussy veterinarians in the world. Though it had declined as a sales event in the early 1990s, Saratoga had made a comeback, largely because Fasig-Tipton, Keeneland's only real sales competitor, had made a deliberate effort to recruit the top physical specimens, regardless of pedigree. This system meant that really good horses that were "a little light on the page" could be offered under the best possible circumstances to a discerning buyer, such as Josephine Abercrombie.

In the short time Two Bucks had been in existence, it had done very well selling at Saratoga, always with athletes that were light on pedigree and naturally near the bottom of the Saratoga catalog rankings. The year before, two strapping colts—a beautiful dark bay son of Unbridled and a muscular chestnut by Lord At War—had brought $125,000 and $80,000, respectively.

By March 1999, the same two consignors, Lane's End Farm and Brookdale Farm, had already agreed to take Two Bucks horses to the spa sale. Lane's End, a premier stud farm owned by the powerful Farish family and a leading consignor at every good sale, had entered a good-looking colt by one of its hot new stallions, Belong to Me. And Brookdale was consigning an imposing filly by the old warrior Crafty Prospector, who stood at Brookdale. Because the sires in both instances stood at stud fees of $30,000, these yearlings were a nice fit for the Saratoga catalog, which Fasig-Tipton liked to keep tilted toward the upper end of the market. The Maria's Mon colt, however, was not. Fasig-Tipton liked to steer the offspring of less expensive sires toward the company's July sale in Lexington, which featured a special section for freshman sires. For the Maria's Mon colt to get into the Saratoga sale, Fasig-Tipton would have to like his physical attributes enough to make an exception, which the horse connoisseurs at Brookdale thought might be possible. Since it had no plans to sell at the Lexington sale, Brookdale was willing to try to get him included in its Saratoga consignment.

"What about Saratoga?" the Two Bucks man asked Galpin. "The Brookdale people said he's so good they would try to take him to Saratoga."

Galpin suggested that might be a stretch.

"For Brookdale, yes, but not for Murray. She could get it done. You get her to agree to put this colt in Saratoga and I'll pay the commission. Ninety-five thousand to me. The deal will be done."

He remembered the rules can be flexible or rigid depending on the horse and its "connections." There is such a thing as an exception for quality. Evaluating racehorses is as subjective as evaluating art. If special treatment can't be applied here and there, why should it exist in the first place? Horses nominated to sales by farms owned by friends of the management or consignors with a history of bringing the sales company "the right kind" of horse often find their way into catalogs even when they are "the wrong kind." So it was worth a try.

The Two Bucks owner could hear the lightbulbs going on inside Galpin's bald head. Of course, Murray might get this deal done a lot easier than could Brookdale, which was a Keeneland loyalist. Murray Smith sold millions of dollars' worth of two-year-olds at Fasig-Tipton training sales each year. The top trainers flocked to her barn, not only to see some of the best-prepared two-year-olds in the world but also to glimpse her famous blue jeans.

Galpin is an eloquent and persuasive man. In a few hours a signed sale contract was faxed to Two Bucks, among its provisions a pledge by Murray Smith to keep the colt in Brookdale's Saratoga consignment, if she could get Fasig-Tipton to agree. That she could was never in doubt with Galpin or the Two Bucks owner. They knew the guys at Fasig-Tipton would try jumping over the moon for Murray Smith.

When the dominant female found out the Maria's Mon colt had been sold so quickly, the surprise evoked her usual cross-examination.

"Who bought him?"

"Murray Smith, a Florida pinhooker."

"Do I know him?"

"It's a her."

"Oh. How much?"

"A hundred thousand."

The deal made sense to her. "Good price, huh?"

Indeed, he thought, especially considering that at another time in his life, maybe twenty-five years earlier, before he became so attached to the dominant female and Regal Band's babies, a woman who looked and acted like Murray Smith might well have gotten the Maria's Mon colt from him as a gift. The fond memories of his own feckless frivolity moved fleetingly through his mind and came to rest in a smile, his having no way of knowing that Murray Smith would soon try to give him back the colt.

The horse transportation company Murray Smith hired to haul her new purchase from Kentucky to Florida employed a twelve-horse semi-van too big to negotiate the narrow gates and sharp turns at Two Bucks. So Two Bucks agreed to deliver the horse to the van, which was parked in a big lot at the Keeneland training center. Mild sedation is in order for a young horse's first van ride, so his legs were wrapped in standing bandages for protection. Horse babies are prone to bang their ankles or cannon bones during initial loadings and Two Bucks wanted the colt to arrive in Florida in the same pristine condition as when the buyer had first seen him.

The transfer from one van to the other went without incident, but because the colt was still a little woozy from the tranquilizer the Two Bucks man suggested the bandages be left on until the colt had fully settled in. "Take them off after an hour or so. I don't think Murray would want him to wear these bandages all the way to Florida. They might slip."

The next day, the Maria's Mon colt got off the van in Florida wearing the wraps. Predictably, one of them had slipped below the ankle, creating a tourniquet effect and constricting blood flow to the foot. A tendon was swollen, the ankle sore, the horse lame. Murray was justifiably furious. Blaming the ankle wrapper, she complained to Galpin, who called Two Bucks.

"I've just had an irate and rather dramatic call from Murray," he said. "We've got a problem. The colt didn't arrive in good order. He's lame and she thinks you shouldn't have wrapped the ankles, so we have a problem."

This made the Two Bucks owner furious as well. Not at Murray Smith or Galpin, but at the idiot who drove to Florida with wraps on the colt.

"I don't blame her a bit for being angry," he told Galpin. "But she ought to be angry in the right direction—at her van company. I told the driver the damn wraps were only intended for my short haul."

"Well, she wonders what you are going to do about it," Galpin said.

The Two Bucks owner knew exactly. Already he was deep into seller's remorse, a postsale regret typical among horse owners like the dominant female who never want to sell—period. It is less common than buyer's remorse, which was what Murray Smith was obviously suffering. A deal that leaves both buyer and seller remorseful should not stand. If Brookdale couldn't get the colt into the Saratoga sale, he would simply switch consignors and put him in the New Sire Showcase in July.

"Just get the vet to treat the horse and as soon as he is able to travel, put him on a van and send him home," he told Galpin. "I'll return the check the minute he gets here. But get a good van company this time, not that numskull outfit that took him down there."

6

To get to Saratoga you must travel one hundred miles north of New York City and one hundred years back in time.

RED SMITH, sportswriter

The best horse-racing writer who ever lived, the late Joe Palmer, once wrote a column about Saratoga Springs, New York, featuring a cocker spaniel that had "rented out his doghouse for the season." That's all anyone needs to know about the place—that it is so coveted an environs during thirty-five days of July and August that anybody who is anybody can't stand not being there—if only for a day or two.

Some of the wealthiest of the horse elite already own one of the proper Victorian homes. Others readily cough up enough rent for one month to pay an owner's mortgage for the year. Anyone who believes they own a horse even remotely good enough wants to race it "at the spa." And the trainers, exercise riders, grooms and wanna-bes of every ilk will live in a cocker spaniel's house, or a borrowed car if necessary, just to be part of the scene. Rich or poor, they take all the nice summer clothes they own, change them several times a day, fight over the good seats at the racetrack, stand in line for the tables at six restaurants and record enough chic memories to keep them warm all winter.

For five days during the third week the visitors all congregate under the big shade trees around the Humphrey S. Finney Sales Pavilion, where they inspect yearlings from the tips of their neatly clipped ears to the ends of their freshly combed tails.

Among them in the summer of 1999 were the owners of Two Bucks—the aspiring breeder and the dominant female—their best summer clothes stashed in the wonderful Adelphi Hotel with its historic 1877 air-conditioning system, and their rented Oldsmobile parked illegally and crossways somewhere near the National Museum of Racing and Hall of Fame a few blocks away.

For folks of such small potatoes, their Saratoga interests were widely dispersed. Five yearlings and two racehorses foaled from Two Bucks mares were also in town, three of whom represented revenue potential for the farm. Among the sale yearlings was a fat filly with bone chips recently removed from both rear ankles in the Brookdale consignment in Barn 3. And across the way in the Lane's End consignment was a nice Belong to Me colt, who had been refusing to enter his stall because it didn't have a proper window like his stall at home. A colt perhaps as persnickety as his sole owner—the dominant female—who'd once seen a cockroach in an Oklahoma City motel at 3 A.M. and moved out instantly, dragging her husband along.

In a racetrack barn a few blocks away from the sales yard was the inimitable Snake, wearing his racing name "Morava" on his halter. Finally he was ready to run in his first race for the patient owner who had paid to put the screws in his ankle and saved him from the glue factory. That such a plebeian horse had found his way to such a patrician setting was due in part to the proven genius of his trainer, the esteemed Michael Dickinson, and the would-be genius of his owner, who had a scheme for Snake that—quite typically—was already a day late and would soon be a dollar short.

Now three years old, Snake had been doing so well at Dickinson's Tapeta Farm in Maryland that the trainer had suggested starting him for the first time in the toughest competition possible—a maiden special on the grass at Saratoga. There was generally such a race in the condition book early in the meet. "He might not win but I can assure you he will not embarrass us," Dickinson told the surprised owner. "On the dirt he is just a horse, but on the grass he is quite formidable."

Having watched Snake grow up running on grass, this was no surprise at Two Bucks—only terrific news. Snake winning a race at Saratoga a week before the Two Bucks yearlings went on sale there would not go unnoticed by buyers, many of whom spend the entire month at the spa. They watch the horses work in the morning, watch them race in the afternoon, and then talk about them over drinks and dinner in the evening. They know their names, their owners and their trainers. Being impressed by horses is what Saratoga is all about. And Two Bucks wanted what every other breeder and owner of horses at Saratoga wanted—to be impressive.

Snake was not the farm's only racing hope there. Among the phalanx of two-year-olds brought by the trainer Todd Pletcher, former assistant to the great D. Wayne Lukas, was the quick and beautiful Unbridled colt that had sold as a yearling at Saratoga the year before for $125,000, a bargain price because he was, like most Two Bucks horses, a little light on pedigree. He now had the exciting name of Wingwalker and an iconoclastic, six-foot-six owner named John Fort, whose life's ambition was to get a horse to the Kentucky Derby and eventually syndicate him as a stallion. Wingwalker looked like he might be the one to turn his young, unproven dam, a mare named Aerobatics, into a Two Bucks profit center. So when the Two Bucks owner saw the tall proprietor of Peachtree Stables towering above a crowd of yearling inspectors in his trademark, broad-brimmed straw hat, he moved quickly to inquire about Wingwalker's progress.

The blood drained from Fort's face. "Haven't you heard?" he replied in a quavering voice. "He died last week. Up here in Pletcher's barn—of kidney failure."

Fort got so choked up, he couldn't say much else other than what the breeder had already heard, that the son of Unbridled had been considered one of Pletcher's top Triple Crown prospects and was expected to start at Saratoga. He left Fort quickly, choking up himself—as much on his own disappointment as in sorrow for Fort, who'd had a hard time in the business. The son of a Harvard mathematics professor, Fort had abandoned a promising career in education to pursue his fortunes in the horse business. But he had had more than his share of bad luck.

The unexpected death of a budding young Triple Crown horse is like a sucker punch to the chins of everybody connected with him. Owner, trainer and breeder are left with an empty stall, dashed hopes and a never-adequate insurance settlement based on whatever the horse had cost originally. The dam, of course, gets another notch of failure carved into her produce record. In this business, even when everything gets done right something can go terribly wrong. Fort, for instance, had come to view his own quest for success the way his father had characterized research into mathematics, "like a blind man in a dark room looking for a black hat that isn't there."

News of Wingwalker's death shifted the Two Bucks Man's attention even more sharply onto the other horses on the sales grounds that he had bred and that were now owned by others. Although he was badly in need of the funds that might be raised by Snake and the yearlings he had entered in the sale, it was the aspects of the horse business beyond his control that worried him the most.

In the corner stall of Barn 9, which faced west on the sale show yard, was the Tabasco Cat colt Becky Thomas had failed to sell in November, back on the sales block, still looking unhappy. Just how unhappy his curious breeder could not tell because the colt had come down with a fever and was too sick to be shown. He would spend the week head hung low behind a closed screen door and would eventually be scratched from the sale.

But directly across the main yard in Barn 3, facing east, no one had any difficulty seeing the regal, impeccably groomed, steel gray yearling standing like a statue, ears pricked forward, looking for all the world as if he belonged there—and not the least bit concerned that some people didn't think so.

Murray Smith had kept both her horse and her word. The swelling had gone down quickly in the ankle of the Maria's Mon colt and with it the inflammation of her temper. Getting him into the Saratoga sale, however, had not been all that easy—even for Murray. She had complained that the inspection team sent to Florida by Walt Robertson, the president of Fasig-Tipton, had not been complimentary of the colt and had been downright "rude" in their efforts to steer him where "he would be a better fit"—the decidedly more blue-collar New Sire Showcase sale in Lexington. But Murray had somehow prevailed, as Murray was accustomed to doing. Her clout as a consignor of two-year-olds weighed far more in the Fasig-Tipton value system than a single horse being out of place in Saratoga. Besides, the Maria's Mon colt was a much better physical specimen than others who were allowed in—like a Pembroke colt from the well-connected Dinwiddie Farm in Virginia, whose dam was now in Kentucky chomping grass in the same pasture with the mothers of all the other Two Bucks horses at Saratoga. A young mare named Storm in Sight, she'd been purchased by the breeding genius at Keeneland the previous November—a bargain at $55,000. And her new owner had been stunned to discover that her yearling son, by a sire even more pedestrian than Maria's Mon, had found its way so easily into the exclusive catalog of 231 Saratoga nominations.

Now, to the chagrin of the dominant female, her husband had taken up residence in the center of the sales yard, with a perfect view of the stalls of two of the best colts—and potentially the best racehorses—he'd ever raised, neither of which he owned anymore. From their lookout spot near the refreshment stand, "the fun couple"—as they were sometimes referred to by their irreverent children—could watch alternately on one end the Maria's Mon colt coming out of his stall repeatedly to be shown to buyers, and on the other the Tabasco Cat colt not coming out at all.

The small size of the Saratoga sale consignment, down to around 200 after the late withdrawals, and the intimacy of the setting meant that all the buyers see all the horses—and often many times over. Eventually every notable found his or her way to Brookdale's small consignment to check out the only Maria's Mon offspring in the sale, each to be identified and commented on by the Two Bucks man for the benefit of the dominant female. He mentioned specifically the grieving John Fort, whom he figured might have liked the Unbridled colt so much he would return to drink from the same well. And he saw the Lexington trainer Johnny Ward, who for twenty years had been buying horses for Oklahoma gas man Jack Oxley, who shopped mostly for fillies. Oxley had been looking for colts lately, however, and at Keeneland the previous September his man Ward had picked out and signed the ticket for a $4 million Mr. Prospector colt named Fusaichi Pegasus for a big Japanese buyer. Ward seemed most interested in Brookdale's fillies, which included the fat one from Two Bucks. He showed no interest in the Maria's Mon colt.

Observing all this allowed the proud breeder of Two Bucks yearlings to fret alternately and needlessly over the future of both the Tabasco Cat colt who couldn't get out of his stall and the Maria's Mon colt who couldn't stay in his. And it provided the dominant female with the opportunity to deliver her typically appropriate and sarcastic commentary on the boring nature of their agenda. She would have preferred spending the afternoon checking out the Performing Arts Center, or perhaps the Lincoln Baths at Saratoga State Park.

Soon she had relegated her husband to a spot among the "typical owners" of horses being sold at big thoroughbred sales by third-party agents and consignors. Conspicuous by their incessant presence, owners tend to skulk behind trees, lounge on benches, and parade endlessly through the barns with no other objective than to gather intelligence on who is inspecting their horses. The instant an unknown looker departs, they rush up to the sales agent like someone in a hurry to use the bathroom. But their urgency is only to spit out the single word burning on their lips, "Whowuzat?"

To discourage this annoying loitering by clients, consignors have resorted to handing out cards to each shopper, asking that they leave their signature. The bigger, fancier sales operations now keep a running tally of the visits, tabulate them on a laptop computer and compile the results into printed reports. There is only one exception, the famous Claiborne Farm, which races most of its horses and sells at auction only rarely. When it does, prospective buyers are never asked to identify themselves because, as the Claiborne man once explained, "We don't care." But Lane's End, the consignor of the dominant female's colt at Saratoga, cares so much it gathers all the information, updates it every few hours and keeps it in a special green and gold binder the color of the Farish family silks. So Lane's End is ready whenever a client like the dominant female drops by to find out how many times her colt was taken out of the stall, by whom, whether they returned for a second or third look, and how many times the radiographs of her horse's bones were inspected by which veterinarians. When she rushes up and asks, "Whowuzat?" instead of saying "Idunno," all Lane's End had to do was hand her a folder full of useless facts. The truth is, the only reliable signal of interest in buying the horse is the arrival of an expensive veterinarian to perform the prospective buyer's proprietary endoscopic examination of the horse's air passages, which usually occurs in the last few hours before the horse goes to the sales ring.

While the dominant female had her own individual Lane's End activity report, her husband did not. Because the two Saratoga horses that most interested him were owned by others, the Two Bucks guy was not privileged to any of the information he regarded as worthless. Therefore he had no choice but to gather his own worthless information by skulking—for two days—interrupted only by the Saratoga social requirements to change attire and stand in line to eat. The vigil—defined by the dominant female as "the monotony of watching helplessly for no good reason"—finally ended with the appearance on the third day of Josephine Abercrombie's farm manager, Clifford Barry, outside the Brookdale barn.

Like Murray Smith, the matron of Pin Oak Stud had kept her word as well. She had sent her man to buy the Maria's Mon colt and claim him for her great racing stable. Like dozens of other potential buyers who had been by to inspect the Maria's Mon yearling, Barry watched him stand squarely. He surveyed his perfect balance, admired the length of his stride, his loose, confident walk, his striking shotgun barrel color, the beautiful head and stallion-quality charisma. Then he sent the farm's veterinarian over to the sale repository where he read the report on his "A" endoscopic throat examination and examined the radiographs of his perfectly aligned bone joints and found a shadow he did not like—a shadow ultimately interpreted to be a "goddam OCD" in his stifle joint, an "osteochondritis dessican" in the biggest part of his big motor—the hip. Hip No. 68.

The radiographs taken by the veterinarian hired by Murray Smith to examine him at Two Bucks before her purchase had shown nothing of negative consequence in any joint. Brookdale Farm said Murray had told them the presale X rays that accompanied him from Florida to Saratoga were clean as well. So even considering his un-Saratoga-like social status, nearly everyone was stunned at what happened when his time came in the sales ring the first night of the sale.

Josephine's man did not bid. Nor did John Fort, nor anyone else's man for that matter. At Saratoga August, as at Keeneland July, blemished merchandise is quickly discarded with disdain. And it was not as if the Two Bucks horse was the only good-looking one at the sale. In fact Saratoga was teeming with far more wonderful prospects to become "the big horse." The Saratogans were saving their money for colts like Ochoco, a son of Mr. Prospector who would top the sale at $3 million.

When hammered down by the auctioneer in the hurry he deserved, Regal Band's best foal had attracted only $90,000, all of it bid by Murray Smith to protect her investment. Later, the consignor, Brookdale Farm, could only shrug at what had happened. They had never seen the colt's radiographs, nor had Murray Smith asked them to support the horse with a reserve bid. Clifford Barry, not wanting to disparage an offspring of a Pin Oak stallion, would only mumble that Pin Oak had not bid because "there was a little something wrong with the X rays."

Yet it took Walt Robertson, the blunt and candid Fasig-Tipton president and chief auctioneer, only a terse second or two to clarify it all for the disappointed.

"That's what happens when they don't belong," he snapped, providing a perspective he'd maintained all along. "We told Murray he didn't belong here. And he didn't."

What did belong, in Robertson's view, were the similarly handsome but better bred colts that were the products of big stud fees like A P Valentine, the son of A. P. Indy sold by the Farish family to Rick Pitino, the famous basketball coach, for $475,000; and the sale's other strapping colt, Songandaprayer, who brought $470,000—the first son of Unbridled's Song to follow his father to the sales ring in Saratoga.

In other words, the product of the mating between Maria's Mon and Regal Band had gotten exactly what it deserved in the sensuous, class-conscious spa—nothing. There, let that be a lesson to you, Two Bucks.

And indeed it was. The other yearling from a Two Bucks mare offered for sale the first night, the Pembroke colt consigned by Dinwiddie Farm, brought only $45,000. Another Dinwiddie horse had brought only $15,000—the lowest in the sale. If there were truly any horses on the grounds that "didn't belong" those two were among them. The Two Bucks man could only wonder if the explanation of Dinwiddie's failure had landed as harshly as that for his own.

When he and the dominant female showed up among "the swells" at the lovely old Saratoga racecourse the following day, the words "doesn't belong here" might as well have been inscribed on a sign around his neck. He even used them himself to describe his beloved Snake, who appeared thin and unhappy while being saddled in the paddock for his first race ever.

With the impeccable timing commonplace in his life of late, Snake's race—a maiden special on the grass one and one-sixteenth miles long—had popped up on the Saratoga schedule on the day after his younger half-brother was to be sold—not the day before. Not only was it too late for a good showing by Snake to help the Maria's Mon colt in the sales ring, Snake did not appear up to the task.

The trainer, Dickinson, known for his superb conditioning of horses, was as usual his most elegant self. At Saratoga all the trainers wear coats and ties to the paddock, but Dickinson is among the few who look like they've worn them before. He had been witty and charming at a lunch, which had been graciously hosted by a bunch of Saratoga regulars, who also owned horses in Dickinson's stable.

But the pride of Two Bucks was not in such fine fettle. In the saddling paddock before the race, all the rivals who had paraded with him down the shady lane from the barns looked bigger, stronger and healthier than Snake. His ribs were protruding. His backbone was razor sharp. There was a noticeable lack of muscle atop his croup around his tailset, a telltale sign of weakness. He looked, well, like he didn't belong. The words had stuck in the front of the horseman's mind like the theme of a bad dream that had been haunting him of late, in which he was perpetually lost.

Soon, it appeared, the words might fit perfectly Snake's racing debut as well as it had his sibling's sale. The first horse ever to carry the new red, gold and green racing silks of Two Bucks, Snake broke well from post position #4 and settled nicely along the rail. Weak and hungry-looking, he was nonetheless skipping along the grass in the effortless fashion expected by those who'd seen him grow up—a "daisy cutter" for certain.

Trainer Dickinson had placed upon Snake's back one of the best turf jockeys in the world, John Velazquez, who had his mount perfectly positioned, "saving ground" along the rail as the field of nine rounded the first turn. As they ganged up going down the backstretch the two leaders—El Temperamental and Decree—began to pull away, while a third horse running in front of Snake on the rail began to tire. Velazquez looked to move around him but was trapped by a gray horse called Sand and Gravel who was moving up fast on the outside. The roadblock in front continued to slow. Snake was pushed back from fourth to sixth, to eighth and finally to last as they turned for home. His ears were pricked. He wanted to run, but he had no place to go.

Up in the clubhouse seats with the dominant female and the swells, Snake's incredibly shrinking owner was looking for a hole of his own into which to crawl. Two rows in front was a very nice man from Lexington named Tracy Farmer who said he had placed a big bet on Snake because he knew the owners. But Snake was about to finish way last—at Saratoga—and in front of everybody at the most prestigious race meet in the country.

Then a tiny thing happened. It was a crack between the rail and the roadblock horse—now going so slow he looked like he was searching for a parking place. Snake saw the opening. So did Velazquez. They went for it at the same time. Snake must have thought he was back at Two Bucks knocking his friend Whacko off the fence. He flattened his ears and dove into the hole, which only the bravest of horses or jockeys ever do, bouncing the slowpoke off the rail. The track announcer, Tom Durkin, began to shout, "Mo-Rava is trying to pick his way through. . . . There is room for Mo-Rava. . . . And here comes Mo-Rava." And come he did. A black bullet had been fired. He passed one, two, then three horses at a time and there he was, even with Decree. Snake pricked his ears and blew by him, bearing down on El Temperamental, who was almost to the wire.

Durkin shouted again, "It's El Temperamental in a photo finish with the hard-charging Morava." Snake had lost by a whisker but everyone there knew which was the best horse. Had the crack appeared a second earlier, he would have won easily. It was the best race of the day and all the talk among the swells.

That night at the concluding session of Saratoga August, the fat Two Bucks filly with the excessive ankle surgery on her resume fetched only $65,000 in the auction ring, a barely profitable proposition. But the Belong to Me colt brought $150,000, a windfall considering that eighteen months earlier his mother had been purchased for $20,000 carrying him in utero.

Clutching her green and yellow binder, the dominant female was effusive in her compliments to her consignor, Lane's End, whose efforts on her behalf she regarded as exemplary. There might well have been in her demeanor even a faint flicker of admiration for her lover and bloodstock adviser, who'd picked the mare for her out of thousands on display at Keeneland two Novembers back and prepared the colt for sale. She would later boast of his prowess in that regard—but only to her friends and out of his earshot. You should not encourage a man who thinks he knows everything and won't follow directions. Neither would he be rewarded financially, not even a commission. Her sale proceeds were squirreled away in the Santa Fe getaway fund.

As happy as he was for his wife, as buoyed as he was by Snake's great race, the Two Bucks man had been dismayed by the whole Saratoga adventure. Snake not only ran his heart out but his back as well, finishing the race, as Dickinson said, "on only two legs." He would have to come home to Two Bucks and spend the fall being fattened up and undergoing back therapy and would not race again that year.

The farm had realized very little revenue—$65,000 for the fat filly and one-third of Snake's $7,600 second-place money. The only horse he'd ever sold by a proven Triple Crown sire, the Unbridled colt, had died without ever getting a chance to race. And the primary reason for going to Saratoga in the first place—the scheme to get the Maria's Mon colt purchased by Josephine Abercrombie—had been just another climb up a beanstalk. Now both he and the lovely Tabasco Cat yearling were still in the hands of pinhookers and headed for the sale for two-year-olds in training.

All in all Saratoga had been a shot in the dark that had hit nothing.

7

Four things greater than all things are,
Women and Horses and Power and War.

RUDYARD KIPLING,
The Ballad of the King's Jest

No matter when or where horses trod the earth, their fates rest with the nature of the humans through whose hands they pass. Like the black stallion of children's literature, they can have good owners who feed and care for them, or bad ones who leave them to starve in the cold.

The best caretakers of horses share the same regard for them as the Koran attributes to their very creator, who when done said to the kind beast: "I have made thee as no other. All the treasures of the earth shall lie between thine eyes. . . . Thy saddle shall be the seat of prayers to me. And thou shalt fly without any wings, and conquer without any sword."

Inveterate horse lovers all are stricken with what the octogenarian Pennsylvania broodmare master Bertram Linder has described as "a compulsive need to be around them." As a heavily decorated American first lieutenant in World War II, Linder even found a horse to ride following the capture of Cherbourg during the Normandy invasion. Commandeering it from a surrendering horse-drawn artillery unit, Lt. Linder rode it triumphantly back into camp in front of a long line of newly taken German prisoners, and as he approached his company, could not resist yelling, "It was nothing, boys."

Linder traces his love of being horseback to his youth in Great Neck, New York, where he remembers being awestruck by watching polo competition, where just like in cowboy movies men rush around on horseback in violent and dangerous quest of something.

The equine ardor of John C. Oxley has similar childhood roots. He believes a lot of people are born with "a horse gene" that kicks in upon contact with the animal and addicts them for life. His own fascination did not have to come from watching others ride or from fashioning stick horses. His family had the real thing, a brown gelding named Ginger that his mother rode to deliver Jack and his sister to grade school in Oklahoma. Later there was a chestnut gelding named Prince and the bay mare Judy. As a boy he fed them and cleaned up after them. Eventually, like Linder, he became infatuated with polo. His father, John T. Oxley, was responsible for bringing the sport to Mohawk Park in Tulsa in the 1950s and played it vigorously until he was eighty-two years old.

When lined up end to end the scrapbooks recounting the life successes of Jack Oxley's father stretch 15 feet. Among the papers and clippings is a meritorious award for being the oldest high-goal polo player in the world and the announcement of his induction into the Hall of Fame. They also include the details of how he made a vast fortune, starting with the founding of the Texas Natural Gasoline Corporation in 1948, which went public in 1953 and was later merged with Union Texas Petroleum. The merged firm went on to become Allied Chemical, one of the largest independent oil companies in the world. Then in 1962, after a short retirement, John T. did it again, this time with son Jack, starting Oxley Petroleum, which is now ranked among the top thirty privately held natural gas companies in Oklahoma.

Like father like son, in polo and in business.

Out in the oil country around Tulsa where it has been spread liberally by the Oxley Foundation among charitable organizations with tax-exempt 501(c)(3) status, the Oxley fortune is considered "a boon to the city's quality of life." Down in the winter vacation land of Florida where Jack and brother Thomas own and operate the Royal Palm Polo Club in Boca Raton, it has been a boon to the sport and the level of recreation among those with the right social status. And back in the bluegrass mounds of Kentucky, Oxley money has been a boon to the people who breed racehorses for a living, whether they have status or not. It was into the last category—the one without status—that Two Bucks would miraculously move as the new millennium began.

Over the past twenty years Jack Oxley has spent millions for Kentucky horses, many of whom are now broodmares grazing on his 220-acre Fawn Leap Farm near Midway. In the view of most, he spent it the right way—on expensive, well-bred fillies who went on to have successful racing careers, including the champion mare Beautiful Pleasure, for which he paid $480,000, then a record. A few years later at the Saratoga sale where Two Bucks' gray colt with the "goddam OCD" went unsold, Oxley spent $810,000, better than two-thirds of it on fillies. The colt he had really wanted was A P Valentine, the eventual Kentucky Derby horse that trainer Nick Zito bought for the basketball coach Rick Pitino. Oxley had thought the A. P. Indy colt would be too expensive, not the kind of sound business investment that had been the hallmark of his adult life. But the $475,000 that Pitino paid turned out to be a pittance when the breeding rights were sold in less than two years for $15 million.

The next year at the same sale, Oxley paid $1.25 million for one filly and $425,000 for another. And a few months later at the November weanling sale he paid $975,000 for a baby female—all of them to be owned and raced by his lovely wife, Debby, in her own set of shocking pink colors. Within the world of wives, this gift is the work of a thoughtful and generous man. But in the world of husbands it is also clearly one with an ulterior motive.

Sometime earlier in his life, Jack Oxley had contracted the dreaded social disease—Derby Fever. It could have happened when he was only nine years old listening to his first Kentucky Derby on the radio the year Assault won in 1946. But more likely he picked it up from direct contact with the other wealthy, ambitious polo-playing men with whom he'd socialized all his life. Early symptoms of the ailment appeared during the oil embargo in the 1970s when petroleum prices and the energy exploration business boomed, increasing significantly the amount of his disposable income available for thoroughbred investment. And the illness reared its head again in 1979 when one of his first good racemares, Yes Dear Maggy, foaled a bay colt named Stalwart that two years later looked like he might become a Derby horse but didn't. It was not until the spring of 1995, however, that Derby Fever began to noticeably ravage Jack Oxley, brought out of dormancy when two colts he owned, Jambalaya Jazz and Pyramid Peak, were running so well that he entered them both in the Kentucky Derby. Their finishing fifteenth and seventeenth, respectively, would have arrested the illness in most men, but not in a son of John T. Oxley. It only made it worse.

Like some other chronic social diseases men often deny having—or at least try to keep secret from their female companions—Derby Fever was not something Jack Oxley wanted his wife Debby to know about. It is an embarrassing disease that has driven giants of world industry and heads of state to expend $13 million on a single horse to win a race with prize money of $1 million, while knowing full well that it can just as easily be won by horses that are raised or bought for peanuts.

The last thing Jack Oxley wanted anyone to know was that he suffered chronically and terminally from something that any moment might cause him to act so irrationally. After all, being neither silly nor foolish had been a hallmark of his entire life. It was one of his attractions.

So while all the expensive fillies he was buying to run in Debby's colors could be justified as sound investment in future broodmares, they also served to cloak the steady, secret advancement of the insidious Derby Fever, which eventually destroys a man's judgment.

Sprinkled among the fillies every now and then was a Derby-type colt to run in his own name and his own blue and maize colors. Because of their minor nature, they were hardly noticed. Instead of trying to buy the expensive A P Valentine at Saratoga, for example, he had settled for a $165,000 Dixieland Band colt, who turned out to be a minor head case.

If nothing else this nondescript purchase marked his return to normalcy only three months after suffering a surprise public attack of Derby Fever at the March sale of two-year-olds in training at Calder in Miami. There, throwing quiet subtlety to the wind, Oxley had paid $950,000 for a fast son of Miswaki with a suspect throat after a spirited bidding war with Roger King, the television syndicator whose brother had bought the Mt. Livermore colt from Two Bucks at Barretts. When finally topped by Oxley, Roger King literally threw his hat in the ring, startling the expensive colt and leaving no doubt to observers as to the nature of the illness from which both combatants were suffering.

What Oxley eventually buys in the sales ring and races is Johnny Ward's doing. He takes only the sales catalog pages that Oxley has approved, looks at the horses for the qualities he likes to train, and makes a short list for his top client to see and then possibly bid on.

Ward's qualifications for picking out a horse are as good as they get. Like Oxley he has been around horses all of his life. His father, John, Sr., and his grandfather, John S. Ward, were both prominent horsemen. His uncle Sherill Ward, who trained the great gelding Forego for a while, was a mentor to him, as were New York training legend Woody Stevens and John Gaver, both masters of their trade. Ward grew up on the family farm near Keeneland and as a youth showed hunters and jumpers with a bunch of horsey-set girls, including his wife, Donna, who all remember him as "cute, nice and quiet and patient with the horses."

At Saratoga in August 1999, the Maria's Mon colt had made no impression on Ward, but six months later when he saw how the colt had covered a quarter of a mile in 22.3 seconds at Calder on February 20, well, that was another story. His time was not all that fast, considering they were blazing at Calder, but it was still plenty fast. More important to Ward, the horse just ate up the ground with long, fluid strides and was still galloping out strong well after the clock had stopped. A week later in the second timed "work," he ran an eighth in 11 flat, a full second slower than the fastest horse, but he still looked good doing it. The colt had a classic shoulder, stood over a lot of ground and had a big motor—all prerequisites for a Ward horse. The pedigree fit, too, perfectly within the parameters Oxley had set for winning the Derby. By now a self-made expert on how a horse must be bred to win the classic mile-and-a-quarter race, Oxley particularly liked the gray colt's distance-loving dam, Regal Band, who went back to Dixieland Band and Graustark. This ancestry was the same as that of Jambalaya Jazz, with whom he and Ward had experienced some success. Overall, there was only one problem about buying the colt—though he had been able to "breeze" under tack, he was having trouble walking at the barn.

The worst fear of his Two Bucks breeder had been realized. All the pounding on the Florida ground that it takes to ready a horse for Calder had left Regal Band's baby with sore shins and a badly bruised foot. No foot—no horse. Not much chance of getting into the hands of a good owner.

Nobody wanted to tell a rich owner he had just bought a lame horse, including New York trainer John Kimmel, who had become interested in the horse on the advice of a Pennsylvania-based company called EQB, one of several scientific consulting services that measure a horse for racing efficiency using modern high-tech sports medicine techniques. EQB offers a combination cardiovascular and gait analysis that when measured against a database of horses with similar conformation and pedigree can provide insight into how efficient a racehorse your sale prospect might be. A keen-eyed horseman like Kimmel can figure out most of the gait analysis stuff on his own, but the cardiovascular efficiency is something else. This type of analysis requires ultrasound measurement of such things as heart size, air passages and blood flow to come up with a better idea of the power of the respiratory pump. EQB ranks cardiovascular efficiency in tiers, the top being a "Tier Five Release." EQB rated Hip No. 10 at this level and also gave him a superior gait analysis, suggesting he had "the heart and stride of a champion." Statistics suggest that even buyers of the most expensive yearlings have only a 2 percent chance of buying a stakes winner, an even less than 1 percent chance of buying a Grade 1 stakes winner who can win at distances longer than a mile. The EQB database suggests that all the champions and most Grade 1 stakes winners have both a gait analysis and a cardiovascular system far different from the average racehorse. In the past EQB had singled out as top prospects Thunder Gulch, Silver Charm and Fusaichi Pegasus, all of whom won the Kentucky Derby. But the cardio analysis of the Maria's Mon colt had provided an unusual finding. Not only did he have a motor that put him in the top 1 percent of horses that could go a distance, it ranked him at the top among sprinters as well. This combination added up to what potentially was an extraordinarily talented and versatile racehorse, one that could compete at any distance on any level.

When informed of the EQB analysis, Kimmel, who was there buying for several top customers, had been duly impressed. "Okay," he said, "that's great, but the horse still has to be able to walk." Which Hip No. 10 could not—at least not very well.

Of all the world's great buyers of thoroughbreds on the scene at Calder, only Johnny Ward kept coming back to look at the ouchy Two Bucks–bred colt, who was not "lame" (in the true sense of the word) but merely "sore"—a not unusual condition for a two-year-old in training.

In Ward's mind, a young horse showing no ill effects of the training stress it takes to go in "10 and change for an eighth" or "22 for a quarter" might have something inside "besides his natural juices"—meaning pharmaceuticals masking his true ailments. To Ward, the Maria's Mon colt being sore was a positive sign, not a deterrent. A veteran buyer like him knew that the soreness might mean he could probably be bought "right"—without much competition from the top tier of trainers and bloodstock agents. It was at this crucial decision-making juncture that the long-standing relationship between the Oxleys and the Wards and their long experience with horses gave them an advantage over others.

Trainers or agents often buy for strangers, for new inexperienced owners, or on "speculation"—with the hope of reselling the horse later. So they all want the same horse—one with the fastest times, no obvious medical problems and the most sought-after pedigrees. These are invariably the highest-priced horses, and the broker's usual commission of 5 percent will be based on such prices. But a trainer such as Ward buying for a twenty-year client like Oxley makes his living off the long-term training fees and purse winnings, not a buyer's commission. Although neophytes might think Ward and Oxley were gambling by buying a sore horse, it was not much of a gamble at all in the scheme of things. Having spent $950,000 for a Derby prospect at the same sale a year before, it looked in fact as if Oxley's outbreak of Derby Fever was back under control. It wasn't, of course. Oxley didn't plan to go to the Derby with a single, gray, sore-footed bullet. He was building an arsenal.

But for a man who'd been dropping a million here and a half-million there on fillies, it was a very quiet buy. In the sales ring, Ward faced very little competition—again most of it Murray Smith's reserve. The $170,000 he paid for a horse that came up sore after running three furlongs in a little over 11 seconds each hardly made a sound.

The big noise and the big money was made by the fastest horses, who ran their furlongs in 10 seconds each and showed no ill effects: A Cherokee Run colt named Yonaguska who brought $1,950,000 from the former British bookmaker Michael Tabor, after being recommended by both D. Wayne Lukas, the trainer who has won more Triple Crown races than anyone else, and Irish veterinarian Demi O'Byrne, who buys more expensive horses than anyone else; and the Unbridled's Song colt Songandaprayer, who brought $1 million from the former Duke and NBA basketball star Bobby Hurley, double what buying ace Buzz Chace had paid for him at Saratoga.

But what about the "goddam OCD" in the Maria's Mon colt's right stifle, the bone blemish that caused Josephine Abercrombie's man and perhaps others at Saratoga to bypass him? The answer is what makes the Two Bucks owner and other thoroughbred breeders bang their heads on the walls of barns and curse Keeneland's invention of the sale repository.

Lo and behold, the "shadow" on the radiograph of the colt's right hip joint—which had been of "no clinical significance" to Murray Smith's veterinarians but had foiled the meticulously laid and executed plan of his genius breeder—was of no consequence at all to the veterinarian employed by John Ward and John Oxley. Dr. Daryl Easley, who makes his living taking care of racehorses and examines all potential purchases for Ward and Oxley, didn't even bring it up. To him it was insignificant.

The future of a Kentucky Derby winner ultimately worth more than $10 million had hinged on the subjective opinion of one veterinarian about one shadow on one radiograph of one joint in a horse's leg—one of thirty-two views taken. No doubt it was his best professional judgment. But it had deprived Josephine Abercrombie of owning the one offspring from her stallion Maria's Mon that would become a good enough racehorse to win the toughest race in the world, the one race certain to make her stallion's career as a sire. This "opinion" also condemned the young horse to the industry's riskiest proving ground where his fate depended entirely on a contrary opinion of the same shadow by another veterinarian and the genius of Johnny Ward's eye.

That the colt could even find his way to Ward and Oxley—who would name him Monarchos after a Greek ruler—is a tribute to the boldness, skill and moxie of the enigmatic Murray Smith, she of the grand blue jeans. Had Smith not been willing to risk $100,000 on the son of an unproven sire and a discounted dam, Monarchos doubtless would have gone through the sale caste system near the bottom rather than near the top. Instead of Saratoga August and Fasig-Tipton Calder, he would have ended up at Keeneland September among the dregs of 4,000-plus yearlings, or at Fasig-Tipton Midlantic, where running into an owner-trainer combo like Ward and Oxley is near impossible. With the "goddam OCD" albatross hanging around his neck, Monarchos would have required the same kind of miraculous stroke of lightning that produced Xtra Heat.

Two months after Monarchos sold in Florida, a similarly modestly bred but well-built filly sold at Midlantic, a lesser sale of two-year-olds in training in Maryland. Xtra Heat was one of three two-year-olds purchased by the same buyer, trainer John Salzman, Jr., for a total of $20,000, so cheap he didn't even bother to have them vetted until after the sale. When he finally did, Salzman found the "goddam OCDs" in both of Xtra Heat's stifle joints that had caused her to be sold twice before at drastically discounted prices—$4,700 as a weanling and $9,100 as a yearling. The consignor who'd prepared her for the Midlantic had been so concerned about the potential weakness in her stifle joints he had substituted swimming for galloping as her exercise. Salzman sent her right to the races in a $25,000 "claimer," which meant anyone willing to put up that amount could own her. She won that race by only a neck. But as of July 2001, she had won fifteen more—sixteen of nineteen overall, all but one of them top-quality stakes races. In her losses, including the Breeders' Cup against the best male sprinters in the world, she finished second, and by year's end had earned Salzman over $1 million. Her estimated value today—$2 million at least.

So it is on such minuscule disparities of judgment, the almost whimsical notions of what might or might not be, that the fate of horses, owners, trainers—indeed entire farms and racing stables—now often turn in the thoroughbred business. The difference between an animal so worthless it sells per pound to "the killers" for foreign foodstuffs and one worth millions can be precisely that between the opinions of veterinarians about the future implications of a shadow.

Horse racing, it seems, is at once a glorious sport of kings and a risky business of fools. So when the news reached Kentucky that the much fretted-over gray son of Regal Band had been purchased in Florida by trainer John Ward for his best owner John Oxley, the breeding "fool" at Two Bucks was only modestly encouraged. For all his experience judging news he still had no idea just how good that news was.

Having met neither trainer nor owner, all the Two Bucks guy had to go on was what he had gone on all those years as a journalist—what he had heard.

What he'd heard about Oxley was all good, mainly that he was a smart, well-intentioned owner, a delightful man who rode horses and actually knew something about them, which elevated him instantly up the owner chart at Two Bucks.

The trainer, however, was another story. All the Two Bucks man had ever heard about Johnny Ward was that he was a Kentucky "hardboot," a term often used by writers who have no clue to its origin. As employed in journalism and literature about racing and the Kentucky breeding industry, it most often conjures up the image of a tobacco-spitting rockhead prone to stupidity and the abuse of horses and people, presumably by kicking or stepping on them in some way with hard boots. It did not seem to fit the soft-spoken gray-haired guy he'd seen on television as the trustee appointed by the court to oversee the treasured Calumet Farm when it had plunged into bankruptcy early in the 1990s. When pressed into service by a court and besieged by a frantic press, Ward had come across as a thoughtful man, experienced in the proper management of both farms and horses.

The "hardboot" characterization, it turned out, fit Ward perfectly, though not because of either temperament, intelligence or skill. Everyone who goes out in the thick Kentucky grass early in the morning encounters the heaviest, wettest dew Mother Nature ever spread upon the earth. Those who wear leather boots, as most horsemen do, will soon find them hard as rocks—thus all become "hardboots."

Contrary to common perceptions, Kentucky horsemen actually apply far less discipline in the raising of horses than those anywhere else. Presumably because they are so valuable, Kentucky horses are in general the most protected, pampered and undisciplined domestic animals in existence. As a result many of them—stallions, particularly—are prone to bite, strike, kick and eat the very "hardboots" who care for them.

Many of the best horse handlers in the industry often referred to as "hardboots" are not Kentuckians at all, but rather cowboys or Irishmen who humanely, intelligently and quickly come to an understanding with the horse on what behavior is permitted and what is not.

So it wasn't the hardboot characterization that made the Two Bucks owner skeptical of the man who would train Monarchos, it was what he'd heard during an automobile ride that day in the fall of 1994. Perusing the *Daily Racing Form* while en route to Turfway Park near Cincinnati for a day of racing, he'd found among the entries Oxley's colt Jambalaya Jazz, making his first start of a career that would eventually include the Kentucky Derby. Naturally it was the horse's breeding—a cross of Dixieland Band with Graustark—that caught his eye. He mentioned the colt to his traveling companions.

"Who's training that horse?" one of them asked. "Johnny Ward, I bet, and he can't train a vine to go up a wall."

"You know what else they say about Johnny Ward," laughed another. "He can't train his own hair to lay down."

Acting on the sage advice of his more experienced friends, that day the breeding fool from Two Bucks left Jambalaya Jazz out of his two-horse "exacta box"—an "exotic" bet picking the horses that finish first or second in any order. And naturally, Jambalaya Jazz ruined it by finishing second. From that point on, Two Bucks bet Jambalaya Jazz every time he encountered the opportunity and won money every time. Jambalaya Jazz was either first, second, or third in twenty of his twenty-eight races and won over half a million dollars.

For certain somebody in the Ward-Oxley camp knew something about how to get a racehorse to the winner's circle. That it might be Ward's wife Donna was sometimes a topic of discussion at meetings of the Kentucky Horse Park Foundation, of which she was a loyal member. The foundation, dedicated to preserving the park as a state treasure, is basically an organization of dominant females, but it also tolerated a few males suspected of being able to raise money or wield political influence on the park's behalf, including the Two Bucks owner, who showed his face only infrequently.

Except for the smile swaps and head nods that typify do-gooder board meetings, he had never had occasion to talk to Donna Ward. But his interest in the future of Monarchos led him to make typical journalistic inquiries about her and her husband. The consensus response was that if Johnny Ward couldn't train a vine to go up a wall, his wife would find a way to get it up there for him.

"Johnny's kind of laid back," said one of the Wards' old horse-show buddies, "but Donna is a bundle of drive and ambition. Smart and tough."

By this time Oxley's fillies were winning big-time races. In 1995, his Gal in a Ruckus took both the Kentucky Oaks, the distaff equivalent of the Kentucky Derby, and the Canadian Oaks, also a Grade 1 race. Four years later Beautiful Pleasure won the Eclipse Award as champion mare, having earned more than $2.5 million. Publicly, Ward had credited the exercise rider—his wife—with much of the success. So the board meeting scuttlebutt amplified: "Donna's the real trainer in that family."

As usual the Two Bucks owner was predisposed to crediting the female influence. His exposure to Donna Ward, limited as it was, had left him with a clear impression. He had no idea if she could train racehorses, but she was obviously strong-minded enough to will the vine up the wall, and good-looking enough to seduce it up there if necessary.

It would be several months before Two Bucks could see for himself how the extraordinary Oxley-Ward combination was working on the steel gray colt, but he was there waiting when Johnny Ward led Monarchos into the Keeneland paddock for his first race in October 2000, his old journalistic skill of observation sharply honed and ready to be employed. The first thing he wanted to see was the horse's feet, the shape and condition of which are sure clues to trainer competence. The next thing he wanted to check out was how well Ward's hair was lying down.

PART 3

DERBY FEVER

8

I'd horsewhip you if I had a horse.

GROUCHO MARX, in *Horsefeathers,* 1932

"This colt has a half-brother named Monarchos that Jack Oxley and Johnny Ward think is a helluva horse. Aiming him toward the Kentucky Derby."

This is the breeder talking to a guy he doesn't know who is inspecting Hip No. 3897 in the lineup behind the Keeneland sales pavilion.

The guy's inspection technique is basically that of a contortionist—as if true quality can only be determined by eyes focused from the apex of a pretzel. The pretzel unwinds long enough to give the breeder a look that says, "Yeah, right," and then contorts some more.

He says he's a trainer named Miracle, which is exactly what the breeder needs at the moment. A Miracle. The 2000 September sale, the biggest in history with 4,652 yearlings—350 per day for thirteen days—is nearing an end and the contortionist is the only human being to show even a flicker of interest in yet another handsome, well-bred son of Regal Band that is about to sell in five minutes—maybe.

Timing is still everything. And the timing of the Two Bucks horse business is still extraordinarily bad. The sale is being held a month before Monarchos is to make his first start, so no one has ever heard of him yet. Snake has won two races but is on the shelf again recovering from a tendon injury. And the market is flooded with yearlings. Yet there are so few buyers at Keeneland that a gun could have been fired down the main aisle behind the sales ring without hitting a two-legged creature. If this were a dove field, the little feathered buggers could dine in peace. Even the consignors are staying away from their own horses out of embarrassment. No one, it seems, wants to see no one looking—except the masochist from Two Bucks, whose tolerance for pain had always exceeded his good judgment.

Early in the September sales the high-priced horses are sold in a leisurely manner. Many of them are on the grounds and available for inspection for nearly a week before they sell. Twice a day the well-heeled buyers are offered a lavish $20 per person buffet in one of the sumptuous Keeneland dining rooms.

But as the sale progresses, the quality of food service diminishes along with that of the stock. The sale slips into overdrive, a ship-'em-in-and-sell-'em pace in which horses are barely on the grounds long enough to dirty up their stalls. Instead of being inspected for days at their barns by the expensive lunch crowd, they are "bought off the line" behind the sales arena, often by people who look like they might have trouble coming up with the price of a cup of coffee.

Having failed to get even his well-heeled, horse-buying friends to look at Regal Band's colt, the Two Bucks man views the attention of this mumbling last-minute shopper as, well, miraculous.

There is no way that this twisting customer, now doing a corkscrew imitation in front of him, has checked out the colt's X rays and throat exam report in the "suppository." So his medical qualifications for racing need to be volunteered and guaranteed.

"Clean as they come," the owner says. "Not a thing wrong with him."

"Except being a Supremo," says the Corkscrew.

The colt's sire, Supremo, is a stakes horse of modest accomplishment but magnificent heritage. A grandson of Mr. Prospector, Supremo is from the same prestigious female family as Regal Band—albeit a different branch. As an experiment in "line-breeding," Regal Band had been bred back to the grandson of her mother's half-sister, Andover Way, a well-respected source of aggressive horses who could run the classic distances of a mile and a quarter and a mile and a half.

One attraction of breeding to Supremo was that his stud fee was only $5,000. Unfortunately this bargain is reflected by the positioning of his progeny in the back of the catalog and by a total lack of respect in the speed-happy, bandwagon-loving commercial market. Despite standing at prestigious Lane's End Farm and having rich owners who were presumably sending him good mares, the stallion's first offspring had not been "precocious"—in other words, they had not run fast as two-year-olds. They didn't get any faster at age three. So though alive and kicking, Supremo was deceased as a commercial sire. Even Lane's End had given up on him, evidenced by the fact that although the farm has consigned the colt, not one of their sales representatives is around to push Regal Band's yearling, so it is left for the owner to do.

For an instant he wishes for the presence of the dominant female, an accomplished salesperson. But on second thought he realizes she might buy the colt back. So it is up to him to pitch the Miracle, who is now squatting in front of the colt like a man taking a dump.

"You'll be making a helluva buy because they say this two-year-old brother [Monarchos] is training terrific. Ward says he could be a legitimate Triple Crown horse."

Ward had never said this, but would have, the Two Bucks breeder reasons, if given the opportunity. He's never talked to Ward but has kept up with Monarchos's published workout times, which have been steadily improving. At this point desperation has gotten the better of precision. And being a journalist and political speech writer, these are not the first words he's ever put in someone else's mouth.

From his squat the Miracle flashes another "Yeah, right" look, and uncoils back toward the sales ring. He takes two steps, plants one foot and corkscrews back around again. "Good-looking colt" is all he says. Effusive as the dominant female.

Five minutes later the Miracle buys himself a half-brother to a future Kentucky Derby winner for $20,000—not bad, even for a Supremo. The Two Bucks breeder is the happy under-bidder, and in fact, the only other bidder period.

His colt has ended up in the hands of Norman Miracle, part-time trainer and full-time Jefferson County sheriff's deputy, and owner Gus Goldsmith, a money lender to the poor—a team typical of those who buy inexpensive racehorses, people who bring to the game enthusiasm, money and good intentions—but little else.

Later that day the Miracle buys another bay colt for Goldsmith, similarly marked with a star on his forehead and a white sock on his left ankle, this one by a stallion named Mi Cielo and out of a mare called Weekend Spree. Despite being equipped with identifying halters when the horses are eventually delivered to his Louisville farm, Miracle can't tell them apart. He promptly gets their identities reversed and trains them for the next ten months thinking one is the other. When it comes time to properly identify and enter them for racing, the trainer compounds his error by tattooing one's lip with the number on the registration papers of the other.

Their official identities now hopelessly confused, he first runs the Mi Cielo colt under the name he had given to the Two Bucks horse by Supremo—Just My Guy. Then he attempts to run the Supremo colt under the name he had given the Mi Cielo colt—Weekend Miracle. Fortunately he is stopped by the racing stewards at Churchill Downs, who by this time have caught on to the mistake even though the trainer hasn't. So then he changes Just My Guy's name to My Guy Gus and corrects his lip tattoo, which enables the Miracle to race him about six months earlier than suits his maturity and at a distance about a quarter mile shorter than suits his breeding.

Names and tattoos aside, both horses run poorly, to the everlasting confusion and the embarrassment of everyone, including the Supremo colt's dam Regal Band and the owner of Two Bucks, who is not the least bit surprised. It is very difficult to keep your horses straight when looking at them through your navel.

When Johnny Ward led Monarchos into the saddling paddock at Keeneland two weeks later for his first race ever, the trainer did not squat, crouch, kneel or corkscrew himself around. And to the practiced eye and everlasting relief of the observer from Two Bucks, his hair was neatly parted and lying nicely in place.

Ward stood evenly and upright on both feet and squarely faced his young charge, but the slate-colored horse did not respond in kind. Monarchos, fat as a melon, his mane askew, the chain end of a shank stretched across his gums, was fit to be tied. Which he had to be in every way necessary to get him saddled. Through the whole process he squirmed around like a worm in hot ashes, the look of terror in his eyes.

Around him dodging expertly were the Wards, Jack Oxley, and a cadre of stablehands. Watching from a safe distance was the Two Bucks man, assuming the posture of casual observer, which is all a breeder can be once he sells a horse.

Though breeding is both the power and financial center of the thoroughbred business, at the racetrack it is not the breeder but the owner and trainer who are considered official "connections." They get the box seats, the paddock passes and the preferential treatment. The breeder of a Kentucky Derby winner, trying to get a parking pass for the Belmont Stakes where the horse planned to run, was once asked by a clerk in horseman's relations: "Why are you calling us? You don't have any connection with the horse. You sold it. Ask the owners for a pass." And when the well-known Arthur Hancock, breeder of the 2000 Kentucky Derby winner Fusaichi Pegasus, went to Pimlico Race Course later that May to watch the horse he'd raised work out for the Preakness, he found himself blocked at the gate because of no "official credentials."

That's why the breeders of racehorses who no longer own them are so seldom seen around the edge of winner's circle celebrations or singled out on television. They don't belong there, unless invited by the new owners. Otherwise they are about as welcome as strangers who show up unannounced to see "the house we used to live in." To the press, the tracks and even sometimes the new official "connections" themselves, the breeders are like an extra testicle on a stud horse—irrelevant and in the way.

So the Two Bucks man felt like an outsider as he stood there watching Monarchos doing a polka in the paddock, the same way he had felt for weeks while skulking around Keeneland to watch him train in the mornings. The horse's breeze times had been nothing spectacular—never faster than 12 seconds a furlong. Although preparing the colt for his maiden race, Ward wisely had never asked him to perform anywhere near the 11-second level demanded of him at the sale of two-year-olds in training.

Monarchos had been included in the small stable Ward had taken to Saratoga in August, where many of the best two-year-olds start for the first time. But because the colt had been so slow recovering mentally and physically from the wear and tear of training, Ward had found it more prudent to wait until he got "home" to race him.

Ward's farm abuts Keeneland. He rents a Keeneland barn so close to his own they all appear to be part of the same complex. Even though he winters a contingent in Florida and travels the New York circuit in the summer, Ward's horses train on the Keeneland track year round. The short walk from their stalls to the saddling paddock is one Monarchos had made many times. Still, he was nervous, wild-eyed and high-headed, which is not unusual for two-year-olds at their first race.

Looking ready to jump over the moon, Monarchos wouldn't leave his feet on the ground even long enough for the Two Bucks owner to satisfy his curiosity about their shape and condition. He wondered if he could still ease up to the colt like he used to do, touch his neck, speak to him softly and have him stand quietly while his feet were picked up and examined the way he had been taught. Probably not. Anyway, this was precisely the kind of meddling that owners and trainers resented, the very reason many breeders were treated like an extra testicle. They wanted to have their cake and eat it, too—sell the horse and still get to fool with it. But Monarchos was Oxley's horse now and the maintenance of his feet was nobody's business but Ward's. The Two Bucks owner edged forward for a closer look anyway.

How a horse moves over the ground can be affected by the way the hooves are trimmed and shod. The trainer's decisions in this regard can also determine the horse's chances of staying sound. Some racehorse trainers, including famous and successful ones, mistakenly believe they can lengthen a horse's stride by cutting down the heels and allowing the toe to grow long. They also were taught—erroneously—that spreading the foot wider made for a more shock-absorbent landing, so they have it trimmed that way, flattening down the frog and leaving a flared circumference. In fact, artificially flared hooves with long toes and short heels only place more strain on tendons and ligaments. And it is the density of the foot, not the circumference, that provides shock absorption. Both misconceptions are big contributors to racehorse breakdowns.

From the safe distance being kept by the Two Bucks owner, the feet appeared to pass his "trainer test," but the colt was still snorting and jiggling around. Like his mother, Monarchos never liked strangers coming too close.

"Reckon Johnny Ward is gonna get his horse saddled," the Two Bucks man, a trained observer, remarked to an acquaintance who had wandered up. The Keeneland paddock is a great place for running into old pals knowledgeable about the game, like the Optimist, who shared the breeder's disdain on a number of subjects.

"Oh, he'll get him saddled all right," said the Optimist. "The real question is, can the old lady stay on him?"

The "old lady" was Monarchos's designated rider, pioneer female jockey Patricia Cooksey, who was nearing the end of her career. The Optimist had assumed that Ward's choice of pilots had been severely limited by the size of the field—eleven entries—and the fact that the first weekend in October coincided with a big stakes event at Belmont

Park. Much of the national jockey contingent was still in New York and would not be arriving for the fall meets in Kentucky until the following week.

Many of the top trainers had stopped giving the Kentucky-based Cooksey mounts on their good horses, but the Wards had continued to do so—which said something admirable about them to the Two Bucks owner. An aficionado of older women as well as horses—especially pioneers—he appreciated the kindness of the Wards' gesture. But not on this horse. Why this horse? Wasn't there someone else? Did the choice of Cooksey as a rider somehow reflect the Wards' low opinion of the colt? Already the inscrutable machinations of the thoroughbred business had begun to devour what was left of his journalist's equilibrium.

Monarchos had drawn the eleventh hole, the far outside and most disadvantageous spot in a seven-furlong sprint. Sprints at Keeneland were almost always won by horses who drew the rail lanes, for the simple reason that track management had them rock hard for the two-year-olds in April and they had baked all summer that way. To get to a quick rail lane, an outside horse had to gun to the lead out of the gate and outrun everybody heading for the rail, which would be tiring and nearly impossible; or else be taken quickly to the rail behind horses and eventually through dangerous, veering traffic by a masterful, gutsy rider, which Patricia Cooksey probably no longer was. That she was a patient, experienced hand who had exercised Monarchos in the morning and that Ward knew would keep his excitable young horse out of trouble would have been little consolation to guys who want to win every race—even had they known it.

"With that post draw and the old lady, your horse has no chance," the Optimist assured him.

Wasn't this one of the guys who'd provided the assessment of Johnny Ward's vine-training ability? The Two Bucks man couldn't remember. But this time the Optimist was obviously on target. The most likely scenario for a first-time starter trying to break his maiden under these conditions is for him to break quick, be forced to run four lanes wide the whole trip and run out of gas long before the finish line.

This blueprint for a dismal beginning filled the Two Bucks owner with an even greater urgency to violate the breeder-meddling rules and introduce himself to Ward and Oxley, neither of whom he had ever met. Ward was still preoccupied with the fidgeting Monarchos, but the smiling, exuberant Oxley looked eminently approachable.

The Optimist, a longtime horseman, volunteered an introduction. "I know Jack from polo."

At sixty-three, Oxley fit the image of a polo player, tidy and taut. But it was easier to envision this smallish Okie elegantly mounted up in Chicago alongside Prince Charles and Michael Butler than streaking across a Tulsa field to crash his horse into the likes of famous Texans Tommy Lee Jones and Will Farish. There is polo, and then there is *polo.*

"How is Oxley at polo?"

"Well, you'd probably say Jack gets the job done. He's always on a good horse on a good team and he'll get where he needs to be. But his old man was a terror. He could still hook a high player and take him out when he was eighty and he didn't hesitate to do it. Jack, he's a lot smoother. He plays like he wants to beat you without hurting you."

Smooth is what Oxley turned out to be, greeting the intruder with a promoter's aplomb, as if he were welcoming an investor into one of his gas-well explorations.

"Well, thank you for breeding this horse," he told the breeder, extending his hand. "We think a great deal of Monarchos. We think he is going to do very well."

Having been gassed so many times over the years, the Two Bucks man had become a pretty good gasser himself. "And thank you for buying him," he told Oxley. "As far as I'm concerned, he couldn't be in better hands."

Of course, this utterance was more prayer than conviction. At this point, what the breeder really wanted to ask was, "Why the hell then do you have Patty Cooksey on him?" Instead, his only concession to candor was only a more prudently put reflection of the Optimist's lament.

"Tough draw today, though. Outside post."

"We just want him to have a good experience," said Oxley. "We don't have high expectations today, the first time out."

It was a good thing. Monarchos broke slowly from the eleventh hole and ran seventh on the outside all the way down the backstretch. By the time the runaway juvenile posse approached the turn, he was still way wide, forced into a much longer route than horses on the inside. By the time they turned for home, he was well-spent and still five wide, finishing eighth, twelve and a half lengths behind.

Leaving the racetrack, the breeder and the owner once again encountered each other. And once more the breeder's interest in the future of Regal Band's offspring overwhelmed his awareness that irrelevant third testicles are usually silent. He could not resist giving unsolicited breeder's advice to Jack Oxley.

"Don't worry about what happened today," he said. "This horse might not run at two. But the Regal Bands all get better with age. So please don't give up on him."

"Oh, we'd never do that. He's going to do very well. Very well."

In his passion to save Monarchos the breeder had just cautioned a stranger against doing something that the man would never consider doing in the first place. Like the horse on their minds that day, there was no give up in a son of John T. Oxley, certainly not in one who is deep in the throes of Derby Fever.

Every autumn the best two-year-old colts on the East Coast stop in Kentucky for a few days on their way to Florida or California, where they'll spend the winter. They come with but one treacherous objective—to further torment the thoroughbred titans whose souls are already burning with Derby madness.

What happens on the Kentucky tracks between Labor Day and the end of November invariably affects what will happen at Churchill Downs when the Kentucky Derby rolls around the first Saturday of the following May. Few horses win the Kentucky Derby without at least having been a stakes contender as a two-year-old. By this time in the racing season two or three colts have already won stakes at Saratoga or Belmont and have established themselves as future stars. A half-dozen others are poised to ambush them in one of three or four big graded stakes races in Kentucky, their owners and trainers acutely aware that a good performance will ensure a winter warmed by coastal sunshine and their own rising temperature.

Jack Oxley and his trainer Johnny Ward were going to Florida as usual, with Ward stabling his horses at bucolic Palm Beach Downs 50 miles north of Miami, not far from Oxley's primary base of operations. But this year it would be different. They were going armed. Sprinkled among Debby Oxley's expensive fillies were more colts than ever before that were reasonably priced and had Kentucky Derby pedigrees and good racing potential. Among them were two certain deadly weapons, both sired by horses that had won the Kentucky Derby during the 1990s: a son of 1995 winner Thunder Gulch named Holiday Thunder, who had been purchased as a yearling for $70,000; and Hero's Tribute, a son of 1993 Derby winner Sea Hero, who had been bought as a yearling for $150,000.

All those encouraging words exchanged with the meddling breeder of the slow-breaking, slow-developing Monarchos had been simply the spewed overflow of two gas bags. Oxley believed that if he made it to the Kentucky Derby in 2001, he would most likely go on the back of Holiday Thunder, the most mature and experienced of his young horses.

Holiday Thunder had broken his maiden in the mud at Saratoga and had overcome a horrible start to finish second in an allowance race against tough company. Three weeks before Monarchos's humble beginning at Keeneland, Holiday Thunder had contested the Kentucky Cup Juvenile (Grade 3) at Turfway Park near Cincinnati in sterling fashion. Running against another Thunder Gulch son, a giant-sized version of his perfectly made self named Point Given, Holiday Thunder got off to a slow start but almost ran down Bob Baffert's best Derby horse from behind to finish a credible second.

The day after Monarchos finished seventh at Keeneland running against nobodies, Holiday Thunder again took on stakes horses in the Grade 2 Lane's End Breeders' Futurity. After being squeezed most of the way, the sleek chestnut squirmed out of tight quarters and went six wide to finish third only a head behind Dollar Bill and another respected Baffert-trained horse called Arabian Light.

But Oxley's rising Derby hopes were also being driven up by his other battle-hardened two-year-old, Hero's Tribute. The strapping bay, Donna Ward's favorite among the colts, might be even more talented than Holiday Thunder. He had broken his maiden at Saratoga, too, a tough place to do it. But then he had stumbled out of the gate in his stakes debut at Belmont in September, losing all chance. He had come back in October, however, with an impressive allowance victory at Keeneland, and on November 4, he scored big in graded stakes company, finishing second in the tough Iroquois Stakes at the beginning of the big November meet at Churchill Downs.

The final big stakes race of the crucial Kentucky fall series was the Grade 2 Kentucky Jockey Club, which is contested on the last weekend of racing at Churchill Downs. Real Quiet, the winner of the 1998 Kentucky Derby, had finished third in the Jockey Club when he was a two-year-old. The winner had been Cape Town, who came back to finish only four lengths back of Real Quiet in the Derby.

The top finishers in the Jockey Club are often as highly regarded among Derby hopefuls as the champion two-year-old. And so few two-year-old champions have gone on to win the Derby that winning the Eclipse Award for juveniles is regarded as a jinx. Winning the Jockey Club is not. And Oxley's Holiday Thunder almost won it, going five wide in the mud and capturing the lead in the stretch, only to be run down at the wire by Dollar Bill.

Their stirring finish vaulted both of Oxley's horses into the forefront of the Derby speculation, along with two-year-old champion Macho Uno and runner-up Point Given, who had finished a similarly close first and second in the Breeders' Cup Juvenile (Grade 1), which that year had been held at Churchill at the end of October. All four colts had proven themselves in tough races over the Derby ground at a mile and a sixteenth, the longest distance contested by two-year-olds.

Of the more than 30,000 thoroughbreds born in 1998, fewer than 100 had gone to the track two years later with hopes of contesting the Triple Crown. And of all the owners and trainers still alive and suffering Derby Fever at the end of November, the owners and trainers of these four had the best justification, for their Derby credentials had been validated in the Derby dirt.

As crucial as these big stakes races appeared at the time, the race most critical to the eventual outcome of the next Kentucky Derby was hardly noticed. On the day before the Holiday Thunder–Dollar Bill battle in the Jockey Club stakes, Johnny Ward took Oxley's other two-year-old—Monarchos—over to Churchill Downs for a second try at breaking his maiden.

The distance was six and a half furlongs, a sixteenth of a mile shorter than the Keeneland race, and the field was a great deal tougher, for it included a speedball named Dream Run. Once again among the spectators was Monarchos's bedeviled breeder—not in the saddling paddock harassing the "connections" with his hoof inspections, but 70 miles away wringing his hands in front of a closed-circuit television monitor at Keeneland. Instead of an "old lady" in the irons this time, there was journeyman Willie Martinez, who did some of his best riding at Churchill. Notice of the jockey switch produced such a conflicting combination of sheer delight and Catholic-school guilt that the Two Bucks man at once felt the need to find a priest to hear his confession and to telephone Patricia Cooksey and apologize to her for not wanting such a lovely person and a competent rider on Monarchos and for being glad she had been replaced by Martinez.

Once loaded in the gate, Monarchos appeared ready to go but wasn't. Breaking slowly again, this time from the sixth hole in the middle of the field, he quickly dropped back to tenth and then eleventh. Dream Run, in contrast, shot to the front to press the pace. He and his fast friends went the first quarter mile in 21.4, which is blistering from a standing start at Churchill, and made the half in 45.3, faster then Monarchos had run even as a two-year-old in training. With the race better than half over, Regal Band's best baby was thirteen lengths behind, farther back than he'd been at Keeneland and almost out of the view of the television monitor. He looked like he might finish last. A terrible thought flashed through the breeder's mind: If Jack Oxley really planned to go to the Derby, it was a good thing he had Holiday Thunder and Hero's Tribute.

Then something occurred on the television screen that the breeder had seen many times before in the pastures at Two Bucks. It made the hair on the back of his neck stand up and liquid emotion rush to his eyes. A son of Regal Band, loping along lazily behind his friends, suddenly looked as if somebody had shot him in the butt with a box of tacks. Somebody had floored the gas pedal. Monarchos was out in the center of the track, his ears flat against his head, each stride longer than the last, eating up the ground, passing horses like they were standing still. Only Dream Run and his fast companion Big Talkin Man were left to be caught. They were too far ahead to nail before the wire came up, but there was no doubt they would have been caught had the race been longer.

In Lexington the people around the breeder watching the simulcast monitor wanted to know, "Who was that fast sonofabitch flying at the end?" And in Louisville, Johnny Ward called Jack Oxley in Colorado to report that Monarchos "had closed some kind of good" and to suggest that maybe he should be sent to Florida for the winter with the other good two-year-olds.

"The horse, the horse! The symbol of surging potency and power of movement, of action, in man," wrote D. H. Lawrence, and indeed, the great author of *Apocalypse* had it right. The symbol of potency and the power of movement are for thoroughbred racehorses and for men, their owners, one and the same. Neither gets to the top of the game running at Aqueduct in December or mired in the Kentucky mud during January. Potency equates with having the power to move. To California, Florida and other points sunny. Not just a symbol of power, it is the proof. Where they are in winter separates stakes horses from the claimers, and those in the thick of the action from the rest in the thin.

Some Kentucky horse breeders make it to Fort Lauderdale for the stylish Gulfstream race meet in January and February, but not the hands-on kind who insist on being present to receive the foals from their mothers in the middle of the night.

This insistence is a cause of consternation to the dominant female of Two Bucks, for whom the Kentucky winters are so dismal she would even flee to Florida, which she hates. Why can't the proprietors of Two Bucks go someplace more pleasant for the holidays? The Oxleys, whose Monarchos carries Two Bucks' hopes on his gray back, are horse breeders yet they go to Florida for the winter. And the Optimist and his wife. They, too, are breeders but frequently away during foaling season—to the Rockies skiing and to Florida for the races.

Yes, yes, her husband concedes all that. But Jack Oxley and the Optimist are both naturally lucky men who pay a lot of very good people to do the hands-on work. Wealth is both their cushion against bad luck and a license to travel.

The hands-on breeder is convinced that if he goes anywhere in the winter for more than two days, Two Bucks Farm will freeze over, the employees will get stuck in the snow and be unable to show up, the barren mares will stay barren, and the pregnant mares will deliver sickly foals that freeze to death. These are all winter things that happen, and if they happened at Two Bucks, he would surely end up the sad topic of sympathetic conversation like poor George Hofmeister.

He did not know "poor George" personally—which is explained by the disparity in the speed of the lanes in which they traveled. But he didn't have to know Hofmeister to feel sorry for what had happened to him.

And it was not as if he had just grabbed a tale of farm woe out of thin air to use as an excuse not to go to Florida in the winter. No, the linkage between the plight of "poor George" and his own had been planted—deliberately—by the hungry realtors on the same day he became infected with Derby Fever.

*

Unlike Jack Oxley, who had been racing horses for a quarter of a century before he acquired the vital badge of permanent industry prominence—a Kentucky horse farm—George Hofmeister had stepped up and taken on the great money-devouring monster right off the bat.

Having made his fortune buying up troubled manufacturing firms and setting them straight, Hofmeister started at the factory end of the horse business—land and breeding. Still short of fifty and flush with assets, the buyer of second-rate companies had decided he wanted to be a seller of first-rate horses, which to him seemed to come only from massive, meticulously manicured horse farms heavy with overhead.

Neophyte horse owners learn quickly that boarding, training and veterinary costs are outrageous. But they are flea pee in the ocean next to the serious money that must be put against mowing, fencing, and maintaining trucks, tractors, weed-eaters—and employees. To the practiced ear, the cost of upcoming equipment repairs can be estimated by the pitch of engine strain heard as the farmhand roars by. And the "goddam insurance" eats up cash flow faster than "goddam OCDs" on a young limb bone. Opening a "premium due" notice on a workers' compensation policy has driven many a horse farmer to the insane conclusion that he would be better off killing the employees before they can hurt themselves on the job.

Prudently, the veteran horseman Oxley had waited until he was in his sixties and management of his gas exploration business had been turned over to an experienced family member before setting up his broodmare operation in 1999. Then, his purchase of lovely Fawn Leap—a ready-made 220-acre operation in the heart of quaint Midway—had been considered "a steal" at less than $15,000 per acre.

But for all his history of finding factory bargains, Hofmeister obviously wasn't looking for any in the horse business. After purchasing a few mares in 1997, he bought 2,350 acres north of Lexington, outside Paris in the immediate neighborhood of Claiborne Farm where Secretariat, his sire Bold Ruler, and Mr. Prospector had roamed the paddocks. Two thousand acres is a lot of farm, which Hofmeister soon learned. But overnight it was completely renovated and set up for horses under the name Highland Farm. Construction was begun on a 35,000-square-foot home, a custom mountain rising on the landscape, more imposing than any building in the county. But Hofmeister had only begun.

Then he started touring some of the biggest, fanciest stud farms in the business, asking what it would take to buy them, too. Among those visited by the affable, red-haired stranger from Ohio was "Alphabet" Jones, owner of Walmac International. What Hofmeister wanted from Jones was a price for all of Walmac, "lock, stock and barrel." Never shy to a buyer, Jones said he'd put a pencil to it and come up with a number. They shook hands and Hofmeister left, promising to call back in due time.

Due time passed. Hofmeister never called. The next thing Jones knew, Hofmeister had bought the breeding rights to 1998 Kentucky Derby winner Real Quiet and announced plans to stand him at a Walmac rival, The Vinery, a stallion farm to the west in Woodford County, where Hofmeister had also acquired "a major interest" in all thirty-one stallions and 250 acres.

Hofmeister still wasn't done. He bought a horse farm in the very far southeast, too—2,500 acres near Scone in New South Wales, Australia. This he called Vinery Australia, and he planned to shuttle his stallions there for Southern Hemisphere breeding duty. Then the former Blue Bird Ranch in Utah was added to the operation. It would be called Vinery West. Not only did he now own land in all directions, he could be seen in all of them as well. At every sale or gathering of the thoroughbred elite, Hofmeister was there, huddling with the big movers and shakers. What could they be selling him now? The answer was not long in coming: Not one more thing—at least for a while.

In the fall of 1998, when most of his fellow titans were shopping for their 2000 Derby candidates, Hofmeister was recovering from a serious automobile accident. En route from Vinery to Highland Farm, he collided with a car whose driver had fallen asleep at the wheel. His injuries were severe—a crushed leg, a broken arm, a "Herman Munster" gash on his forehead—requiring weeks of hospital and rehabilitation time. While he was laid up, his businesses—fifty-eight plants employing 8,000 workers on three continents—obviously missed him. Cash flow slowed down. Creditor demand speeded up.

By this time, Hofmeister owned 120 broodmares, a number beyond the worrying capacity of even the most conscientious of hands-on breeders. In 1999, he began selling as fast as he had bought. Vinery Kentucky and Vinery Australia were sold to German investors. Blue Bird reverted to its former name and former ownership. So when John Oxley was sending his small band of Derby contenders to Florida for the winter, George Hofmeister was cataloging his large equine collection for future dispersal. Highland Farm, including a $9 million horse inventory, was about to go on the market for $60 million.

This was the nature of the talk among the horse farm realtors, who are to the horse industry what mob lawyers are to the mob—consiglieres. They own and race horses, show up at every gathering, and know everything that is going on. But they don't own farms—at least not long enough to get "premium due" notices and tractor repair bills. This wisdom is the root of their counselor's cachet, a license to go to Florida for a few days in winter, and when they return, to lounge away the afternoons at Keeneland watching the races from Gulfstream where they have just been.

Like all returning travelers they bring back titillating tidbits of inside information—and the germs of disease, both of which they spread through close contact in the stuffy, simulcast rooms. And it was here, undoubtedly, amidst musings on which two-year-olds were hot at Gulfstream and which real-estate consigliere might benefit from the massive debacle about to befall "poor George" that the proprietor of Two Bucks first contracted Derby Fever.

The infection was doubly ominous. The carrier was a farm consigliere fresh from Gulfstream and hot on the trail of new farm listings, presumably those he suspected might be going under. First he mentioned Hofmeister's massive Highland, about which he seemed knowledgeable. Then, drawing closer within certain germ-spreading range, he whispered, "What about Two Bucks? I heard you might be ready to sell, too."

The Two Bucks owner blanched. Did signs of his own impending doom already have him in the category with "poor George"? Probably. The consiglieres read the auction results like tea leaves. At the time Two Bucks had relatively little debt but also matching revenue.

"It is always a possibility in this business," the owner replied—but dismissively.

"Well, if you do decide, you've got my number."

"Yes, thanks," though wanting to say, "Yes, and you sure as hell have mine."

Then came the point of infection.

"By the way, I saw your horse at Gulfstream."

"Yeah. What horse is that?"

"What horse is that? Monarchos."

The consiglieres, many of whom double as bloodstock agents, even know who bred which obscure horses.

"I thought Ward trained at Palm Beach Downs."

"Well, he does. But Donna's running that barn. This year Johnny's got the Derby horses at Gulfstream. They say Monarchos is really Oxley's Derby horse."

"Hell, he hasn't even broken his maiden yet."

"No problem. He'll break it by a mile. He's the one."

The consigliere backed out of infection range. "Don't forget me now, on that other thing—okay?"

Okay.

Monarchos a Derby horse? Who was he kidding? This had to be filed under typical consigliere bullshit. The Two Bucks proprietor had long ago grown skeptical of authoritative pronouncements by members of the real-estate profession, which had been the business of the dominant female when he met her.

But what about selling Two Bucks? There the consigliere might be on target. Sure as hell the 2000 balance sheet would show that something at Two Bucks needed selling. Needing to sell something is a common condition of the horse business. Needing to sell everything in a hurry is most common to neophytes for whom the glorious sight of thoroughbreds grazing bluegrass pastures veined with black oak fence can easily become an irresistible attraction to overextension.

Only if they can last long enough at horse raising will things get better. Not that the urgency to sell will ever go away. It won't. But it will come with an option—the farm or the horses. For him, if not for "poor George," that option was still alive.

9

If I had a stallion like you have right on your farm, I'd hang onto him with hooks of steel and build a barrier around him as high as the wall of China to keep anybody else from getting him. The one I refer to, of course, is Celt the son of Commando.

W. S. VOSBURGH, eminent turf journalist,
in a letter to his friend A. B. Hancock of Kentucky, in 1912

Reaching the state of delirium that accompanies having two winter book favorites for the Kentucky Derby had cost Jack Oxley a lot of money. But among the industry titans struck with Derby Fever, he was merely a piker. The three colts he'd sent to Florida with Johnny Ward had cost him less than $400,000. Among those intent on winning the most difficult race in the world, the idea that Oxley might do it with a "hardboot" training a trio of cheap horses was pretty much a joke.

Men more wealthy, more powerful and more driven had invested far more in the same quixotic quest. By any measure—personal ambition and ego, the number of horses, dollars invested or scope and depth of motivation—Jack Oxley, wealthy and successful as he was, was a peon.

Although history suggested that a Derby winner could come from almost anywhere, those truly serious about winning the big one in the big money millennium were going about it in a really big way. They all knew that "horses are like strawberries, good one day and gone the next," so you couldn't just start out with two or three runners and realistically expect to have one the following May.

The sheikhs of Dubai would have more than a hundred to start with, the Irish fifty or more. Prince Ahmed Salman, a member of the Saudi Arabian ruling family, had built and dedicated an entire corporation to the task of winning all the classic races in the world.

At the July Keeneland yearling sale in 1999—the same year Oxley purchased his Derby favorites Holiday Thunder and Hero's Tribute for a total of $220,000—Sheikh Mohammed, the most active of the Dubai brothers, had shopped the higher-end market in search of Derby winners. He bought thirteen yearlings, ranging in price from $200,000 to $1.4 million, for a total of $9 million, and still he was not the sale's leading buyer.

That distinction went to a "new man"—Satish Sanan, an India-born, English-educated eradicator of Y2K computer bugs, who spent nearly $12 million for fourteen horses. The July before he'd done the same thing—fourteen at a cost of $13.4 million. What a way to celebrate success. The year the world would use his software to avert Y2K disaster, Sanan planned to win the 2000 Kentucky Derby. From those fourteen yearlings surely would emerge the "the big horse." Sanan predicted it would be the most expensive of the lot—the $2.2 million Pleasant Colony colt that was his favorite. That hadn't happened.

But nobody could accuse Sanan of trying to play this man's game in short pants. Since 1997 he and his wife Anne had spent $44 million on seventy-two yearlings and built a $15 million farm and training facility in Florida, to which the Hall of Fame trainer D. Wayne Lukas had moved his headquarters.

But with the 2001 Derby less than six months off, the only two-year-olds Lukas had on the stakes trail belonged to others. At the same Calder sale where Oxley had bought Monarchos for $170,000, Lukas had picked out the fastest and most expensive two-year-old on the grounds, a horse named Yonaguska for $1.9 million, but for the Irish—not Sanan. So the computer whiz still didn't have a Derby horse for

2001. Obviously, he had not spent enough. It seemed you could not spend enough.

Yet from the arid deserts of the Arab Middle East to the emerald fields of Tipperary in southern Ireland, from the old Hapsburg dynasty in Austria to the islands of Japan, international titans of politics and industry were still hard at the task.

Owning and breeding the thoroughbred horses that win America's Triple Crown races has long been a personal obsession of kings and queens and sheikhs and power mongers of all descriptions. Along with a handful of famous European races like the Epsom Derby in Great Britain and the Arc de Triomphe in France, they constitute the measuring stick for a "who's got the biggest" contest among some of the world's most competitive men.

But more is at stake than bragging rights and penis envy. The true measure of success in the thoroughbred business is the same as in any other—money. And the only way to make real money in racing is with the most valuable breeding stallions, and value can be most quickly, surely and profitably established by successful competition in world-famous races. In the 300-year history of the sport, the rewards have always gone to the people who own and breed the winners at the highest level.

For the past seventy-five years, owning and standing the successful stallions has been synonymous with industry control. And as Jack Oxley moved his relatively small but potent stable of Derby contenders to Florida for the winter, control of the long-troubled thoroughbred industry was being fiercely fought over by a handful of powerful interests intent on domination.

At first glance, they all looked to be sportsmen like Oxley—ambitious, wealthy and consistently successful men simply trying to leap over yet another impossible hurdle in search of yet more achievement and personal glory. But among his most powerful international rivals were men driven by such a sense of burning nationalism that they had long ago weighted down their individual hopes with the pride of their homelands. Their horses carried not only their own vast fortunes and egos into these battles but the hopes and reputations of their small countries as well. And without exception, all were veteran and brazen gamblers who believed that if they invested enough in the game it could eventually be bought.

No one horse or single race would determine if they could or not, but there was no better place to start than with a stallion that wins the Kentucky Derby.

It was a typically sweltering July night at the Keeneland yearling sale in 1998 and the big eye of the thoroughbred world was focused on a mysterious, pony-tailed figure wearing little round dark glasses, whose appearance reporters likened to that of an aging Samurai warrior or the object of an FBI counterintelligence investigation. He was in fact a Japanese businessman named Fusao Sekiguchi, one of his country's so-called "bubble gentlemen" who during the 1980s economic boom came up with overnight fortunes of seemingly hollow centers. He had just bought for $4 million a yearling colt that symbolized potential racehorse and stallion success as much as any horse since the wondrous Secretariat. In the process Sekiguchi had outlasted a coalition of opposing buyers as unusual in makeup as he was in appearance—the Irish powerhouse Coolmore and the dark, soft-spoken Sanan.

It was not Sekiguchi's first Keeneland spending spree. Two years earlier, having made a fortune with a company that outsourced engineering and technological support services to burgeoning high-tech companies, he had bought seven July-sale yearlings for $5.75 million. But when he returned home, he discovered that his business partners, upset with his heavy racehorse spending, had ousted him from his job as chief executive officer, which had paid him the equivalent of $250,000 a month. No longer able to pay for his purchases, Sekiguchi turned them back to Keeneland but soon kept his promise to compensate the sale company for any losses incurred in their reselling.

Now rolling again, swarmed by an anxious, sweat-drenched press corps and pridefully hiding his pidgin English behind an interpreter,

Sekiguchi insisted on thanking everyone he felt responsible for his good fortune, including the $4 million colt's breeder and seller, Arthur B. Hancock III, and trainer Johnny Ward, the man who had found the colt for him and done his ring bidding. During the hectic, impromptu press conference, Sekiguchi spotted Ward and his wife Donna in the crowd and summoned them to his side.

"This is the man who advises me best," said Sekiguchi through his interpreter. "He knows horses."

It hadn't taken a lot of genius on Ward's part to find or buy this handsome son of Mr. Prospector, one of the two most prolific producers of expensive racehorses in history. Because he was nearing the end of an illustrious career at stud, every son of Mr. Prospector was sought out and closely watched over from birth. Ward had first seen this one as a weanling on Hancock's Bourbon County farm and had checked on him regularly. Everybody went to see Arthur's high-priced stud colts. Not only was he one of the few people in history to breed and race two Kentucky Derby winners, he had stood the ornery, hard-knocking Halo, one of the few stallions that ever sired two. Arthur's grandfather and namesake, A. B. Hancock, was one of the most influential men in the history of American horse racing. Over two generations, he and Arthur's father—known as "Bull"—had been primarily responsible for moving the thoroughbred breeding industry from Europe, where it had resided for a century, to the limestone knobs of central Kentucky, where it has resided ever since. They moved it piece by piece, by picking off the best breeding stock. Not only did they cherry-pick the European yearling market, for years the Hancocks and their Kentucky brethren bought the continent's best racehorses that they believed would make the best sires. The share and season prices the horses could command in rich, rapidly industrializing America allowed them to pay so much for the best horses that Europeans could not afford to keep them. In the past century, the three generations of Hancock men probably have laid their hands on more great thoroughbred bloodstock than any single family on earth, even though much of it ended up being owned in partnerships or held individually by their well-to-do clients.

In recent years Arthur, who owns and operates his own farm called Stone, and his younger brother Seth, who controls the family's legendary Claiborne Farm, have not exactly held on to their best stallions with "hooks of steel," as their grandfather was advised to do by the wise Mr. Vosburgh nearly a century earlier. Periodically they have come face to face with the same reality that the Europeans and their forefathers did from time to time—that it is sometimes better to save the farm by selling the horses. After his Halo-bred stallion Sunday Silence won the Kentucky Derby, Arthur sold him to a Japanese buyer for $10 million before he ever saw a Kentucky mare close up. Arthur said the sale kept him out of bankruptcy. Halfway through the decade his brother Seth duplicated the sale, sending the promising Mr. Prospector son Forty-Niner to stand in Japan as well and replacing him with another wonderful income producer, the 1990 Kentucky Derby winner Unbridled.

So anybody with the money could have bought Arthur's exciting Mr. Prospector colt when he was a weanling on the same terms as was offered to Johnny Ward—$1.5 million or $750,000 for half. Though Ward declined, the price was not as unreasonable as it sounds. More than thirty Mr. Prospector offspring had brought $1 million or more at public auction. And this one was physically superior to most in that he was free of his sire's most often passed-down trait—front legs that grew unpredictably in several directions.

By the time he got to the yearling sale, the only unknown about Hancock's colt, by now nicknamed "Superman," was how much the stallion hunters would be willing to cough up for him. Many of the usual suspects, including D. Wayne Lukas and the Coolmore tandem of John Magnier and Michael Tabor, were hot for him. Everyone was in awe of the colt's physical attributes, including his unmistakable look of intelligence. But some veterinarians had questions about his throat. Of the four who looked at him for Coolmore, only the esteemed surgeon Paul Thorpe passed him without reservation as to his ability to race. Some commented on his pinched heels and his low-slung pasterns, that section of leg bone connecting the ankle to the hoof.

Photo by Suzie Picou-Oldham

The author, the dominant female and Al the Jack Russell at Two Bucks Farm.

Joseph V. DiOrio/Horsephotos.com

Security guards clear the path for thoroughbreds on their way to the auction ring at Keeneland, the world's most important seller of racehorses.

Photo by Lee Thomas

Regal Band and the breeding genius.

David Stephenson, *Lexington Herald-Leader*

Maria's Mon, the sire of Monarchos, with his owner, Josephine Abercrombie, and her farm manager, Clifford Barry.

Courtesy of the author

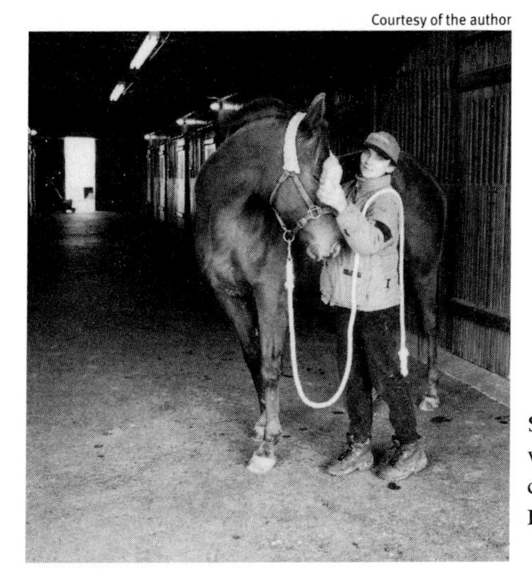

Sigita Budrikaite provides X-chromosome care to the broodmare Knoosh at Two Bucks.

Photo by Cheryl Manista

Monarchos when he was three months old, already practicing for the Kentucky Derby.

Photo by Anne M. Eberhardt

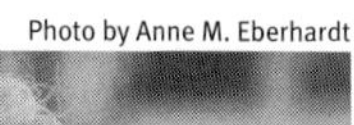

Murray Smith, the pinhooker who started Monarchos under saddle.

Michael J. Marten/Horsephotos.com

The "swells" inspecting yearlings at the "spa" in Saratoga.

Michael J. Marten/Horsephotos.com

Fusao Sekiguchi, owner of the 2000 Kentucky Derby champion winner Fusaichi Pegasus, in the winner's circle.

Four Footed Fotos

Morava—a/k/a "Snake"—defeats an expensive stakes horse named Three Wonders at Churchill Downs on June 15, 2000.

Michael J. Marten/Horsephotos.com

Debby and Jack Oxley, owners of Monarchos.

Michael J. Marten/Horsephotos.com

Trainer John Ward grazes Monarchos.

Michael J. Marten/Horsephotos.com

John and Donna Ward with Jack Oxley's Eclipse Award-winning mare, Beautiful Pleasure.

Janet Worne, *Lexington Herald-Leader*

Not far from Keeneland stands the infamous "castle"—a monument to failed expectations in the bluegrass.

Courtesy of the author

Al the Jack Russell at risk in the SUV.

Joseph V. DiOrio/Horsephotos.com

Sheik Mohammed of Dubai (*left*), the world's leading buyer of race horses and his longtime international rival, the Irishman John Magnier (*below*).

Joseph V. DiOrio/Horsephotos.com

Courtesy of *The Blood-Horse*, photo by Bill Denver/EQUI-PHOTO

The Blood-Horse cover following Monarchos's victory in the Florida Derby on March 10, 2001.

Michael J. Marten/Horsephotos.com

Bob Baffert and his "big red train," Point Given.

Joseph V. DiOrio/Horsephotos.com

Point Given's owner, Prince Ahmed Salman of Saudi Arabia.

Vincent Dusovic/Horsephotos.com

Congaree bests Monarchos in the Wood Memorial in New York, April 14, 2001.

Joseph V. DiOrio/Horsephotos.com

Hall of Fame trainer D. Wayne Lukas inspects a yearling at Keeneland.

The Courier-Journal

Bob Baffert and his fiancée, Jill Moss, atop a Jaguar at Churchill Downs.

Photo by Suzanne Depp

Jack Oxley listens politely to the pre-Derby observations of Monarchos's breeder.

Photo by Barbara Livingston

Monarchos, with exercise rider Bryan Beccia aboard, watches the track traffic at Churchill Downs with his companion pony Mouse and Johnny Ward's assistant, Yvonne Azeff.

Michael J. Marten/Horsephotos.com

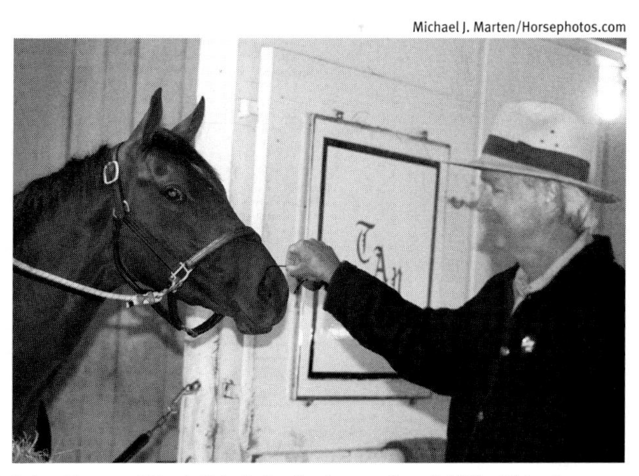

John Fort and Invisible Ink, the horse that fulfilled his dreams.

Four Footed Fotos

Monarchos winning the Kentucky Derby. His time of 1:59.97 was the second fastest in history.

Photo by Anne M. Eberhardt

The author and the dominant female became known as the Twin Spires Squires after Monarchos's victory.

Michael J. Marten/Horsephotos.com

Jorge Chavez with his "dream" horse.

Michael J. Marten/Horsephotos.com

Debby and Jack Oxley with the spoils of victory.

Four Footed Fotos

The author on the edge of celebration, barely.

None of this concerned Ward in the slightest. Perfect or not, he had Hip No. 228 valued at $2.2 million for Sekiguchi when he arrived in Lexington. But he sent his flamboyant visitor, complete with entourage, to Hancock's sale barn with the warning that the colt would likely cost considerably more.

No matter to Sekiguchi, who knew when he laid eyes on the prize yearling that for him there could be no other. This was a man who collected rare race cars, staged the first bullfights in the Orient, wrote a best-selling book on business acumen and wanted to invest 1 billion yen (about $10 million) in the horse-racing business. To a horse breeder he was a buyer from heaven, a bidder not to be denied. He wore his pajamas to a meeting with aides back at his hotel and declared, "I want that horse. I don't care how much he costs; I want that horse."

Naturally, Sekiguchi was certain his new purchase was destined to win the Kentucky Derby and predicted it, despite the fact that no son of Mr. Prospector ever had and neither had any horse sold at public auction for more than $1 million. In fact, only four sale-toppers from the July Keeneland sale and none in the history of Saratoga August had ever even earned back their purchase price on the racetrack.

In a refrain peculiar to men who have been driven by Derby Fever into an unreasonable expenditure for a young, untested thoroughbred, Sekiguchi offered the only possible explanation for his compulsion: "When I saw him I felt this enormous power and that's when I made up my mind."

An animal of such magnitude needed a magnificent name, so one was concocted by adding the Japanese "ichi"—meaning number one—to his own name Fusao and coupling it with the name of the mythical Greek horse with wings: Fusaichi Pegasus.

In fulfilling the dream of the ecstatic visitor from the Far East, breeder Hancock and trainer Ward, both in their fifties and third-generation Kentucky hardboots, were doing exactly what the Irish, the English and the French had done before them—aiding the transfer of their best-bred, best-conformed stallion prospects into the hands of wealthy foreign interests. And they were driven by a passion equally as compelling as Sekiguchi's—survival in the business they loved.

Sekiguchi's aptly named wonder horse was destined to become the second foreign-owned Derby winner of the decade, the star of an international horse drama that would define the importance of the Kentucky Derby to the thoroughbred world like nothing else. He would become the most glaring symbol of how well-planned, nationalism-rooted strategies—particularly those of the Irish and the Arabs—are quietly but significantly dismantling American domination of breeding and racing worldwide.

The day Fusaichi Pegasus won the 2000 Kentucky Derby, assuring his career as a stallion, Sekiguchi made it clear his star would set in the West. "He is an American horse and belongs in America," he said.

But when it came time to sell him, Sekiguchi still faced financial difficulties. Already he'd had to hock a minority interest in all his horses, including "Fu-Peg," to Shadai Farm, the Japanese horse empire of Teruya Yoshida and his family. So Sekiguchi did what the Kentucky hardboots had been doing for years, what Arthur Hancock had done when he sold Sunday Silence and what younger brother Seth had done by selling Forty-Niner. He sold out to the highest bidder.

After refusing to bid more than $4 million for him as a yearling, the Irish investors from Coolmore turned around and bought him back from Sekiguchi in a deal valued at upwards of $68 million. The mere possibility of this kind of instant uptick in equity in such a short time frame is how normally sharp-penciled, tough-minded businessmen justify paying a fortune for an eighteen-month-old horse they've never even seen run across a field.

The last stallion of this magnitude and potential to go to stud in Kentucky was the 1992 Horse of the Year, A. P. Indy, who was Japanese-owned as well. When A. P. Indy's racing career was over, he ended up as the premier stallion attraction at Lane's End in Woodford County, Kentucky, where he had been bred and raised. In traditional fashion, he returned there as property of a syndicate put together by the farm owner and longtime friend of the George Bush family, Will Farish, currently the U.S. ambassador to Great Britain. The Hancocks had handled their most successful horses this way for years. The financial arrangement did not hinge entirely on the market value of the horse (foreign interests would have undoubtedly paid more) but put more weight on the personal relationship between his Japanese owner, Tomonori Tsurumaki, and the diplomatically talented Farish, a former chairman of Churchill Downs and arguably the single most powerful figure in the American racing establishment.

Farish wanted the horse to come home and Tsurumaki, a friend of the West, made sure that he did, which was not welcome news to the fledgling but promising Japanese racing industry, or to the sire-poor Europeans. Over the years the deal turned out to be a smashing success. Now perhaps the second most valuable stallion in the world, A. P. Indy commands a $350,000 stud fee—with no guarantee of a foal—and even at that price a place in his book is very difficult to come by.

Like A. P. Indy, Fusaichi Pegasus began his stud career on a magnificently maintained breeding farm in Woodford County, Kentucky. But not on a family-owned farm on the strength of a deal among pals, but rather at the imposing Ashford Stud owned by the Irishmen. Like the horse himself, the farm was a trophy of their business acumen and burning ambition.

At Ashford, the ownership of which Coolmore took as restitution for an unpaid American debt, access to Fusaichi's coveted semen won't be doled out on the basis of lifetime friendships and neighborhood familiarity, but rather in accordance with an international promotion and marketing strategy to virtually anyone with a mare and money on any continent. Rather than stand in reserve for an American farm owner and his breeder friends as he once would have, "Fu-Peg" had become the best-marketed, best-looking, most expensive and incontrovertible evidence of the most effective stallion strategy ever executed by horsemen not named Hancock. If the Coolmore pattern held, he would stand his first two breeding seasons in Kentucky before departing each summer for double duty somewhere in the Southern Hemisphere, and eventually to Europe to stand a season or two in Ireland or Great Britain, or even Japan.

So as the competition for the 2001 Kentucky Derby began to take shape on the winter tracks in Florida and California, the 2000 winner stood in the eyes of many as a glaring symbol of everything that had gone wrong. Precisely the kind of horse upon which Kentucky superiority had been based, this paragon of breeding genius had already passed through the hands of one foreign owner into the hands of a second whose sworn goal was to return the base of thoroughbred breeding to Europe.

And now, as the Kentucky elite looked forward to the next great race sure to make a stallion, the 2001 Kentucky Derby, there was a distinct possibility that the same thing was about to happen over again.

Ironically, their best hope of preventing it lay with the same Kentucky "hardboot" who had found and bought Fusaichi Pegasus for Sekiguchi—Johnny Ward. Everyone had felt bad for Ward when Sekiguchi had shifted the promising son of Mr. Prospector to the barn of another trainer, Californian Neil Drysdale, and even worse when Drysdale won the Derby with him. Derby horses don't come along all that often for small stable trainers like Ward. It said Kentuckians can find the horse for you, but you better get a California trainer if you want to win the Derby. But this year, in what surely had to be some balancing act of fate, Ward had three promising "Derby darlings," all belonging to Jack Oxley. Even though Oxley was an Oklahoma oilman who spent a lot of his time somewhere else, he paid taxes in the Bluegrass, had three other stallions standing stud on Kentucky farms, and had been supporting Ward's stable for more than twenty years. That was enough to qualify him as a hometown boy.

For sure if Ward and Oxley could win the 2001 Derby, there would be no reproduction of the galling picture the race had presented to the world the year before, when the near-perfect son of Kentucky's most famous stallion had arrived to fulfill his destiny at the Kentucky Derby with a Greek-Japanese name that few hardboots could pronounce, accompanied by an owner in a garish yellow jacket who traveled with a bevy of fancy geishas and who showed up in the winner's circle in gangster pinstripes out of a 1940s George Raft movie—an owner whose own tongue-twisting name would be mangled on global television by a Kentucky governor who has trouble pronouncing "equestrian"; an owner who would—God forbid—have to accept the magnificent Kentucky Derby winner's trophy through an interpreter.

10

So did this horse excel a common one
In shape, in courage, color, pace and bone,
. . . What a horse should have he did not lack,
Save a proud rider on so proud a back.

WILLIAM SHAKESPEARE, *Venus and Adonis*

Yvonne Azeff wore the look of a Middle East guerrilla fighter, one of those dark, wiry, female officers with laser eyes, close-cropped hair and bandoliers across her chest. Television news depicts them brandishing automatic rifles at border crossings or directing mortar fire and tank maneuvers. Mysteriously alluring women, they speak only to give curt orders and are never seen in anything but smartly cut camouflage uniforms, which if removed would surely disgorge empty shell casings.

Whatever Azeff's level of passion for war, it ran high for good racehorses. And by the time she went to work as an assistant trainer for Johnny Ward in Florida that December, she had seen more than a few of them. A former exercise rider and jockey from the Maryland and Delaware tracks, she had served training apprenticeships under Stanley Hough and Randy Bradshaw and finally the master himself, D. Wayne Lukas, for whom she monitored the training of two Triple Crown horses, Cat Thief and High Yield.

Ward had been trying to hire Azeff for some time. She was perfect for his new Kentucky Derby strategy. Ward wanted to complete the training of his Derby horses at Churchill Downs, the site of the race, rather than at his usual base at Keeneland 70 miles away. If a legitimate Derby candidate emerged from the rigors of Florida winter conditioning, he would be sent directly to Churchill to train. But a first-rate assistant would be needed to live with the horse night and day. And though most of the Florida horses would be housed in his winter barn in Palm Beach, the trainer wanted to experiment by sending Oxley's Derby hopefuls along with a few others—a "short string"—to train at Gulfstream Park, the site of the Florida Derby, an important spring prep race. True, the Gulfstream track had a reputation for being hard and tough on the legs of young horses, but there were offsetting considerations. The hustle and bustle of the place and the close proximity of the track and paddock to the noisy stands made it perfect for preparing a horse to deal with the mania of the Kentucky Derby.

Azeff knew that mania inside and out and knew what kind of a horse a trainer must have to get there. While getting acquainted with the population of Ward's stable in Palm Beach, the young woman spotted one she hoped would be among the string sent to Gulfstream the following month for her to train.

"John, am I going to get this little gray colt?" she asked her new boss. "I think he's going to be a star."

By the time she led him over to the Gulfstream paddock for his first Florida race a few weeks later, Azeff was sure of it. Starting for the first time as a three-year-old, Monarchos—now nicknamed "Sparky" by Azeff's barn staff—again broke slowly from the gate—eighth out of eleven. But this time he had a great rider on his back, the little Peruvian Jorge Chavez, who knew all about slow starts in life. Chavez, an orphan from the streets of Lima, hustled Monarchos quickly up close to the front of the pack, which covered the first quarter mile in 22.2 seconds. A blistering quarter of a mile later, Azeff's budding star had eased into the lead in a race for the first time in his life, and when asked to do so by Chavez, ran away from them all.

Returning to the winner's circle aboard a six-length winner that had just destroyed a good field of Florida maidens in the time of 1:22.1, Chavez realized the significance of what had just happened. The crowd waiting for him in the winner's circle did, too. As Chavez dismounted, his agent Richard DePass smiled, gave owner Oxley a knowing look and wondered aloud, "My, my, what do we have here?"

Waiting for Chavez on the ground, Azeff already knew the answer, or thought she did anyway, and had whispered it to the groom Tammy Holtz when she assigned Monarchos for her to rub. "Nobody knows it yet," she told Holtz, "but this is our Derby horse."

So certain was Azeff of Monarchos's future that shortly after New Year's she had telephoned her mother, Barbara Barnhill, a former exercise rider herself who lived in Citra, Florida, and gave her a heads-up: "Mom, make your plans now to go to the Derby, because we've got a shot to win with this gray colt we've got."

A horse's route to the Derby is so treacherous and fraught with uncertainty that believing in January it has "a shot to win" in May is something a knowledgeable horsewoman like Azeff would confide only to her mother or whisper to the horse's groom.

The only certainty at this point was that while working for D. Wayne Lukas, Azeff had caught a wonderful case of Derby Fever and was capable of spreading it throughout Ward's operation to horses and people alike.

The rider who gets on a racehorse every day is just as important as the one who rides it once a month in a race. And the week after Jorge Chavez rode Monarchos home a winner, the horse got a new exercise rider named Bryan Beccia.

A "contract rider," Beccia was accustomed to getting on fourteen horses a day—$10 a horse—just to clear $700 a week. Azeff knew him from her time with Lukas. Beccia had exceptionally strong hands and was known for his skill with difficult-to-handle horses, perfect for the rambunctious colts Ward had entrusted to Azeff's care. A former assistant trainer himself, Beccia knew that as a rider he possessed the trainer's most valued tool—a clock in his head. If a trainer wants his horse to go five-eighths of a mile in "1:01 and change"—which means a little more than 1 minute and 1 second, but less than 1 minute and 2 seconds—Bryan Beccia could bring back close to the right change. Some of the best race jockeys have no idea how fast they're riding. Beccia always did.

Azeff's offer—four or five mounts a day for around the same money—was too good for Beccia to pass up. But the job had to be only temporary. Miami stayed too hot too long for the forty-two-year-old Connecticut native, and Beccia had already purchased an airline ticket to California. Another trainer, James Chapman, had hired him to prepare the sprinter Caller One for the big million-dollar race in Dubai later in the spring.

The first time Beccia got on Monarchos he got off thinking the gray colt was okay, a nice horse but nothing special. But each day the rider liked him a little better, especially his long, efficient stride and the way he seemed to enjoy running. Monarchos galloped as hard as most horses did in a full breeze, and the longer the run the more fluid the horse became under him.

Ward does not ask his horses for exceptional speed in their prerace workouts. He wants them to run steady and hard but under control. Teaching racehorses to "rate"—or run at a speed dictated by the rider—is the most difficult aspect of training. Five days before Monarchos was slated to make his second start of the year, he "breezed" five-eighths of a mile in a pokey 1:04.2. Of the twenty-six horses that worked the same distance that day at Gulfstream Park, Monarchos was the slowest—an unintended result, no doubt, of the most important training lesson he had gotten from Azeff and Beccia. Monarchos had become accustomed to traveling at whatever speed his exercise rider dictated. And that day it had been Chavez in the irons, not Beccia, and the Peruvian had no idea he was traveling so slowly. Before the race Beccia had to rev Monarchos up again in an unpublished "blowout."

But on race day, it was again Chavez, the street urchin turned millionaire master-jockey, who climbed aboard Monarchos. At 4-feet–10, he was more than half a foot shorter than Beccia, and the difference was in the length of their legs. Chavez sat perched atop a horse like a pea. What he lacked in size he made up in expertise and enthusiasm. Gifted with perfect balance and incredible endurance, Chavez had a distinctive riding style that earned him the nickname "Chop-Chop" after the short, rapid thrusts of the whip which he delivered judiciously from a statue-like stillness above the horse's withers. It was Chavez' touch and stability that had first impressed Donna Ward a few years earlier, then in search of an especially gifted rider for her difficult-to-handle mare Beautiful Pleasure. Both mare and jockey won Eclipse Awards, the Oscar of racing, in 1999.

Aboard Monarchos, Chavez had two missions even more important than winning. One was to get his colt out of the gate quickly again, and the second was to settle him to "rate" behind the leaders, a racing strategy called "stalking the pace." The allowance race would be his first going a mile or more and around two turns of the track. Until now, all Monarchos had ever done was sprint to make up ground.

When the gates opened this time, Chavez gunned Monarchos out of the three hole and to the front of the pack. Distilled, a quick horse carrying big-time Derby hopes, broke even more sharply from the outside followed by a companion, and Monarchos settled into the third spot along the rail, exactly what Ward was hoping for. Here his horse could get dirt kicked in his face by the frontrunners for a while and still be in perfect position if and when they tired. The early fractions were moderate, but not suicidal—24 seconds for the first quarter, 47.4 for the half—about what Monarchos was used to in his gallops under Beccia but slower than in the sprints.

Three-quarters of the way through the race, which was one and a sixteenth miles long, Distilled decided to pull away. Another Kentucky Derby hopeful, Thunder Blitz, moved up on the outside to go with him. Only after Thunder Blitz had poked his head in front of Monarchos did Chavez loosen his hold. Under him the stride of his mount lengthened instantly. Three or four jumps later Monarchos had caught and eased by Thunder Blitz on the inside. As Distilled led the pack through the turn for home, Chavez cut Monarchos an inch more rein slack and tapped him lightly on the shoulder. The resulting bolt forward excited the track announcer, Vic Stauffer, who began to shout. "Monarchos cuts from the rail . . . and he is coming now with a sustained run."

Heard 800 miles north, the urgency in Stauffer's voice sent chills up the spine of the hands-on breeder from Two Bucks. Satisfied his farm was sufficiently safe from the dangers of winter, he had driven the ten minutes to Keeneland to see the simulcast, accompanied by the dominant female, who was now well into her "It's February so I will go anywhere—even Keeneland" mode. Though the expression on her face still said, "I don't belong anywhere this depressing," the call of the track announcer had obviously enlivened her vigorous instinct for winning. She inched closer to the monitor, while her husband stood dumbstruck, as if some movement or show of emotion might bring a halt to Monarchos, who had begun to pull away.

"What a classy performance," Stauffer shouted, "Monarchos waited for Chavez to ask him to go and now he is going. . . . Monarchos is three in front and Distilled is left in his wake."

Chavez was still sitting "chilly"—motionless—barely tapping the rocket he was riding with the tip of his stick.

"A star in the making here, folks," Stauffer declared. "Monarchos wins by four and a half."

The crowd around the simulcast monitor erupted into shouts and applause, not because they'd all won a bundle on the 3 to 1 favorite, but because it was Johnny Ward's horse. They had watched a Keeneland horse—a hometown horse—beating horses in Florida they didn't know. Very few of them were as tuned in to what had happened as the "consigliere" realtor in their midst. He had spotted the Two Bucks breeder the minute he came in the door and had rushed up.

"I'm here to watch your horse, too," he had announced. "I'm gonna drop a bundle on him. I believe he's the one."

Now the grinning realtor was back in the breeder's face again. "See, I told you he's the one. You've got yourself a Derby horse, buddy."

The Two Bucks breeder cautioned the dominant female against believing what she'd just heard, in favor of what he'd been reading. Despite what she had just witnessed, Monarchos was only the third-ranking Derby prospect in the Oxley-Ward stable. Both Hero's Tribute and Holiday Thunder were far more likely to make the Derby.

Characteristically, the dominant female questioned the source of such an authoritative pronouncement. "Who says?"

"The horse press. All the reporters who are down there on their winter vacation with the rest of the big shots. They know what's going on. It's way too early to think Monarchos is a Derby horse. Forget it."

Veteran scribe Steve Haskin, the Triple Crown reporter for the industry's weekly "bible," *The Blood-Horse*, had not even mentioned Monarchos as a possible Derby contender until two weeks prior to the allowance race. With both Holiday Thunder and Hero's Tribute already high in his "Derby Dozen," he had slipped Monarchos into a category called "knocking at the door" and then into slot number 19 of his "20 to watch."

Having lived with a journalist for twenty years, the dominant female's regard for the press was similar to her husband's esteem for real-estate brokers.

"What do they know?" she asked.

"Plenty," he replied.

But down at Gulfstream, it was the guy who climbed on Monarchos's back every day who knew plenty. Bryan Beccia called his trainer friend Chapman in California and quit the job he'd planned to take getting the sprinter ready for Dubai. Beccia wasn't going anywhere, which flabbergasted his prospective employer. Beccia had always been a man of his word. But in light of what was happening, Chapman understood. Horses that can change a man's life come along so rarely; how could Beccia possibly leave one as special as Monarchos?

*

The day Monarchos destroyed the allowance field was the day of the Donn Handicap, the first big race of the year for older horses in America. All the important turf writers, and some not so important, were at Gulfstream. Going to Florida in the winter is proof of their potency, too, so most of them try to get down for the Donn in mid-February and stay through the Florida Derby the second weekend in March.

Like the horse owners, the leaders of the horse press are mostly old or middle-aged men from cold climates like New York, New Jersey and Chicago, so they need the warm sunshine, fresh orange juice and camaraderie of Gulfstream to get their sap rising in the spring.

But unlike the rich owners, the press denizens need to justify their Florida excursion to their employers, which are mostly daily newspapers and industry magazines and newsletters. Better find a good racing story, or it's back to Frozen City.

To their dismay, there was none at Gulfstream. The Donn was a dud, mainly because the ranks of older handicap horses were unusually thin. Aside from Fusaichi Pegasus, the 2000 crop of Triple Crown horses had been unexciting. Like Fusaichi, they'd retired to stud, or like the Preakness winner, Red Bullet, and the Horse of the Year, Tiznow, were still laid up with injuries.

The best the Donn offered was a virtual match race won by a perpetual runner-up named Captain Steve over a late bloomer called Albert the Great, whose best days as a racehorse were yet to come. As a story, it worked for a day or two, but only because of the matchup of top trainers: Captain Steve was trained by California wonder boy Bob Baffert and Albert was in the barn of New York favorite Nick Zito.

But what to do after the Donn? The one news story that normally sustained employer interest and justified reporter expense accounts for another three weeks—the Kentucky Derby buildup—was nonexistent. Never before in memory had so many reporters been in search of so scarce a Kentucky Derby story at Gulfstream in the spring.

Frank Stronach's two-year-old champion Macho Uno had been on the shelf all winter with undisclosed "growth problems" and was not at the track. Neither were the Arab horses, who were doing their preparation in Dubai. The training of the West Coast contingent, including Point Given, who'd given Macho Uno a tussle in the Breeders' Cup Juvenile, had been hampered by terrible California weather. None had been slated for the Florida Derby. The biggest-name three-year-old in Florida, A P Valentine, had been the biggest flop at the Breeders' Cup and was still suffering from the sore shins that were now blamed for the flop.

In the face of journalistic urgency for expense account–sustaining stories, the press usually depend on the same three loquacious big-name trainers that owners flock to in their efforts to win the Triple Crown races—Lukas, Baffert and Zito. But none of them had a credible entry in either of the two upcoming Derby prep races at Gulfstream, the Fountain of Youth stakes or the Florida Derby. Zito was the only one around, but his famous and expensive nonparticipant, A P Valentine, could not be hyped any more.

So the press had to make do with what they had. Overnight, the biggest Kentucky Derby stories at Gulfstream became the horses trained by two competent but heretofore unheralded trainers, John Dowd from New Jersey and Johnny Ward from Lexington.

They weren't celebrities like the Big Three, but they would do in a pinch. Dowd was particularly useful because his horse, Songandaprayer, was big, good-looking and had cost a million dollars. Even better, it had an almost-celebrity owner, the former basketball star Bobby Hurley.

Ward's profile was a bit harder to raise, but it could be done. There was a great angle. Ward, affable hardboot, had picked out and started under saddle the 2000 Derby winner, the famous Fusaichi Pegasus, but had been displaced by Neil Drysdale. Now he was back with not one but three potential Derby horses belonging to a single owner. Two of Ward's horses were already high in Haskin's Derby Dozen and the third, Monarchos, had just dazzled everybody with his Donn day victory.

Two weeks later the Fountain of Youth pitted Songandaprayer and the number-one horse in Ward's barn, Holiday Thunder, in the first showdown of the year for three-year-olds, with the victor certain to become the favorite for the $1 million Florida Derby three weeks later and a winter book favorite for the May run for the roses in Louisville.

The speedy Songandaprayer made a mockery out of the Fountain of Youth, going right to the front and never looking back. Holiday Thunder made a brief rally but his lungs bled under the pressure of his rush, shutting down his stretch drive. He finished sixth.

On the undercard that day, Ward's other leading Kentucky Derby candidate, Hero's Tribute, made his three-year-old debut in an allowance race and won impressively. Among those he beat was another horse making his first start of the year, Zito's much ballyhooed A P Valentine, who was still so highly regarded as a Derby candidate that he had been made the second choice in the first Kentucky Derby Future Wager.

Churchill Downs begins taking bets on the Derby in February of each year, but only during three betting periods called "pools," in which the odds are determined by the money wagered during the period. Pool 1 opened the Friday before the Fountain of Youth, and as usual, the chances of selecting a horse that would make the Derby starting gate were about as slim as those for picking the winner.

The Derby field was so muddled at the time that all three of Ward's horses were granted "individual wager" status, which meant each had his own odds when the pool opened. Holiday Thunder's were the shortest at 15 to 1 but shot up to 30 to 1 after the race, when it was learned that he had bled. Hero's Tribute, and surprisingly, Monarchos, both opened at 19 to 1, but their odds began to drop as the press hype rose in the wake of their allowance victories. In keeping with the Ward stable's official public position that they had no internal pecking order for Oxley's three colts, Yvonne Azeff placed Pool 1 bets on all three.

Hero's Tribute immediately became one of the favorites for the Louisiana Derby, another important step along the Kentucky Derby road, which would be contested in New Orleans on March 11. And in the mind of the press and the professional horseplayers, the big Florida Derby, traditionally the most important of all the so-called "prep races," quickly became a shootout between two swift, charismatic colts with headline-making names—John Dowd's Songandaprayer and Johnny Ward's Monarchos.

The Blood-Horse moved them both into their weekly Derby Dozen, at eighth and twelfth, respectively, and the authoritative Haskin, articulating what was becoming the general consensus of the horse racing world, wrote of Monarchos: "If he's right there in the Florida Derby, he's on his way to bigger and better things. Everyone is searching for a star to emerge. If he should win, he could be the one."

Back in Kentucky at Two Bucks Farm, the lifelong news addict began each day gleaning from every possible source and Internet site every phrase uttered and sentence written about Monarchos on the "Kentucky Derby trail," proclaiming all the while to anyone who would listen that not a word of it could or should be believed.

Still, on the day Pool 1 of the Kentucky Derby Future Wager closed, he drove over to Keeneland and bet $100 anyway, at 17 to 1 odds, on the Regal Band foal he knew full well had no chance of making it to the Kentucky Derby.

But down at Gulfstream two people who knew better—exercise rider Bryan Beccia and groom Tammy Holtz—bought themselves a little piece of that action, too.

11

A horse! A horse! My kingdom for a horse.

WILLIAM SHAKESPEARE, *Richard III*

On Versailles Road between Keeneland and Two Bucks there is an honest to God medieval castle that has been a target of gossip and scorn from the day of its celebrated groundbreaking in 1969. That's when the inimitable grande dame of Derby parties, Anita Madden, engraved it in horse country lore by observing, "There are rumors there will be orgies in every turret. . . . Let's only hope they are true."

The idea made the breeder of Monarchos smile every time he passed the castle, which he was about to do when the cell phone went off in his SUV. In more ways than one, the castle is a structure out of *Don Quixote*. From the highway, where the tourists stop to take photographs, it appears complete, from the massive front gates to the dozen "orgy" turrets and four towers along the 12-foot-tall stone walls. But inside it is unfinished—a partially hollow, never-ready wedding present from a too-soon-broke husband to a too-soon-gone bride. Located prominently in an historic preservation area hopelessly zoned for agriculture, the castle has stood empty and for sale for twenty years as a monument to failed dreams.

The man who had just placed a $100 bet on a horse to win a race he most likely would never enter stopped here to take the cell-phone call, an appropriate site, it turned out, for the conversation that followed.

The caller was Sam Ramer, gravel-voiced head of the United Thoroughbred Trainers Association, who had obviously lost his mind. Sam had been reading the racing press and had decided that *Backstretch*, the slick quarterly magazine he edited and published for the UTTA, should keep and publish a journal that chronicled the training of one of the Kentucky Derby horses from beginning to end. It would be posted two or three times a week on the magazine's website and eventually published in article form.

"I think Monarchos is the most likely one for us to follow," said Sam, in the distinctive growl of a man with a defective larynx. "And since you the breeder are also an editorial adviser to the magazine, I thought I better check with you and see if maybe you'd want to keep the journal yourself."

The breeder hated the idea almost as much as he liked and respected Sam. But he was shocked by his reasoning for the instinctive dislike of Sam's idea when he heard it coming from his own mouth.

"Damn, Sam, you're gonna jinx him is what you're gonna do. You're gonna jinx the hell out of Monarchos."

Jinx him?

This from a man whose lack of respect for superstition was as old and deep set as his love for horses. All his life he had walked under ladders, all around black cats, and he thought nothing of setting off around the world on Friday the 13th. To him, superstition was the religion of fools. Now, suddenly, he was arguing that writing about Monarchos two or three times a week was going to "jinx him"—somehow result in his being injured or running so badly in the Florida Derby that he would never contest the Triple Crown.

"Well, I haven't even talked to Johnny Ward about doing it yet. He might feel the same way you do. But if he goes along, you're not interested in doing the journal yourself, I take it."

"Definitely not. I don't think the Wards would take kindly to the breeder hanging around interrogating their employees."

The angst he'd felt trying to talk to Ward and Oxley in the Keeneland paddock the previous October was enough to override his burning curiosity now for every detail of what was going on with a horse he felt sure would any day be declared out of the Kentucky Derby for some reason or another.

"I hear you, I hear you," Sam laughed. "Believe me, I understand perfectly."

That Sam understood perfectly meant only that his twenty-five years as a thoroughbred trainer had clearly pushed him over the edge of reality along with everyone else in the racehorse business. The breeder found that amusing, and laughed out loud after Ramer hung up, arousing a sleeping dog from the back of the SUV. Conditioned to suspect that any sound or movement from his owner might mean food, a Jack Russell terrier named Al landed like a paratrooper in the front seat and promptly assumed his begging position, resting upright on his haunches with front paws neatly folded across his chest in anticipation of certain reward. Unlike his owner, Al was never burdened by either superstition or unrealistic expectation.

Trapped on the shoulder of the road by passing traffic, the driver and his companion were forced to consider the turreted eyesore now framed in the window of his Toyota. The fantasy of mass fornication along its stone walls matched the absurdity of its juxtaposition with an historic preservation route. How ironic that it rested as a traffic hazard at the end of an 80-mile-long, four-lane political debacle known as The Bluegrass Parkway, a limited-access road originally intended to connect Interstate 65 halfway between Louisville and Nashville with Interstates 64 east to Ashland and 75 heading north to Cincinnati or south to Atlanta. The connection was never made for the same reasons the castle remained unfinished and unsold—lack of the money or political clout necessary to get around zoning laws protecting quadrants of two counties that hold the heart of the thoroughbred industry. No matter what direction the Bluegrass Parkway might be aimed from the castle, it had no place to go except across the sacred grounds of Keeneland or up the gut of thoroughbred farms belonging to the most powerful owners and breeders in the business. They might as well be trying to take it right through the boardroom of the Jockey Club in New York.

To the locals the castle was a monstrosity, but to the smiling occupant of the SUV its grand but ridiculous nature symbolized the spectacular, comical adventure that had been his life. What more appropriate setting than an empty castle at the end of a road that goes nowhere in which to assess the current chapter of a Two Bucks horse on the Derby trail? And who better to discuss it with than his trusty pal, Al the Jack Russell, who often came in for such duty because he loved riding in the SUV and was less likely than the dominant female to pursue disagreement for the sake of amusement?

Matters of logic and high finance, such as those before him this day, were best unencumbered by the complications of boy-girl relationships. Al's objectives were no more complicated than food and sleeping in the front seat. Besides, he was particularly suited for consultation in this instance because his namesake and breeder was Alice the Farm Accountant, so the very sight of the lovable little bugger on the seat beside him brought to mind the sound reasoning and fiscal prudence demanded by CPAs.

The overriding issue facing this unlikely pair of jacks was the inexplicable abandonment of long-held principles that had up to now prevented life from becoming the "risky scheme" that politicians and preachers were always warning about on TV.

Three hundred miles down the parkway from the castle was the breeder's hometown of Nashville, where nearly six decades earlier he had been inoculated against risk-taking by having nothing to risk. Except for a few penny poker games in his college days that invariably left him guilt-ridden, the resulting immunity to taking chances had held up.

What had appeared to be risk-taking in his professional life had in reality only been rather obvious choices between sure things. And the monument to thirty years of risk-free indenture to two respectable employers was the castle of his own only three miles away, Two Bucks, pristine and complete, where he felt like Cervantes's mythical hero—a king by his own fireside "as much as any Monarch on his Throne." The farm and a perpetually new SUV ride for Al the Jack Russell were hard evidence of the benefits of long dedication to rational existence and the dictates of a good conscience burdened with guilt by any extravagance. The first time he'd ever spent frivolous money on a horse—$10,000 for a paint filly in 1982—she immediately had become a literal nightmare, the cause of sleep loss for weeks.

Now he was dreaming of horses and losing sleep again—but not for good reasons like anxiety and regret. The thoroughbred world and its Monopoly–money economics had changed him. His risk-averse nature had dissipated exponentially, and with it, disturbingly, his long intolerance of debt.

Two Bucks had just completed its first substantial losing year ever: Half his mares were barren for 2001, which did not bode well for the future, and his bank account looked, well, like he'd been getting his business advice from a Jack Russell.

But, instead of belt-tightening, his response had been a departure from a lifetime aversion to gambling into nonsensical skylarking betting on horses. Over the years he had learned to handicap a horse race as well as anyone and had prided himself on his modest success. At Keeneland and Churchill he often picked winners for the fun of it. But always with no money at stake. Not burdening either the horse or his decision making with the weight of his personal gold was the kind of cold reasoning that had made him successful in journalism. But now, on the basis of a press frenzy and the musings of a real-estate broker—"Hey, buddy, you got yourself a Derby horse"—he had just made what was basically a casino bet—17 to 1—that an obscure horse from the perimeter of the thoroughbred establishment was somehow going to win the hardest race in the world to win.

A $100 horse bet might not seem like much to some people. Two hundred thousand dollars borrowed against a $2 million farm wasn't much debt either. But three hours down the road to Nashville, in a military cemetery, was a World War II vet who had risked everything as a forward observer in the Battle of the Bulge and then spent the rest of his life earning a factory wage that never left him an extra $100 to chance on anything. The principle, it seemed, had now been buried with his father.

Its demise was what should have been keeping him awake nights, not the horse. There were 35,957 thoroughbred foals registered the year Monarchos was born. That this one off his farm could end up among the fifteen to twenty that would line up in the gate at the Kentucky Derby was about as realistic as what he and Al were looking at through the truck window—a medieval castle in Versailles, Kentucky. Not "Ver-Sigh," mind you, "Ver-Sales." The Kentucky colonials had so hated the British that they gave their towns French or German names. But they still gave them English pronunciations.

This was the kind of adulterated logic that had come to rule his life.

His pal Al was probably just about to weigh in on the situation when the cell phone went off again in the SUV. This time it was the dominant female.

"Where are you?"

"Sitting in front of the castle."

"What are you doing there?"

"Talking to Al."

"What about?"

"The farm economy."

Sam Ramer was not confident that Johnny Ward would go for a published daily journal on Monarchos. No trainer wanted his work scrutinized in print every day, especially on the most important of all races.

The generation of traditionalists from whom Ward had learned his trade hated the press. Their work was hidden behind closed stall doors and dropped stable awnings, and sometimes even their horses were hidden, too.

Old Silent Tom Smith went to great lengths to trick reporters prying into his training of Seabiscuit, a popular public hero of his time and the subject of intense press attention. Smith often trained Seabiscuit in secret—sometimes in the middle of the night—while employing his star's slower, carbon-copy sibling as a double and parading him around the press and the public.

Sports have always been a bastion of superstition, and even now no profession is more mindless in heed of it than racehorse trainers. Racing is so bereft of reason and rife with the inexplicable that good and bad luck have become justification for the routine. Taking up horses in any capacity is a license to become a kook. Likely sooner than later something will happen that will make you a believer in fate. Sam Ramer's belief had been confirmed early in his training career when the friend of one of his owners had showed up at Churchill and violated one of racing's most sacred taboos—by photographing a horse on the day of the race. Ignorant of tradition, the owner's guest had pulled a camera out in the saddling paddock and captured the trainer giving the jockey a legup mounting the horse.

"That is the kiss of death," Sam declared, shaking his head and calming his startled horse. Indeed it was. The filly threw her rider in the post parade and ran through a retaining fence, bowing a tendon. She never raced again.

So Sam would not have blamed Ward for refusing to entertain a regular snooper around his barns. But Ward surprised him. During his days as the court-appointed overseer of the Calumet Farm bankruptcy, Ward had developed an unusual comfort level with the press. The death of the farm's top stallion, Alydar, who was euthanized after breaking a leg under strange circumstances, coupled with the surprising suddenness of the farm's financial collapse, had imbued the story with tabloid-level mystery, which put Ward in a tough spot. Any reluctance on his part to communicate would be instantly perceived by the press as further cover-up. He quickly learned the advantages of candor and returning phone calls.

Ward had gotten an even more relevant education watching the battle only a year earlier between the racing press and the California iconoclast Neil Drysdale, who had succeeded him as the trainer of Fusaichi Pegasus. A stone-faced Englishman and son of a British Royal Marine officer, Drysdale was a consummate horseman and a distinguished trainer. But he had no patience for media attention and little time or inclination to explain his methods to anyone. In fact, he'd rather talk about art or life in general than horses, and his view of the Triple Crown was different from that of most other trainers, to say the least. In 1992, Drysdale had scratched Horse of the Year A. P. Indy from the Kentucky Derby on the morning of the race because of a bruised foot, and he had declined to run him two weeks later in the Preakness.

When Fusaichi Pegasus won the Derby as expected, the press naturally began promoting him as a likely Triple Crown winner, which the industry wanted more than anything else. Only eleven horses in 126 years had won the Kentucky Derby, the Preakness and the Belmont Stakes, and none had done so since 1978. But Drysdale didn't like the Triple Crown idea any better the second time around, especially the 24-hour-a-day spotlight accorded the centerpiece. He took his horse to the Preakness this time but refused to house him in the newly refurbished and accessible stakes barn, deciding instead to shield him from the press in an obscure corner of the most rundown part of Pimlico Race Course. When, as the overwhelming 1 to 5 favorite in the race, Fusaichi Pegasus was pushed wide in the mud and upset by Red Bullet, the press lowered the boom on Drysdale. Again he responded by keeping his horse as far away from the press as possible at the Belmont Stakes, housing him instead at Aqueduct. There, before training a step, Fusaichi cut his heel on the sharp edge of a stall door and was scratched from the race.

Ward shared Drysdale's concern about the toll that running three big races in five weeks takes on both animals and the people who train them. But Drysdale's approach had helped neither his horse nor the industry. Four other Derby winners had undergone the same Triple Crown press scrutiny in the decade, all of them trained by two other California trainers whose attitude toward the press was drastically different from Drysdale's. Bob Baffert and D. Wayne Lukas hadn't won the Triple Crown either, but their pursuit of it had been good both for them and for the racing business. Between them they had won five of the last ten Kentucky Derbys, and Ward had watched them handle the press as well as they had handled their horses. Along with New Yorker Nick Zito, who had won a Derby and a Preakness, Lukas and Baffert had through the combination of talk and action established themselves and their training methods as models for how to do it.

Baffert and Lukas did things a little differently from Ward and his hardboot contemporaries around the Midwest. They had barns, horses and assistants all over the country. Their strength was in numbers, organization and marketing. And not the least of their tools was a good handle on the information-hungry, superstition-threatening press. The success of these press-savvy trainers at winning the big races had drawn increasingly to their barns the best horses and the wealthiest owners. Meanwhile, their training methods and media relations had become blueprints for dozens of up-and-coming young copycat trainers who themselves were beginning to dominate the Kentucky Derby entries. One former assistant to Lukas, Todd Pletcher, had saddled four of the twenty horses that started the 2000 Derby, while his mentor had saddled three. Baffert had entered only one for the first time in years.

Ward figured that if Baffert and Lukas could get their horses and themselves through the Triple Crown meat-grinder, so could he. And in doing so he might strike a blow for the dozens of other good but relatively obscure hands-on horsemen and, more important, for their way of doing things. Allowing his friend Sam Ramer to do a daily journal on Monarchos would be good preparation for what was to come should any of Oxley's horses make the Derby. Having reporters grilling him and his help every day would harden them for the Triple Crown just as training at Gulfstream was doing for his horses.

A few days later a young writer-handicapper from Athens, Georgia, named Andy Plattner began shadowing Ward's training operation in Florida for *Backstretch.* Plattner became friendly with Yvonne Azeff, Bryan Beccia and Tammy Holtz. Soon the *Backstretch* website was reporting what they all ate for breakfast, and how quirky Monarchos preferred to mix his own. He liked to take a mouthful of water from the bucket and squirt it into his feed tub. Then, he swished it all around a portion of his grain with his lips, ate the wet part and went back for another swig of water. But if someone else tried to put water on his feed, he not only rejected it but took offense at the intrusion.

The personality that emerged fit a profile familiar at Two Bucks. Monarchos was indeed his mother's son, a moody eccentric that snubbed you one minute, tried to nip you the next and would rest his head on the shoulder of the right person, but only at the right time.

Plattner reported how Monarchos pranced and swished his tail en route to the track and how he habitually tried to eat Azeff's tennis shoes and menace Mouse, the companion pony. He wrote about Azeff's mother, about Ward's relationship with his wife, Donna, about the sire and dam of Monarchos and his low-budget beginnings at Two Bucks and about the long, unconventional daily gallops that would become the controversial centerpiece of his unlikely journey to Churchill Downs.

Nowhere was Plattner's journal more eagerly awaited or thoroughly scrutinized than back in Kentucky at Two Bucks, where the appetite for news from Gulfstream was insatiable, and where day by day even more long-held principles were being violated and more aversions abandoned—and where risk was rapidly becoming a way of life.

On his knees at the front door of the stall, the bearded young veterinarian ran the sensor of his sonogram machine back and forth along the mare's belly, stopping when the ultrasound image on the computer screen showed clearly the ominous layering of dark and light lines inside the womb.

"We've got a problem here," Dr. Michael Beyer told the Two Bucks breeder. "The placenta is already separating from the uterus, which means she could have a premature birth at almost any time."

Regal Band, dam of the now "highly regarded Monarchos" and almost certain entry in the Florida Derby, was still forty days shy of her March 11 foal date and her pregnancy was in serious trouble. Foals born that prematurely—even under perfect circumstances—have less than a 50 percent survival rate. Beyer suggested she be shipped immediately to one of the two blue-ribbon veterinary hospitals in Lexington.

Her owner hated the idea. Years of experience had taught him that foals were usually better off when born on the farms where their mothers lived and to which their immune systems were already attuned. Simply moving the mare could induce the early delivery they were trying to avoid.

But a premature foal would most certainly constitute a "red bag" birth, which means the placenta completely detaches before delivery and the newborn requires immediate oxygen and other emergency care. But at the clinic, chances of prolonging the pregnancy might be better and a premature foal might have a better chance of survival. There was no choice, therefore, but to send Regal Band to the maternity ward at Hagyard-Davidson-McGee—especially in light of the fact that the owner of Two Bucks and the dominant female had cast aside another principle and were planning to be away from the farm.

That's right. Leaving town in the winter after all—and to Florida no less, with the big shots, to watch the horses run at Gulfstream—particularly Monarchos, if he made the Florida Derby.

Despite all the ink being given Monarchos, no one in the horse press was even sure he would. From his winter headquarters in Palm Beach, Ward was still being coy about Oxley's "Derby darlings," refusing to say which would run where or when, or to rank them in any order.

"I don't list them in any kind of order myself," he insisted from his barn in Palm Beach. "Each horse is loaded with assets."

And at that point, at least, all of them had the same jockey—Jorge Chavez. He had ridden both Hero's Tribute and Monarchos to victory in the Florida allowance races and was listed as the rider of both in the upcoming stakes races—the Florida Derby on March 10 and the Louisiana Derby the following day. Yet Holiday Thunder was still considered by many as the most experienced and mature horse of the three and the most likely to be under Chavez when the Kentucky Derby gates opened.

The jockey conflict alone was sufficient grist for the analytical-genius proprietor of Two Bucks to continue to downplay the chances of Monarchos ever making it to Churchill Downs in May.

"Only one of Oxley's horses will make it to the Kentucky Derby and he's third in line right now," he assured everyone.

All the more reason, he rationalized, to accept an invitation from friends on the South Florida coast to visit on the Florida Derby weekend, despite the bad timing of it all. Florida Derby weekend coincided perfectly with the end of Regal Band's precise 342-day gestation period. Her expected delivery date of March 11 was the day after the race. They could go watch the first Two Bucks horse ever in a graded stakes race, or stay home for another Regal Band foaling, which for five consecutive years had been routinely uncomplicated—until now. Now, it was extraordinarily complicated, and very much in keeping with the mind-boggling asymmetry of horse raising and racing.

If Regal Band waited to deliver on time, her owners would be gone at the time of a risky "red bag" birth. If she foaled early, the baby would be to some degree premature, and therefore, leaving its care to others would be irresponsible.

It was always like this. Horses get hurt on the eve of big races or the day before they are to sell. Mares go for years without producing a runner, then a year after they die or are sold, a hot offspring surfaces that would have shot up their value. By the same token, mares with a history of perfect health often get sick or become unproductive immediately after becoming valuable. The mother of the 1999 Kentucky Derby winner, Charismatic, died after one more foal. Regal Band had always remained the picture of health throughout her pregnancies—fat, bright-eyed and with a coat shiny enough to provide a reflection (when it wasn't mud-covered), but her hair this time had suddenly gotten dull and the daily check of pregnant mare rumps had detected a slight but not alarming vaginal discharge.

Regal Band was just upholding tradition. With a perfect reproduction record since coming to Two Bucks, she was experiencing her first difficulty the very month she had a runner headed for a $1-million Grade 1 stakes race—or was he really? That would not be known until the actual entries were made three days before the race—just the right amount of time to ensure that the airline tickets to Florida would cost enough to require a second mortgage.

"That's why the wealthy have private planes or spend all winter in Florida," observed the dominant female, brandishing her travel expertise. "Either one is cheaper than flying back and forth to Florida in the winter to see your horse race on three-days' notice."

Damn the expense, responded her husband. Damn the possibility that Regal Band might foal while they were out of town, or that Two Bucks would be buried under a 14-foot snowfall.

A Derby horse happens only once. Before another Monarchos came along the Two Bucks man might be forced to sell out, as Poor George Hofmeister had been, or just as likely, be run over on the treacherous Kentucky backroads. The former threat hung constantly overhead like a sword of Damocles, and the latter danger daily confronted him and Al the Jack Russell as they traveled about in the SUV.

The farm roads in central Kentucky were little more than lanes, with narrow shoulders lined by ancient, immovable oaks. And every family owned big trucks and tractors, viewed by the men as penis extensions but which the women sometimes had to drive, obviously not without fear of running off the road and into the trees. So, each for their own reasons, both male and female drivers kept their monster machines squarely in the middle of the road, wedging out oncoming traffic to either side like bowling pins. And it was all done courteously and with good will, the drivers smiling as they approached, sometimes waving or signaling acknowledgment by lifting a single finger off the steering wheel. When he first came to Kentucky, the Two Bucks man believed his neighbors were greeting him hello as they passed. But now after a dozen Hofmeister-type near misses, he knew they were simply bidding him goodbye, in case he didn't miss the oaks.

So it was folly to sweat the small stuff. The parameters of risk associated with breeding horses in Kentucky were no longer in doubt. He was bound either to go broke, or be killed by an oak tree. It was just a matter of which came first.

12

All the king's horses and all the king's men
Couldn't put Humpty together again.

HUMPTY DUMPTY, Anonymous

The point beyond which the disease could no longer be arrested probably occurred with the purchase of first-class airfare to Palm Beach. That it was now contagious at Two Bucks was evidenced by the fact that the tickets were ordered by the dominant female, a travelmaster whose compulsion to outcheap the airlines usually resulted in shopping for seats in the corner of the baggage hold or hanging by handstraps beneath a wing.

Obviously her husband's case was further along. Leaving town at the height of breeding season to go to a horse race strongly suggested that even his proud work ethic had been undermined. The dam of Monarchos was still at the veterinary clinic and expected to foal any minute. Yet when her pregnancy reached 335 days, he declared "the scary part" past and confidently predicted that she would deliver a healthy full-term foal, thereby relieving him of any worry about leaving town. Secretly, his peace of mind had been delivered in a personal commitment from his old friend Doug Byars, head of medicine at Hagyard-Davidson-McGee, to oversee the blessed event. Dr. Byars's house was so close to the clinic he could walk to the maternity ward, and his interest level in Regal Band had been validated. On the door of her stall, alongside the notice that a dangerous "red bag" foaling could be expected, was a press clipping noting that her offspring Monarchos was "a favorite in the Florida Derby."

This assurance did not mean Florida travel would be carefree. Travel with the dominant female never was. Earlier he had seen her packing lethal weapon number 1 for trip destruction—her portable Global Positioning System (GPS). Her compulsion to be properly geographically situated at all times had wrecked more than one pleasant journey, and bringing the infernal contraption along was an open challenge to his resolve.

Another racing excursion, a trip to Belmont Park, had resulted in his taking an oath to never again get into an automobile that contained both the dominant female and a GPS. This remark had not been one of his idle threats like feeding Al the Jack Russell to the coyotes. Only a truly strong marriage could survive what had happened two blocks from La Guardia Airport. In a corporate rather than marital union, it would have been "a deal breaker."

A reporter who had tracked Martin Luther King, Jr.'s, assassin from Memphis to Lisbon and had found his way through the streets of Moscow, Beijing and other difficult cities did not need a GPS to get from La Guardia to Belmont Park. It's this simple: Take the Grand Central Parkway to the Cross Island Parkway and get off at exit 26B.

But the travel guru, who prided herself on her innate pathfinding ability, had had no faith in that of her husband since the day he fessed up a small part of the dream that had been plaguing him for years, the part in which he wanders aimlessly and futilely through a giant hotel in search of his room so he can dress for a speech. The dream always ended before he found his way, but never before he wished he were dead.

"All that means is that you have no sense of direction," she said, dismissively. "And we knew that already."

So she had insisted on programming and bringing along the portable GPS—plus four map printouts downloaded from an Internet site. When the car she had rented contained its own GPS, she insisted on implementing that one, too, as "a backup."

As the designated driver he had already memorized the maps as instructed: highway to highway to exit. But as they left La Guardia, the dominant female began to orally relay instructions from her portable GPS. All the while the recorded voice in the rental car GPS—also female—took up the same task.

So as the driver attempted to follow signs directing him to the Grand Central Parkway, the voices of two obviously dominant females began issuing directions. And not once did they agree.

"Turn left at the next corner," instructed the one in the seat next to him, while the one in the GPS box ordered, "Proceed three-tenths of a mile to expressway entrance." Soon he was obeying first one, and then the other. Within half a mile of the airport exit he was hopelessly lost and confused in Queens. A quick turnaround to retrace his steps only angered both GPS announcers and made matters worse. The dominant female's portable appeared to react the most rapidly. "Keep going straight now until you intersect the Grand Central Parkway," she ordered. But the rental car GPS lady was even more adamant about the alternative route she had selected. "You are now heading in the wrong direction. Turn around and proceed four-tenths mile to right turn."

It was at this point the veteran world traveler surrendered to the hijacking. Stopping the car, he turned the wheel over to "whichever one of you two geographically positioned and authoritative ladies would like to drive. Me, I am walking back to the airport, which fortunately I can still see."

The silent anti-GPS oath he'd sworn that day was obviously now about to be tested by the same unexpected and unavoidable development in his life that had already trod on a wide array of personal covenants. Now he was going somewhere he shouldn't be going, under circumstances he could not abide for reasons he could not rationalize. Someone else's racehorse was running over his life, through his dreams even, and—most disconcertingly—threatening the emotional cocoon that had long insured his happiness.

For years he'd wrapped his life in the protective cover of a journalist's detachment, feelings waterproofed by decades of lessons learned in the role of impartial observer. Because news is inevitably the product of excess—in speed, greed, ambition, apathy, love and hate—the experience had restricted his ups and downs to middle range. No peaks, no valleys. A life of moderation meant a deprivation of ecstasy, but the payback had been a safety net of lowered expectations. He might catch a fever now and then but he carried the antibody to disappointment.

Through thick and thin he had remained a third-party chronicler of his own existence: astounded by achievements, forearmed for failure, his balance unaffected by either. Except where his children were concerned, he had avoided a rooting interest even in his own life. Now the success of a thoroughbred horse from his farm had suddenly become as compelling a concern as the welfare of his own offspring.

So on the eve of the Florida departure, once again he made a vow: that all of what was going on could not and should not be. Beginning with this obviously frivolous trip to the Florida Derby, he would resume watching the progress of Monarchos the same way he had watched himself—Don Quixote riding off on Rocinante.

So it was with a renewed respect for the preservation of oaths taken and a sustained personal equilibrium that he replaced the live new batteries in the dominant female's GPS with old dead ones; covertly notified the rental car company at the Palm Beach airport that despite his "Gold" customer status, under no circumstances should he be rented a car equipped with a GPS; and began looking to pack in his own luggage what he would need most for the trip—a set of worry beads once given to him by his mother.

The musings of the real-estate consiglieres were proving clairvoyant. Could these drive-by Peeping Toms be oracles after all?

The Florida splurge had come at a time when Two Bucks was operating on borrowed money and revenue derived from the sale of assets. Anticipating a decline in future yearling sales, the already small broodmare band had been reduced from fifteen to ten. Among the culls was a profitable producer, sold for no other reason than to raise operating capital. Furthermore, an enticing offer to sell Two Bucks itself had materialized. Getting out of thoroughbreds entirely was no longer beyond the realm of possibility.

Hoffmeisterdom might well be near. Yet it could at the same time be postponed indefinitely or rendered altogether marvelous because the realtor wisdom had been correct on Monarchos, too.

Despite all the public declarations that Oxley's three Derby hopefuls had no particular pecking order, inside the Ward camp Regal Band's baby had jumped to the head of the line. This made the Florida Derby all the more critical.

One reason was that money earned in stakes races is the main criterion for getting into the Kentucky Derby if there are more than twenty entries, which is often the case. Having never competed in a stakes race, Monarchos needed the earnings. Equally important was Oxley's personal goal of winning the most important stakes race in the state where his interest in horse racing had actually taken root.

The Oxley family had spent the winters in Florida for years. Long before he ever owned a racehorse, Oxley was watching and betting on them at Florida tracks. He considered the experience his "master's degree" in a long equine education. Twice he had tried to win the Florida Derby and failed. His colt Jambalaya Jazz was the favorite in 1995 but had finished fifth. Five years later he had tried again with a horse named Scottish Halo that finished out of the money. New Yorkers like to win the big races at Saratoga and Kentuckians want to win at Keeneland, in front of their friends and neighbors. Oxley viewed the Florida Derby as the biggest race run in his "hometown" and knew that Monarchos, who had been brilliant all spring at Gulfstream, had a chance to do it. He had dreamt of Monarchos coming from behind, circling the field and sweeping to victory.

Rather than steeling himself against disappointment as the horse's breeder had done, Oxley was girding himself for victory. He had also bewitched the opposition by donning his lucky underwear. In the enchanted land of racetrack superstition, at least, Monarchos could run every step down the Derby road fueled by the limitless enthusiasm of his owner while freed by his breeder from the weight of all unrealistic expectation.

In the real world, meanwhile, the horse was sitting on ready. Since the allowance win, he had been training sensationally. Two weeks before the race, with jockey Jorge Chavez watching from the sidelines, exercise rider Beccia breezed Monarchos five furlongs in 1:00.1. A week later in his final tuneup with Chavez aboard, he did the same workout in 1:00.3. Both times he went "easy"—without being pushed—and galloped out another quarter of a mile without urging. All week long before the race, he gave his handlers a bit of the "Sparky shuffle"—a little sideways two-step jig to and from the track which they had come to equate with readiness. A fit horse who couldn't wait to prove it.

"If they intend to beat this guy Saturday," Beccia told Azeff, "they better come with their shoes clamped down."

On their own, the tourists from Two Bucks would have had a hard time just obtaining a good seat at the Florida Derby. Gulfstream's best attended event, the race provides a perennial test of the track's patience and facilities, especially accommodations reserved for swells, who for the fiftieth running would be coming in record numbers.

Fortunately his host and friend Smoot Fahlgren—not a fictitious name—was a veteran high roller, a Florida winter resident, and therefore in charge of arrangements. An advertising industry legend, Smoot was savvy enough to recruit the ultimate Gulfstream insider, the octogenarian Hash Weinstein, as an advance man. Hash had sent gate passes, the name of the maitre d' from whom he'd gotten reservations and a slip of paper with "the name of the guy who'd have some box seats." Hash said to be sure to "use the valet parking because it's the quickest way in and out."

En route to the track, Smoot laid it all out for his party of six, which included his clearly better half Judy, the two "Kenturkeys"—a term of affection—and a couple of New Yorkers, a guy named Rock that Smoot said was the smartest ad guy in the world and his girlfriend.

Smart Rock was something all right, dapper and charming—but also delusional. He claimed that at a charity function once in New York Princess Diana had tried to seduce him. Came right out and told him, "I want you now," and suggested she was ready to shed her entourage—among other things. The guy was so-so good-looking, but old enough to be her father. Come on. Smoot and the male Kenturkey figured that at least half the story had to be untrue because Smart Rock insisted he had turned the princess down cold. His girlfriend said she believed him, which suggested she might be delusional, too, but more likely just accommodating. The dominant female, however, swallowed it hook, line and sinker, but probably just for the sake of argument. The disbelief of her husband and Smoot, she argued, only meant their own moral compasses were permanently askew.

While waiting in the line to valet park, in a Mercedes wagon borrowed from an anonymous friend of Smart Rock's, Smoot handed out the free admission passes Hash had sent him. Printed clearly on each one was "Good for all Saturdays but March 10—Florida Derby Day."

The Two Bucks breeder immediately took this as the final omen regarding Monarchos's chances of winning and wrote him off. Sort of a last straw. First, due to an unusual set of circumstances, Monarchos had been made the 7-to–5 favorite to win as part of a two-horse "entry." Because Oxley also owned a share in another respected contender, Invisible Ink, Florida law required that they be coupled in the betting—numbers 1 and 1A. Monarchos got the "A." If that wasn't jinx enough, rain clouds were blowing up again in the distance. It had rained earlier in the morning and nobody knew how Monarchos would run on a wet track. But the rain never returned and the hospitality outlook improved when little bald hometown guys in pastel coats started yelling "Hey, Smoot" the minute he got out of the Mercedes.

Except for the invalid gate passes, the strings pulled by Hash all worked. The box seats he'd arranged were in the middle of the swells, near the finish line. Ted Bassett, the Keeneland chairman, was seated just to the left. And off to the right was former Kentucky Governor Brereton Jones exchanging pleasantries with a Florida magazine publisher and what the male Kenturkey incorrectly identified as a cluster of off-duty exotic dancers. Leather vests and hip-huggers do stand out in a crowd of citrus-shaded ladies in last-word suits and alluring wide-brimmed hats that probably reminded Smart Rock of a princess.

Soon, the Oxleys and the Wards arrived and sat down nearby to smiled acknowledgments from the crowd. Having seen Oxley only once, the Kenturkey had foolishly and mistakenly pointed out a look-alike in the Palm Beach airport to the dominant female, who had insisted on wishing him luck with Monarchos. "I'm not Oxley," the man said. "But I wish I had his horses."

From her box-seat observation point, the dominant female could not understand how her husband could have made such a mistake. "Oxley is much more handsome," she said. As restitution she secured the promise of another introduction so she could again extend her best wishes, this time to the real McCoy.

Meanwhile, the Kenturkey made another serious mistake. Little planes were flying over Gulfstream tugging banners touting "Inky," the nickname for Invisible Ink, the race cofavorite with Monarchos. The managing partner of the stable that owned Invisible Ink was tall, big-hatted John Fort, the man who had choked up at Saratoga while relating the death of the potential Derby horse he'd bought from Two Bucks. This year Fort's fortunes had improved. Invisible Ink had nearly died, too, from an infection that resulted in colitis, a deadly diarrhea that caused him to drop several hundred pounds. Only after responding to a diet of putrid buttermilk did Inky miraculously recover to become a good racehorse and a better story.

Spotting Fort towering stylishly among the swells in a Great Gatsby suit, the Kenturkey had sought him out, congratulated him on the recovery of his horse and wished him well in the race. It was the sportsmanlike thing to do. Competing owners and breeders are always doing that, with the understanding that the wish is for a safe trip and second place. Fort graciously accepted. He related what a remarkable horse Inky had been, how well he had trained coming up to the race and why he could be expected to win. The implication was clear, at least to a man on his way to paranoia and dementia: respect for Inky was what had made the double entry the favorite.

Their conversation lasted several minutes. Not once did Fort acknowledge the Kenturkey's connection with the cofavorite. So consumed was Fort with the prospects of the horse he had purchased and now managed that he never even mentioned Monarchos.

The slight left the Kenturkey grumbling. "I'll be damned. I can wish him luck, but he can't wish me luck? What's wrong with that guy?"

The saddling paddock of a big stakes race is a congregation of swells and wanna-bes. Special admission credentials are necessary so there will be room for the horses. Betting experts and horsemen want to be there so they can assess the condition of the animals—to look them in the eye (or examine their feet). A lot of others want to go because it is an exclusive place to be and to be seen. The fences that separate those inside the saddling paddock from those outside is a demarcation line of privilege. At the Florida Derby, for example, the exotic dancer look-alikes were inside with the owners and trainers. The Kenturkeys managed to get only close enough to the demarcation line to determine which horses were remaining cool in the Florida heat, a kind of demarcation line in itself. Horses who fret and "wash out" in the paddock or during the parade to the post often come up short in the race.

A late entry sent from California by D. Wayne Lukas, and thus feared by the Kenturkey, was dripping wet and obviously distraught in the paddock. Two horses had dark streaks across their shoulders and were lathered up between their haunches. One was basketballer Bobby Hurley's speedster Songandaprayer and the other was polo player Jack Oxley's Monarchos, whose wet rump Smart Rock somehow managed to photograph from a distance.

The sight of Monarchos losing liquid in the paddock naturally validated the prospects of doom for the Kenturkey. The whole thing could come crashing down in two minutes. All Monarchos had to do was run badly and out of the money and his Kentucky Derby prospects were toast. Favorites were not supposed to sweat in the paddock. Hell, he didn't even like Monarchos being the favorite. And certainly not a favorite wed in the betting with another horse owned partially by Oxley and managed by a guy who refuses to mention Monarchos's name. None of it boded well.

On the other hand Jack Oxley indulged no ill omens. When the dominant female dragged the Kenturkey over to the box to keep his promise of introduction, Oxley seemed to know he was about to have a dream come true. He was glad to finally meet the dominant female he was sure had played a major role in the breeding of a horse about to win the Florida Derby.

"And when this race is over," Oxley told her. "You know where to come."

He thoughtfully extended the same invitation to the owner of Monarchos's sire, Josephine Abercrombie, who had just arrived from Kentucky in time to see the first Maria's Mon offspring in a major Grade 1 stakes race, and to several others in nearby boxes.

"He just invited us all to the winner's circle, you know that, don't you?" the dominant female informed her Kenturkey escort, obviously doubtful of his perception.

"Oh yeah, well, you notice he didn't say the word 'winner's circle' because he's been around this game long enough to know it would jinx his horse. Now, you have jinxed his horse even more than it was already jinxed."

"Hmmph. Some people are positive, you know. They don't believe in jinxes. If Monarchos wins, I'm going."

"Going where? Say it again, so you can jinx him some more?"

"Hmmph. Down there." She pointed.

*

His horse breaking out in a sweat in the paddock had bothered Johnny Ward, too. Monarchos had some troubling quirks. He didn't like visitors eyeing him from a particular angle outside his stall, and he hated the raindrops pinging on the aluminum barn awning. Unrecognizable noises sometimes provoked what Yvonne Azeff termed "a Sparky moment." When the shower had hit earlier that morning, Ward's crew had smothered him with female attention to calm him down. By this time Azeff and Tammy Holtz were living with Monarchos, catering to his every whim. Ward had figured out that this particular horse "responds well to the Y-chromosome." What he meant, of course, was the X-chromosome, but so what if he had his chromosomes mixed up? He did have his hair nicely arranged, and he knew Monarchos liked girls the best. It was the way the horse had been raised. Growing up at Two Bucks, Sigita, the Lithuanian barn boss, had lavished him with attention, too.

Monarchos flared again en route to the paddock. At Gulfstream the hoopla of Florida Derby day (the Grand Funk Railroad in concert and a band seated near the winner's circle) provides a scaled-down rehearsal for the bedlam that horses will ultimately encounter at Churchill Downs. But again Azeff and Holtz were able to regain the colt's attention, which is the secret of great horse handling. By the time Chavez hopped aboard his back and headed for the track post parade, Monarchos had relaxed. So had Ward. The sweating had not been enough to affect performance. To the 28,000-plus patrons, however, this was not readily apparent by the way the race began.

Monarchos broke cleanly from the middle of the thirteen-horse field, but Chavez had slowed him down before the pack passed the clubhouse. By then he was eighth and dropping further behind. Led by longshot speedsters Trailthefox and Radical Riley, they ran the opening quarter mile at a modest pace—23.1 seconds. Going around the first turn, Monarchos had only two horses beat. A quarter mile later, he was still eleventh, twenty lengths or more behind, not normally a good place to be. Gulfstream is known as a speed-favoring track, with a loose sandy top and rock-hard bottom that allows speedsters to skip along effortlessly without tiring. When the time comes to sprint at the end, the leaders often have enough left that closers can't make up the ground.

From the swell seats, the Kenturkey could see all his dire predictions coming true. All Monarchos had to do was to finish as lethargically as he had begun and it would all be over. A lot of other horses heavily hyped during a Florida winter by a snowbird press had proved to be frauds the first time they tackled stakes-quality competition. And at the moment, the Two Bucks horse looked like he could get branded as one, too.

Across the infield pond, on the opposite side of the track, the man upon the gray's back knew better. When Monarchos had won the allowance race a month earlier, Jorge Chavez had declared him "my Derby horse." Chavez knew his stuff. He had ridden the sprinting champion Artax to record-shattering victories. He had demolished the best mare competition aboard the massive Beautiful Pleasure, who could run a mile as fast as any horse could. And he had ridden a lot of horses that had no chance at all. Chavez knew when he had a lot of horse under him and when he didn't. At the moment he felt like he was sitting on a keg of dynamite, and he couldn't wait to light the fuse.

The "speed" horses way ahead had not been traveling a killing pace, so they'd have kick left. Chavez knew he would need an early start to catch them. With almost half a mile left in the race, he decided to ask Monarchos to close the gap. When he did, the horse bolted sharply underneath him. Instead of the steady acceleration the jock wanted, the horse had hit passing gear.

From the box seats at least two sets of binoculars were focused on the move. The Kenturkey saw it and breathed a sigh of relief. At least he was going to make a race of it. But a few boxes away Johnny Ward gasped. He thought Jorge may have pulled the trigger too soon. Some fire-breathing sprinters who run only six-furlong races can really turn it on for the last half mile. But in races of a mile or more, most good horses have at best a quarter mile of all-out run in them at the end. Only "freaks" like Secretariat could accelerate steadily for a half mile and not be wobbling at the end.

Monarchos had fired so quickly that track announcer Vic Stauffer missed it. At the three-quarter pole—three-eighths of a mile from the finish—Stauffer noted that "Monarchos is being pushed along now by Chavez." An understatement. Four horses had already been passed. And by the time the words echoed through Gulfstream, Monarchos was roaring five wide and had wiped out the rest of the field on the turn. As he collared the leaders, Stauffer caught up with him: "Here comes Monarchos with an eye-catching middle move."

North American racehorses run counterclockwise and take the turns on their left lead, which means their left front leg is extended, hitting the ground before their right in a three-beat gallop. At the top of the stretch horses normally switch from their left lead to the right, which is like shifting into overdrive.

Monarchos came out of the turn still on his left lead. Inside him, shifting gears of their own, were the toughest of the other horses. The runaway Songandaprayer had wanted to go early and his jockey, Edgar Prado, had been unable to stop him. Having run wide all the way against the brilliant sprinter City Zip, "the Song" was sung and had only the prayer left. His measure was being taken at the moment by two determined finishers, Fort's Invisible Ink, and a bred-for-distance horse called Outofthebox. Aboard Outofthebox, the world's leading rider, Jerry Bailey, saw Monarchos coming and tried to go with him. But the best Outofthebox could manage was to hold his place on the rail in front of Invisible Ink, who was blocked from moving out by the tiring Songandaprayer. It didn't matter. Monarchos was flying—still on the wrong lead.

Chavez jerked his horse's nose to the outside and again asked for a lead change. Monarchos hit the overdrive gear and was gone. He won by four and half lengths and was still putting distance between himself and the others well past the finish line.

Against his better judgment the stunned Kenturkey headed for the winner's circle, heeding the dominant female's interpretation of protocol: "We can't not go." Shock having left him not quite up to speed, she beat him there by a Monarchos-like margin. Adrenaline had already propelled Jack Oxley out into the middle of the track, where he was circling aimlessly, a man beside himself.

Meanwhile the victors returned majestically, a stick-waving painter's palette of color; the jockey's leathered face, Oxley's blue and yellow silks, the horse's gun-metal coat, red saddle towel and track bandages, his distinctive white Sur-win Australian bridle, all now splotched tan with wet Florida sand. A circus horse that had gone through a mud puddle.

Tammy Holtz hooked a lead shank on the dirty rainbow and led it in a circle in the middle of the track with Oxley following. Then Yvonne Azeff led the horse a few rounds before finally handing it to Oxley, who had been persistently trying to catch up with his circling horse. Every time he reached for the shank, one of the women led the horse out of reach.

Finally, all were united with the Wards in the winner's circle for the photographs, where Chavez explained his early move: "I might have gone a little early, but my horse exploded. I felt like a king."

A winner's wreath of orchids had been thrown across Monarchos's withers and when the sand-caked jockey alighted, he came down with a handful of snatched blossoms.

Before accepting any congratulations, the jockey dropped to one knee and offered them up to his wife, Margarita, and their two daughters, Matilda and Julie.

It was a defining gesture, typical of what Chavez had become after a miserable start in life. Having just won one of the most important races in his life aboard a horse he now knew was about to give him a chance at his ultimate goal, Chavez's attention was on his family. A tiny king genuflecting to honor his most important court, offering up a blossom to a child. The Wards and Oxleys understood, for they knew that he was as extraordinary a human being as he was a rider. Accordingly, they broke into applause and were joined by others, unknowing, who could only admire what they were seeing.

Once again the track announcer Vic Stauffer saluted the winner of the fiftieth Florida Derby. He yelled the horse's name at the top of his voice. And as the word "MONARCHOS" resounded over Gulfstream, the crowd rose to its feet and cheered, no one louder than the former agnostic Kenturkey in the winner's circle, who still did not want to believe that one of Regal Band's babies was going to the Kentucky Derby but could no longer help it.

Privileged accommodations put the party of six among the first in line to claim their car from the valet parking. This position had the Kenturkeys in a perfect spot to accept accolades from other swells familiar with the winning horse's genetic beginnings. Former Governor Jones and his wife, Libby, the owners of Airdrie Stud, for example, knew his dam Regal Band was in foal to Siphon, Airdrie's hottest new stallion.

"I'll give you $600,000 for the mare and foal right now," said Brere Jones, always looking for a good deal. This made his wife snigger.

"Don't you dare sell him that mare for that," she told her good friend, the dominant female. "She's worth a million and he knows it."

Somehow the governor's car was retrieved first. So was Ted Bassett's, and that of the magazine publisher and the girls mistaken for exotic dancers. After a half hour Smart Rock began to worry about the whereabouts of the borrowed Mercedes wagon and went to inquire. The keys were missing from the valet stand. No one knew where they were, and the car to which they belonged was also missing.

Smoot and the male Kenturkey began to suspect the thief-favored Mercedes wagon was already being disassembled somewhere. Feather-brained with triumph, they began to make jokes about it being driven aboard a pirate ship bound for South America and how Smart Rock would go about explaining that to the owner. No one knew the license number of the Mercedes. There was even disagreement as to its color.

Behind the party of six the number of people waiting in line was dwindling. John Fort, the managing owner of the third-place horse Invisible Ink, turned in his claim check and his car appeared magically. He went by the Kenturkey like he was passing shrubbery. Obviously in a snit, Fort could be heard telling companions that Inky had been foiled by bad racing luck. Trapped on the rail, he had been "unable to go with the other horse." Not "Monarchos" but "the other horse."

"If Inky had gotten in the clear, it would have been different."

Amidst the incredible elation, the Kenturkey felt a another twinge of irritation at Fort. He wanted to say, "Oh, yeah. I heard that. My horse can whip your horse any day."

Only it wasn't his horse. It belonged to the Oxleys, who were long gone, too, having floated by on a cloud to a waiting limo that did not have to be retrieved from a valet park.

The Mercedes wagon finally appeared, its mysterious delay explained only in hasty Spanish that no one was able to decipher.

"What did he say?" Smoot wanted to know.

The Kenturkey's mind was still hopelessly lost in combat with the departed owner of Invisible Ink.

"He said Monarchos only won because his horse was caught in traffic."

What was wrong with that guy Fort anyway?

Nothing, except that his fever had progressed to a significantly advanced stage the Kenturkey could not yet fathom. Once a horse becomes a serious candidate for the Kentucky Derby, a wondrous whirlwind develops around it that builds like a spring hurricane as it moves north toward Louisville and the first Saturday in May. People are sucked in like fans drawn to a team or a human athlete chasing a record or a championship. The interests gathered along the way range from the casual on the fringe to the obsessed in the center. It is there at the heart, among the people closest to the equine hero, where the stakes are the greatest. And when giant personal egos, national interests, trainer reputations, careers and large sums of money are laid on the line, sportsmanship becomes a matter of lip service. On the surface, the Kentucky Derby is a sporting event, to be sure. But beneath, it is a war of skill, gamesmanship, marketing and media manipulation where winning means everything and losing demands a good excuse.

PART 4

MONARCHOS RULES

13

The move—and that's how they'll refer to it in the future, simply as "the move"—was devastating. One second Monarchos wasn't on the radar map, . . . the next he was, . . . demanding you consider him one of the favorites for the Kentucky Derby.

DAVE JOSEPH, *Fort Lauderdale Sun-Sentinel*

Finally the turf writers had what their perpetually hero-hungry sport needed for the 2001 Triple Crown: a star. The time in which Monarchos won the Florida Derby—1:49.95—was nothing to write home about. But the way he won—the winning "move"—was the stuff of legends. He had gone from last to first in about 30 seconds, making up ten lengths on good horses already rolling. After running a half mile, he'd scorched the next quarter in 23.1 seconds. Despite going eight wide around the turn, he still managed to run the final eighth of a mile in less than 13 seconds. Then he ran on for another eighth of a mile past the wire, and when Chavez tried to pull him up he had grabbed the bit in his teeth and kept going.

This performance left experts like veteran Steve Haskin of *The Blood-Horse* sputtering superlatives. "Monarchos was a million lengths the best," he wrote. "This was as impressive a performance as any we've ever seen in a Kentucky prep."

He had crowd appeal, too. Among the heavily Hispanic backside population, he had developed a fan club from which had come yet another colorful nickname—"More-nachos."

Oxley's horse clearly had the style and turn of foot to win the Kentucky Derby. And fortunately the press and the race already had another favorite, the imposing giant Point Given, who had been resting all winter and was about to reemerge on the West Coast. Monarchos may have the highfalutin name and a regally named dam but Point Given was fit for a king in every respect, from looks to ownership. Standing over 17 hands and weighing 1,240 pounds, he was bigger than the great Secretariat and believed capable of perhaps even running as fast. His pedigree for the job was superb. His father, Thunder Gulch, had won the Kentucky Derby in 1995, and his dam's grandsire, Alydar, had finished second in 1978 in an epic struggle with the great Affirmed.

As the ancient sport limped into the new millennium, it suddenly had what had always served it best—a rivalry. Horse racing had been reborn in America in 1938 with a press-contrived match race between Seabiscuit, "the people's horse," and the fabled War Admiral. One horse from the east, one from the west; one aristocratic, one blue-collar; one good-looking, one not; and both able to flat-out carry the mail. The story had everything necessary to entertain a Depression-weary public then badly in need of a rags-to-riches model.

Seabiscuit was an ugly castoff who had failed early as a racehorse and as a three-year-old ran in cheap claimers instead of the Kentucky Derby. Ratty-tailed and knob-kneed, he had been rescued from the scrap heap and turned into the terror of the newly constructed tracks on the West Coast. In perfect contrast was War Admiral, an exquisite equine specimen and the epitome of the blue blood that ruled the traditional eastern tracks. The most beautiful and celebrated son of Man o' War, this ebony powerhouse had won the Triple Crown handily and had broken his sire's track record at Belmont Park in the process while running with a bloody foot.

Their epic struggle at Pimlico Race Course, won by Seabiscuit in a record-setting performance, was the most highly publicized sports event of the era and is still widely regarded as the greatest horse race of all time. As a marketing triumph for racing, it has since gone unmatched while the sport remained perpetually in search of equals, its economic health riding a roller coaster of superstar horses and great rivalries. Now, with the emergence of an exciting come-from-behind closer like Monarchos to challenge the awesome Point Given, the approaching Kentucky Derby held the promise of both.

In a strange twist of irony the Seabiscuit legend was about to be revived in a celebrated new historical account by Laura Hillenbrand, a book already destined for the movie screen. Not coincidentally, publication of the book, which was entitled *Seabiscuit: An American Legend,* was timed for the beginning of the Triple Crown season, and the book's potential for stirring public interest was eagerly being anticipated by a thoroughbred industry continually trying to reinvigorate itself.

Similarities between the famous old race rivalry of 1938 and the new one building in 2001 were striking. Though separated by sixty-three years, both featured the divisions, class distinctions and differences in training styles that have long permeated the thoroughbred industry. All four horses had been born in Kentucky. But Point Given, like Seabiscuit, had gone west to seek his fortune, while War Admiral and Monarchos had done all their running in the east, each in their time becoming a regional hero.

Both of the West Coast–based horses had owners new to the game bent on cracking the top echelon of the thoroughbred establishment that had long been closed to anyone without the right ancestors and generations of old money. Although privileged all his life, Seabiscuit's owner, Charles Howard, had become socially prominent only with the rise of the automobile age, his new wealth derived from selling train-loads of Buicks in San Francisco. As a rich, upstart "outsider," Howard could have no more perfect modern-day counterpart than Point Given's owner, Ahmed Salman, a forty-two-year-old prince of Saudi Arabia who had begun buying racehorses while attending the University of California at Irvine. The prince returned home to live in a palace and supervise the family publishing business, but not before he established a training farm in Bradbury, near Santa Anita, and a global racing company called the Thoroughbred Corporation.

Prince Salman had to earn his industry spurs the same way Howard the Buick king had—by beating the best establishment horses in the biggest races. In this sense they were direct opposites of the owners of War Admiral and Monarchos. Samuel Riddle, descendant of a textile magnate, and Jack Oxley, an oil and gas man, were both chips off sturdy old blocks of U.S. industry, lifelong horsemen and longtime breeding enthusiasts. Either was welcome to any table set by the thoroughbred elite the world over, including the exclusive Jockey Club in New York, where both were awarded membership.

Even the trainers from the distant eras offered sharp distinctions that could be milked for colorful copy by the racing press. The trainers of Seabiscuit and Point Given were both westerners, too, and relatively new to the top level of racing. And each had a unique personality and a different training style that raised eyebrows among their more established peers.

Plainsman Tom Smith, who conditioned Seabiscuit, had started out training cheap stock horses to race in rodeos and wild west shows. Because of his startling turnaround of the temperamental Seabiscuit, who had been given up on by "Sunny" Jim Fitzsimmons, the most celebrated racehorse trainer of his time, Smith was automatically suspected of being a "joint" or "machine" man who used unethical electrical gadgetry to get his horse to run. Teaching a horse to react to electrical shock or a noise associated with it was the most common way of cheating in those days, especially on the lower-level tracks where Smith began, and the technique was undoubtedly one he knew.

Likewise, Point Given's trainer Bob Baffert came off the quarter-horse tracks of Arizona, where he was called "Snake" and where "lighting up a horse" is not all that uncommon. Even where there is not a scintilla of evidence other than an enviable record, any unusual burst of success by a young or previously unheralded trainer swirls in rumors of modern wizardry, such as "chemistry" or so-called "designer drugs." And no one had ever gone to the top of the thoroughbred training ranks as quickly or with as much aplomb as Bob Baffert.

In less than a decade he had risen from nowhere to become the most successful and best-known thoroughbred trainer in the world. In no time he had supplanted legends like D. Wayne Lukas and Bobby Frankel as the leading trainer on the West Coast. More important in the overall scheme of things, he had gained equal status with Lukas as the trainer to hire to win the Kentucky Derby. In 1996 the first horse Baffert ever brought to the classic, the gelding Cavonnier, lost by a nose. Then Baffert, joking that he was bringing horses with longer noses, won two in a row with Silver Charm in 1997 and Real Quiet in 1998, both bargain-basement colts. Ever since, his barns have been filled with choice runners belonging to top owners.

Rumors being an inevitable offspring of envy, they proliferate around any trainer as successful as Baffert. But whatever his methods, they produce fast horses that stay relatively healthy, even over the hard California training tracks. And like Smith six decades earlier, Baffert represented both a challenge and an alternative to his long-established counterparts rooted in Kentucky, New York and Florida. But unlike the intruders Smith and Howard six decades ago, Baffert and Prince Salman had no resemblance to underdogs. Baffert's horses were routinely the betting choice in virtually every big race they entered, and the prince owned some of the best horses in the world. To win a Triple Crown race, Baffert had become the trainer everyone had to beat and his owner had the horses that could do it.

In his day Tom Smith said so little he was known as "Silent Tom." But he was press savvy, and aided by the image-conscious owner Howard, turned Seabiscuit into a national hero. He managed his horse's racing career like it was a political campaign, traveling 50,000 miles by train and parading him for crowds of reporters at whistle-stops.

Baffert, by contrast, is the star in his media events, with horses changing around him year to year and track to track like supporting actors. Whether he's merely walking to the track or boarding a jet for the opposite coast, no journey is complete without a gaggle of press and entertaining commentary from the trainer—some self-deprecating, some sharp-barbed and well-aimed at competitors.

Smith and Baffert had differing styles for different eras but the end goal was the same—to aggravate the opposition and leave them envious and guessing. Together they were the antithesis of George Conway and Johnny Ward, the soft-spoken men of modest achievement and proven methods who trained War Admiral and Monarchos. In the offbeat, unconventional and often comedic world of horse trainers, Conway and Ward were definitely straight men, not easily picked out of a crowd or uncomfortable when lost in one.

Unlike them, Baffert at forty-nine was a man with crowd appeal. Compact and perennially tanned, he makes the most of his prematurely white hair, a large shock of which he rakes across his forehead above eyes usually hidden behind little oval-shaped, pitch black glasses. Contrived or not, it is an image made for the television camera, in front of which he is both glib and comfortable. A marquee horse like Seabiscuit, Secretariat or Cigar comes along once in a while, but Baffert provides racing with constant celebrity. His involvement alone was enough to insure that the instantly hyped Point Given–Monarchos rivalry would provide a story smorgasbord for a news-hungry racing press.

A week after the Florida Derby, while preparing Point Given for an easy opener against a thin field in the San Felipe Stakes at Santa Anita, Baffert defined his oversized, long-backed running machine as "a Big Red Train ready to roll." And roll he did, unfocused but fleet anyway, romping away from an overmatched field.

Point Given and Monarchos were installed immediately as 5 to 1 Derby cofavorites in the minds of both the *Daily Racing Form* handicappers and Churchill Downs oddsmakers. The rivalry was set. And nowhere did its outcome mean more than in the training barns of

Louisville and New York and on the breeding farms of the Kentucky bluegrass. Of the last ten Derbys, six had been won by California-based trainers—three by D. Wayne Lukas, two by Baffert and one by the Englishman Neil Drysdale—and two others had been won by the New Yorker Nick Zito.

Although two Lukas wins—with Grindstone in 1996 and Charismatic in 1999—were applauded in Kentucky because of local owner-breeder connections, only Mack Miller's victory with Sea Hero in 1993 was considered one for tradition. A popular Kentuckian, Miller was the private trainer for Paul Mellon, son of Andrew W. Mellon, the financier and steel magnate. Together Sea Hero's owner and trainer made superb representatives of the thoroughbred aristocracy, true sportsmen who bred to race and maintained relatively small, boutique-quality racing stables. Paul Mellon and Mack Miller were the kind of horsemen the industry preferred to see in the winner's circle at Churchill Downs. No mob suits, geisha girls or interpreters, no open-collar shirts or "Miami Vice" dark glasses—and no playful stunts with the winner's trophy. Baffert tended to wear the hardware on his head whenever possible.

But it was not simply the lack of neckties or decorum that galled the lovers of tradition. It was the new formula being established for winning the Kentucky Derby. The success of Baffert, Lukas and their trainer protégés had turned it into a numbers game. Their rich, ambitious new-breed owners sent them more two-year-old Derby prospects in a year than most trainers had horses, period. Being sent thirty to fifty each year was not uncommon. Their "factories" then turned out enough "survivors" to dominate the juvenile races and return to Louisville as three-year-olds to fill most of the Derby entry spots, one of them almost certain to win the world's most important race and perpetuate the trend. These ever-shifting odds meant a permanent tilt in the balance of power. The hundreds of hands-on trainers with stables so small they fed their own horses every day no longer had much chance against the half dozen or so who issued directions by cell phone from a jet to assistants on both coasts.

For breeders, the racing game was headed in a similarly disturbing direction. The new owners spending the most money to dominate the Triple Crown were in fact foreign breeders—the Japanese, the Irish, the Arabs—all with the ultimate common objective of supplanting Kentucky production dominance. The most powerful and well-heeled of horse buyers—the Dubai sheikhs, the Coolmore monolith and now Prince Salman of Saudi Arabia—made no secret of their goal of gathering so much top bloodstock that the winners of the world's great races could be bred in their homelands. Another member of the Saudi royal family, Prince Khalid Abdullah, owner of Juddmonte Farms, was already established as a world-class breeder, and horses bred by the Arabs and the Irish had regained domination of the great European grass races. Similar success in the American Triple Crown, particularly the coveted Kentucky Derby, could mean only one thing: that the concentration of the great stallions and mares on Kentucky farms—the heart of the American breeding industry—would eventually be diluted and dispersed around the world.

In the best tradition of Seabiscuit and War Admiral, two horses had been set against each other in the minds of the press and the industry, their images fixed as representative rivals of east and west, old and new.

Point Given and Monarchos were both twists of good fortune, extraordinary products of the imagination of vastly different men. They now ran for the same glory but along paths of prince and pauper carrying the hopes and aspirations of opposite extremes with all their contradicting implications.

Point Given. Poster boy of what thoroughbred racing had become, a speed sport survivor of a celebrity owner's numbers game, prepared by a media-star trainer for the television era and eventual stardom as a high-priced stallion never accessible to the average mare owner.

And Monarchos. Blue-collar hero of meager beginnings, throwback to another time, a people's colt saddled with nostalgia, certain to go to stud in Kentucky at a reasonable fee, a local standard-bearer who when compared to Point Given and the others appeared to be decidedly a horse of a different color.

Not surprisingly, the Two Bucks man still looked to newspapers for his caution flags. The big headline on a Florida Derby column in the *Fort Lauderdale Sun-Sentinel* said, "Wow—but don't get too excited," making the point that only two of the previous eleven Florida Derby winners had gone on to win the Kentucky Derby.

Aboard his return flight from Palm Beach to Versailles, this warning was heeded by the editor-turned-horsebreeder and considered worth sharing. Who better to appreciate commonsense journalism than his traveling companion? He clipped the headline from the newspaper and waved it for the benefit of the dominant female, whose expectations he suspected might have been aroused by victory.

"See, this guy's got it right," he said.

No response. She was preoccupied with the Sunday financial section of the *New York Times*. Obviously there was no need to bridle enthusiasm that never came unbridled. Although the quickness of her own "move" to the winner's circle had been noticeable to Smoot and the others, she had remained typically stoic in the bedlam, public shows of exuberance being a violation of her serious Czech-Catholic upbringing. Dignity was paramount to daughters of immigrants. "It's a matter of how you were raised," she liked to say.

Still, he knew how much more she liked winning than losing. Was it possible she was deliberately carrying her *New York Times* financial section wrapped in the front page of a Florida paper bearing a huge color photograph of the winning jockey Chavez and the striking gray colt that had grown up on their farm? Was it the winning race or the declining economy she'd been discussing with the strangers in the Atlanta airport? Interest rates most likely, or the future of high-techs on the Nasdaq.

The Blood-Horse magazine called on his cell phone before they made it home, wanting to photograph Regal Band so a picture would be in hand should Monarchos win the Kentucky Derby. The query at once rankled his old skeptical journalist's side and pushed his newly sprouted superstition jinx button.

"Isn't this a little premature?" he asked, knowing full well the request was standard print media procedure. He recognized his response as disingenuous the minute it left his mouth, the first surface crack in a personality being split like a chasm. Despite the sensational performance of Monarchos, he wanted the bridle he had long ago slipped on his own enthusiasm to remain in place—at least for *The Blood-Horse* to see. But beneath this cool patina of restraint his exhilaration had broken loose with the bit in its teeth, his psyche a runaway bound for schizophrenia.

He had become a real-life version of the conflicting portraits that decorated his library at Two Bucks. Above the fireplace was a painting, a present from the dominant female on his fiftieth birthday, portraying him astride the champion paint mare bought as a baby in 1982, the year they married. Commissioned from a photograph she had taken on the farm, it depicts her husband as a common cowboy sorting cattle, a simple occupant aboard the vibrant, dazzling animal intended to showcase the artist's talent. The portrait was his prize possession, not only because of sentiment and beauty, but because it so accurately reflected his self-image—a man lucky just to be along for the ride.

On a coffee table before the fireplace was a magazine bearing a full-page color reproduction of the same horse in the same glorious action. In this one, however, the artist, Oleg Stavrosky, had altered the rider, hiding his face beneath a slouch hat, draping the torso in a duster and placing a blazing Winchester carbine in his hands. This portrayal was a life metaphor, how he had always lived.

The man on the horse was him all right, but not really. The real man was hiding beneath a disguise, watching someone bolder doing something more exciting; a docile cowhand transformed into a fierce and mysterious "Shooter on a Paint" by a few strokes of genius, or as was now happening with Monarchos, strokes of something that could be mistaken for it.

The familiar ticking in his brain was surely the clock running again on that fifteen minutes in the spotlight everyone was supposed to get in life. Whose allotted quarter hour was he usurping now? His own had come and gone long ago and he kept exhausting time rightfully belonging to others. Maybe the spotlight kept returning because he never acknowledged it as his own.

The last horse he had had in a big race was named Ross Perot, and it was a run for the Rose Garden, not the roses, that he had navigated as media adviser. But even that had not been as it appeared. Perot's campaign for president had been a crusade for reform, quixotic from the start. Had Perot been an equine, he would have had the speed and heart of a champion. But he would also have balked at entering the gate and never would have tolerated a jockey, run in a straight line or accepted training of any kind. Perot was the people's horse in his contest, too. But like many capable thoroughbreds, he would waste a lot of their time and a lot of money and never win a race.

Monarchos was a better bet than Ross Perot. His perfectly balanced physique, four-barrel carburetor throat and oversized heart gave him the wind and speed to be a successful racehorse. That combination, along with the harmony of his marvelous name, metallic color and winning personality, had already produced a media star—a hero with the potential of Seabiscuit. But in the still seriously conflicted view of his humble yet proud breeder, Monarchos still looked a lot like Don Quixote's horse.

Someone who didn't know horses once said they are dangerous at both ends and uncomfortable in the middle, none of which is true if you get to know horses like the Two Bucks man had, if you come to an understanding with them. He had gotten to know dreams, too, but with them had reached neither understanding nor comfort. Even more so than horses, aspirations were at one end all too easy to climb aboard, but at the other too often dangerously disappointing. And with his notoriously poor and recently deteriorating sense of direction, there was always the likelihood of getting lost in the middle.

The dream of breeding a Kentucky Derby winner held no more

promise than one of electing a president of the United States or winning a Nobel Prize. So he stayed put on the ground, clinging to the solace of the observer's perspective from which he could merely watch his favorite figure from literature, a mythical man on a mythical mount in ridiculous pursuit.

The dam of Kentucky's new equine hero looked considerably more imposing now that she was worth at least $600,000—ten times her value the day before the Florida Derby. Her eyes were brighter, she held her head up more confidently, her haunches looked more powerful. Money will do that for a girl.

Regal Band had waited to produce her 2001 foal until after her famous son had won a million-dollar race and her feckless owner had returned to take up his responsibilities again. He'd gone directly to the clinic from the airport, where he found his most predictable mare in her pre-foaling good humor. When she came voluntarily to the stall door to nuzzle, he knew she'd foal by midnight and foretold it. She did.

The birth was indeed of the dangerous "red bag" nature expected of a mare whose placenta had begun to separate prematurely. But the veteran foal deliverer from Two Bucks was himself poised at the scene along with all the available medical assistance that could be summoned to the Hagyard-Davidson-McGee veterinary clinic's "maternity ward" a half hour before midnight on a Sunday. This team included the head man, Dr. Doug Byars, who kept his promise of hands-on supervision. Regal Band's "red bag" was promptly opened and the biggest, best-looking and most robust foal of her broodmare career arrived to smiles and sighs of relief.

Within two days this fat bay filly, with the charisma and athleticism of her big brother, was running circles around her mother in a paddock at Two Bucks for the benefit of *The Blood-Horse* photographer.

"Are you sure this isn't a little premature?" the owner asked, unable to resist milking the charade for another drop.

"No, we're taking pictures of several of the Derby dams just in case. We do it every year."

A "Derby dam" on the farm had resulted in a significant increase in SUV traffic. Bloodstock agents with a keen sense of smell for impending sales commissions knew farms the size of Two Bucks are usually anxious to cash in their lottery ticket. Most came bearing the conventional wisdom that "Derby dams" and "siblings of a big horse" are never worth any more than they are in the days right before the Derby. "If Monarchos wins, the price might go up a little," they all said, "but if he doesn't it goes down a lot."

They could all get the struggling small-farm owner "four to five hundred thousand today," assuming of course that Regal Band was successfully bred back and in foal to a popular stallion. Throw in the impressive new foal and they could get $750,000 for the package. "But that's if we act now. After the Derby, well you know, the Derby is unpredictable. The best horse doesn't always win. Monarchos runs bad in the Derby and all bets are off."

Similar offers were coming in on the cell phone directly from respected breeders and friends who owned shares in the best stallions, like Seeking the Gold and A. P. Indy. They knew Regal Band would be ready to breed within thirty days, so their offers to buy the mare or "foal-share" were timely, well intentioned—and risky. A "shared" foal from the dam of a horse that wins the Derby could be worth a million dollars. The foal from one who finishes twelfth might have trouble recovering the stud fee. Horse breeding is a gambler's game even at the top.

If there had to be dilemmas in life, this was the kind to have. There in his lap was one worth waiting for. A contract to buy the farm had been sitting on the table awaiting his signature. Now he had a mare and foal obviously worth more than he'd paid for the farm. A man realistic about the future of the thoroughbred business and his own pygmy place in it would do the prudent thing: Take the money and run.

For years now the dominant female's heart had been in the art colony of Santa Fe, where she wanted to build a dream home in a ritzy gated community. Her desire to go there had become a monotonous hum.

"Now's the chance," he told her. "We can sell the farm, sell the mare and we're out of the horse business."

She was intent on her laptop, the Nasdaq probably under scrutiny again. CNBC's constant lament on the U.S. economy droned on the television in the background. She was piddling with declining stocks and he was trying to present her with a $3 million deal that made them irrelevant.

"Surely, you wouldn't sell Regal Band. Not now," she said, finally.

"Now is probably the best time to sell her. She may never be worth more. The time to sell horses is when people are standing in line to buy them."

"Well, you can't sell her before the Kentucky Derby. What if Monarchos wins? She'll be worth a lot more."

"What if he doesn't? The odds are better that he won't win."

"But he might. I think we ought to wait."

"And bet our future on a horse winning the Kentucky Derby?"

"Sure, you've said yourself that once the gate opens any of them have a chance to win."

Spoken like a dedicated investor in the new global high-tech economy. Suddenly the dominant female was a faith-based gambler, betting it all on the come, missing a chance she had been waiting for.

Retrieving their existence from its regrettable backslide into the agricultural age had been her passion ever since the French cattle debacle, when the bulls wrecked Two Bucks.

This was before thoroughbreds, back when he had been into raising those damn "beefalo"—the miraculous cross between bison and bovine that was supposed to produce meat so lean it would solve the world's cholesterol problems and reduce heart attacks.

The business was so promising that Two Bucks had been crawling with beefalo heifers, and there was talk of a monstrous bison bull from South Dakota that never showed up. Had he ever arrived, the buffalo could not possibly have wreaked more havoc than his last-minute replacements had—the two French Saler bulls "borrowed" from a guy in the north end of the county. They were supposed to be docile and easy to get along with, but the old big one, Francois, refused to stay with his heifer band on the front of the farm and had led them on a rampage to the back of the property.

The next morning when the dominant female went out to walk the dogs, she found fences in splinters and metal gates twisted into figure eights. Francois and his young rival were still squared off in the creek on the back forty, steam rising off them like locomotives that had crashed head-on repeatedly throughout the night.

Thankfully, the owner hauled off Francois forthwith, but his young rival spent the summer with the heifers, futilely it turned out. Not a single female turned up pregnant, resulting in the bull thereafter being called "Defective," in recognition of the eventual veterinary evaluation of his reproductive equipment. That's what the vet concluded: a "defective penis."

During the roundup of the barren heifers, which were all sold at a loss, Defective compounded his misery and embarrassment at Two Bucks by charging a cutting-horse mare who wheeled and kicked him between the eyes, knocking him unconscious.

What was it with her husband, the dominant female had often wondered, all this breeding of animals? Was it ever to amount to anything?

Now, finally, with the horses, it had. Here was her chance to get out once and for all, yet the dominant female was inexplicably reluctant. What was it with her? Was she coming down with Derby Fever? Nasdaq disorder? Ameritrade account dysfunction?

Vexed, the Two Bucks man retreated to the safe haven of proven modern corporation management principles: When unable to forge a consensus on what to do, don't do anything.

This plan effectively put life on hold and increased the insurance premiums. Newly inflated assets could not wander around in the spring storm season uninsured while everyone waited to see how much they were worth.

14

Goin' to de races. . . . Ain't dat great
Postman worked . . . in Fo'ty Eight.

WALTER BRENNAN'S Academy Award–winning character
Blister Jones in the movie *Kentucky,* 1938

The reign of Monarchos as the press favorite for the Kentucky Derby ended a month after it had begun, his fifteen minutes of fame over when the press spotlight moved from Florida to California. There on the first weekend in April Bob Baffert rolled his Big Red Train out onto the track again, this time for the Santa Anita Derby, another in the series of "preps" that are to the Kentucky Derby what playoff games are to the Super Bowl. Winning the preps is not essential for a horse to go on, but those that do not run well in them are generally eliminated. The preps determine the field and set the odds for the Derby. Traditionally the Grade 1 $750,000 Santa Anita had determined "the best of the west" just as the Grade 1 Florida Derby settled the standard-bearer from the east.

Both of Baffert's previous Kentucky Derby winners—Real Quiet and Silver Charm—had finished second in the Santa Anita, Real Quiet in 1998 behind a horse named Indian Charlie that Baffert had considered number one in his barn at the time. Publicly describing Indian Charlie as "the perfect Derby horse," Baffert had tongue-whipped him into a favorite's role to the point that Real Quiet's victory had appeared a surprise even to his trainer.

That was a mistake Baffert would not make again. Although another of his horses, Congaree, had only a couple of impressive allowance wins to his credit, his trainer began to talk him up as the only horse around who might prove a challenge to Point Given, whose prowess already had driven all the other good California three-year-olds to the Florida, Louisiana and Kentucky preps. Instead of testing his star stablemates against each other in the Santa Anita as he had done before, Baffert entered Congaree in the April 14 Wood Memorial at New York's Aqueduct Racetrack a week later, where the then still "mighty Monarchos" was scheduled to run in his final Derby tune-up.

Point Given, meanwhile, was sent out to decimate a tiny field in the $750,000 Santa Anita, in what amounted to a match race against a second-tier sprinter named Crafty C.T., whose pedigree and lack of stamina gave him no chance at the mile and an eighth distance. The feeble nature of the opposition, however, had no effect on Baffert's normal level of humility. "Point Given was really something, wasn't he? . . . I don't have to worry about the fitness of this guy. The others [his Derby winners Silver Charm and Real Quiet], I was worried they'd get the distance."

Point Given's winning time of 1:47.3 was more than 2 seconds faster than Monarchos's time in the Florida Derby—a distinction not lost on handicappers or the racing press. More important, he had earned a Beyer speed figure of 110, while Monarchos had been awarded 105. This figure, an index rating developed by *Washington Post* turf writer Andy Beyer, is calculated from a number of factors including the type and condition of the track, the weather, the quality of competition and the difficulty of traffic problems the horse may have encountered. Many trainers, writers and handicappers rely heavily on Beyer numbers and the even more arcane "speed" calculations of privately purchased services, such as Thoro-Graph and Ragozin.

"Point Given was simply amazing in the Santa Anita Derby," wrote James Scully in the *Bloodstock Journal*, a daily Internet racing news service. "The chestnut couldn't be any more impressive physically and won for fun Saturday, galloping to the lead on the far turn and drawing off to the easiest of victories in a very quick time. After watching his performance, it was difficult to imagine anybody beating him in the Kentucky Derby."

Speed. It was now the prevailing influence in horse racing, like money in politics and home-run power in baseball. Its sources are mysterious, unexplainable and therefore automatically suspect; its implications are controversial and unknown. Nobody knows for sure why some horses run faster than others. Why they are quicker one afternoon than the next, swifter on one track than another. And how some trainers can get a horse to run harder than it has ever done for someone else.

Half the good horsemen in the world argue that nothing can make a horse move faster than he is naturally capable of moving. The other half rolls its eyes in disbelief, convinced that the same chemicals that give men a superhuman shot of adrenaline or reservoir of energy will produce super-equine efforts as well. They believe a lot of racing is bravery, motivation and a more efficient respiratory system—all of which can come from a syringe or a bottle. But among trainers and handicappers alike there is no dispute that identifying the source and implications of speed in every race can put you in the know and thus in the money.

One certain source of speed for athletes, human or equine, is wind sprints. When the legendary Horatio Luro, who trained Northern Dancer, wanted to "put speed" in a horse, he would run him all-out for five-eighths of a mile, then loosen the saddle and walk him around until he got his wind back. Then he would tighten it again and send him another three-eighths.

Not many modern-day trainers can wind-sprint their horses for three-quarters of a mile on a hard track twice in twelve days leading up to a big race and still win it. But on Tuesday, April 9, Baffert sent

Congaree out on the Santa Anita track for his final workout prior to getting on a plane to New York for the Wood Memorial. He sailed six furlongs in 1:11.2—that's nearly 12 seconds a furlong, or about 38 miles per hour. Of the fourteen horses that worked that distance the same day, Congaree was the fastest, as he had been six days earlier when he finished in 1:11.3. At this point even Point Given had never worked that fast. When horses are the fastest of all those who work the same distance on the same day, they are awarded a "bullet," or a black-dot designation, in the past performance history published before a race. Bullets become the badge of speed.

While California racing and work times are routinely faster than those in the rest of the country, this kind of racing preparation is seldom followed by top trainers elsewhere. Monarchos, for example, never had a timed workout either that far or that fast in his life. Ward favored slower five-furlong sprints and two-mile gallops. In the five weeks between the Florida Derby and the Wood Memorial, Monarchos "worked" three times—never longer than five furlongs nor in "splits" under 12 seconds each.

But for Baffert speedy workouts were as routine as the cockiness with which he predicted that his lightly raced number two horse would easily handle the Florida Derby winner in the Wood. His begrudging assessment of Monarchos as "a good horse who stepped up and mowed 'em all down in Florida" sounded downright disdainful when he added, "Congaree should win the Wood unless Monarchos turns out to be a complete freak."

One of the mysteries about Baffert was whether his mouth was geared as strategically as his training methods or just ran out of control. But whether being rated toward a specific end or simply running "loose on the lead," his incessant boasting had the same infuriating effect on opponents, who would rather beat him than anyone.

Baffert was immediately suspected of trying to bait Ward into pushing Monarchos harder. So far, in accordance with Ward's usual style, he had been kept to a regimen of long, sustained gallops to build endurance for the long stretch run demanded for the Derby at

Churchill Downs. If lured into "speed" training and an eventual stretch duel with Congaree in the Wood, Monarchos might "go over the top" in his training and not have enough left in Louisville three weeks later.

Whatever Baffert's motivations, his boasts were taken in the Ward camp as an obvious lack of respect for both the Florida Derby champion and his trainer. They also laid the foundation for a running public feud between Baffert and Ward over training methods and the eventual anointment in the press of Point Given as the second coming of Secretariat.

While Baffert blazed his two Derby hopefuls in clock-stopping wind sprints on the hard ground of California, Ward shipped Monarchos and Hero's Tribute to Churchill Downs where he galloped them long distances on a track sloppy from rain and melted snow. Publicly he explained to the press how coming to Churchill early and getting experience over a variety of conditions was the best way to ready a horse for the Derby. Some members of the press regarded Ward's comments as the first shots of a colorful word war in the making—a Kentucky trainer who'd never won the big race sniping at a California trainer who'd already won two and barely missed a third. All Ward was really doing was laying a foundation in defense of his own style. He knew what was coming during Derby week when the press descended on Churchill Downs, and he was already drawing lines in the clay between the old way and the new. Privately he regarded Baffert's fleeting tongue and blistering workouts as nothing more than "showtime" for a racing press already too obsessed with "speed" and the idea that great trainers were those with a dozen Derby prospects in their barn.

"We will not ask either of our horses for speed," Ward said repeatedly.

To any layman or casual fan, a trainers' dispute over fractions of a second differences in wind-sprint training is boring and inconsequential. And indeed, it might well be irrelevant. No one has gathered any scientific or medical evidence that shows a horse is more or less physically fit, or more or less physically damaged, by how fast or slow they train for a particular race. Nor has any reliable research been done on what kinds of surfaces horses can most safely travel.

But trainers and other industry insiders instantly recognized the Baffert-Ward spat over the speed and distance of a workout as metaphorical—a microcosm of vast differences in separate universes of horse racing. The minute distinctions in how hard these two men drove horses toward the most important race in the world was in miniature the rivalry between east and west and the deep division between the traditionalists and the numbers-game trainers over the long-run implications of speed.

The wear and tear of the exercise regimen over time and the nature of the ground over which it is conducted clearly matter. Young horses pushed too hard too early on any surface are more likely to break down, and no matter what the age of a racehorse the continuous stress of exercise takes its toll. Hooves, joints, tendons and muscles all simply wear out eventually. And so does the will and desire of the horse, if it must endure pain in the process.

Ward is among the most thoughtful, articulate and outspoken of the "breeders' trainers"—a contingent that wants rules, track surfaces and drug laws geared to keeping horses sound and running long enough for them to become heroes and television stars. Trainers with small stables need their horses to stay in the game. The "numbers" guys always have a replacement.

As obscure and arcane as the argument might appear, it cut right to the heart of the issues dividing the industry and threatening its future. Training regimens, racing surfaces, licensing procedures, medication regulations and gambling laws differ greatly from jurisdiction to jurisdiction. Horses that win in California and Florida often have trouble in Kentucky and New York. Even nearby tracks have their differences: Horses have to be prepared one way to run at Aqueduct and Keeneland, another at Churchill Downs and Belmont Park.

To have a chance at the Kentucky Derby Ward had been forced to train Monarchos all winter on the hard, speed-favoring surfaces in Florida. He knew his home track at Keeneland, though muddy all winter, would have its rail lanes rock-hardened by the training-sale horses by the time the Bluegrass Stakes rolled around in mid-April. Long before he knew who his opponents would be, Ward had selected the Bluegrass as the final tune-up for Hero's Tribute and the Wood for Monarchos, mainly on the basis of the track surfaces. Keeneland would be "fast," meaning that front-running horses like Hero's Tribute would have an advantage. They would not tire enough to be caught by closers like Monarchos. The history of Aqueduct's track was that it tended to be loose and sandy and didn't necessarily favor one kind of runner over another. But already there were rumors that Aqueduct was firming up its track surface in hopes of helping a speedy New York horse named Richly Blended sprint his way into Derby contention. Unless he won the Wood, New York would not have an entry to call its own.

The trend was distressing to Ward and the others for whom he spoke. In the quest to revive itself as a television sport, horse racing had seriously begun trying to emulate the success of stock car racing. The National Thoroughbred Racing Association—the NTRA—was taking its marketing lessons from NASCAR, which had successfully turned its schedule of races into a television series with point standings and world championships. The thoroughbred tracks seemed to be taking their cues from race cars, too. Going fast, crashing and burning was the ticket to television viewership. A speed-hungry world liked to see spectacular speed duels and record-setting performances. Yet despite all the wind-burning done at the training sales for two-year-olds and the earth-scorching workout times at Santa Anita and Hollywood Park, thoroughbreds had not been going any faster in the big races. Track records in the Kentucky Derby, the Preakness and the Belmont Stakes were all a quarter of a century old, mainly because of pressure from the eastern-based trainers. The deep, loose track surfaces that preserved those records also preserved the easterners' ability to compete. Tradition demanded that those horses who rush to the lead and wind-sprint for three-quarters of a mile pay a price. If the trend was not reversed, the Triple Crown races in Louisville, Baltimore and New York would permanently belong to the speed merchants from Texas and California.

There was no better time or place to raise the issue than this year at the Kentucky Derby, on the one track where speed never held up in the stretch and in the only race the world always watched.

Regardless of differences in training styles, Johnny Ward took the superlatives Bob Baffert was laying on his red horses to be true. He was particularly impressed with what he'd heard from others about Congaree, who was nearly as big as Point Given, better put together and maybe even faster. After finishing sixth in his first start, Congaree had won two in a row by a total of thirteen lengths.

Yvonne Azeff had seen Congaree's last allowance win at Santa Anita and had reported to Ward that he looked to be extremely gifted. The only question was his Derby pedigree. Could he go the mile and a quarter? His sire, Arazi, had been brilliant but had still had trouble with the distance. There was no question, however, about the Wood, shorter by an eighth of a mile.

But it was "speed"—both Congaree's natural quick turn of foot and the Aqueduct racetrack surface—that was the real concern. Still, Ward stuck to his training regimen. Two weeks before the race, on April Fool's Day, he worked Monarchos a lazy five-eighths of a mile in the mud at Churchill and let him gallop another quarter mile in 14 seconds per furlong. Even at that pace Monarchos looked a little tired afterward. "That's fine," Ward said. "We haven't been asking him for anything much. We won't, either."

Despite goading from the press, Ward refused publicly to attach much significance to the race with Congaree. "The Wood is a prep for the Kentucky Derby," he said. "Nothing more than that."

A week later, he worked Monarchos another five-eighths more briskly, just a tick over a minute flat—12 seconds a furlong—and shipped him to New York with Azeff. Shortly after takeoff from Louisville, the jet, which was carrying five other horses, including It's So Simple, another Wood starter, hit an air pocket and dropped a couple of hundred feet, startling Monarchos. Again the "X-chromosome"—Azeff—was nearby to settle him. At Aqueduct, Azeff thought Monarchos liked the track okay and looked comfortable moving over it. But it bothered her that a stray black cat kept walking up and down in front of his stall.

Ward would not go to New York until the morning of the race. He had remained behind in Kentucky to train Hero's Tribute right up to the Bluegrass. In Ward's mind the best thing that could happen to Monarchos on the day of the Wood Memorial would be for his stablemate to run well in the Bluegrass Stakes later the same afternoon at Keeneland. Like Baffert's two horses, Hero's Tribute was a big, physically imposing animal that liked to run up front and bang around on other horses. He had run all over Dollar Bill in the Louisiana Derby. It was a role Ward and Oxley had envisioned for him on Derby Day—to press the pace and take up space behind the front-running speedballs. This strategy would make the going tough in the spot where Point Given and Congaree would be laying. But Oxley wouldn't send Hero's Tribute to the Derby just to take up space. He would have to earn his spot.

As Ward saw it, if Hero's Tribute came through, he'd gain a strategic advantage over Baffert. The California trainer had two powerful owners—Stonerside Stables and Prince Salman—each expecting a Derby winner. Their horses had similar running styles and Baffert could not afford to compromise either by using them to complement each other. But Ward had one owner with two horses—a front-runner and a closer—and a single goal. Their strategy had been laid out and agreed on for some time. Churchill Downs had a long stretch run and a century of history that says winners come from behind, which favored Monarchos.

By sending Monarchos to New York, Ward hoped to repeat the winning route Fusaichi Pegasus had taken the year before, when an easy Wood victory had set him up perfectly for the Derby. But Baffert had checkmated Ward by entering Congaree, who had not raced in six weeks. Baffert might be able to bring his fresh horse back for the Derby in three weeks from a gut-wrenching, all-out wind sprint to win the Wood, but Ward would not try it with Monarchos.

On the day of the race, Ward's riding instructions to Jorge Chavez called for a repeat of the Florida Derby. He was not to join Congaree in a chase of Richly Blended, whose style was to lead wire to wire. Nor should he allow Monarchos to engage Baffert's horse in an eye-to-eye stretch run. Trainers believe that when horses "hook up" and battle each other stride for stride it takes more out of them. Some horsemen believe the winners and losers even remember which they were. Ward wanted neither a physically and psychologically drained loser nor a confident winner with an empty tank.

Having been made privy to John Ward's strategy concerning Jack Oxley's horses, the backseat driver of the Monarchos bandwagon had embraced it wholeheartedly.

Well-wishers who called were warned not to expect a win in the Wood, even though Monarchos was going off the 4 to 5 favorite over Congaree, who was 8 to 5. Don't bet on it, he assured them. That he and the dominant female weren't even going to New York for the race but planned to watch it on television at Two Bucks was to be taken as evidence of its long-run insignificance.

By now he'd gathered evidence to support his charade. As a reporter he'd always demanded evidence.

"Monarchos has won three in a row already this year. Horses rarely win four, almost never five. So we're not worrying about the Wood. We're aiming for the Derby."

"We" of course had nothing to do with it. Was this the editorial "we" or did he have a rat in his pocket? "We" were onlookers like everyone else, except that they were no longer themselves, he especially.

Such public posturing was so reminiscent of his years covering politicians that privately he was ashamed of himself. Of course the Wood was important. Deep down he believed Monarchos should never lose another race. A horse with his heart, his turn of foot, his impeccable breeding would blow by Congaree like he was in neutral and shut Baffert up once and for all.

He had taken Baffert's typical braggadocio in the cool perspective expected of a veteran journalist, expert in the recognition of meaningless rhetoric.

"Did you see what this arrogant sonofabitch Baffert said about Monarchos?" he had shrieked in the direction of the dominant female. "He said Monarchos would have to be a freak to beat Congaree. I hope Monarchos blows his doors off. Beats him by twenty lengths."

This was becoming his customary attitude now when hearing or reading of the racing prowess of any Kentucky Derby contender other than the horse from which he had sworn emotional detachment, the one on which he was just along for the ride. Earlier that day he had been lambasting another horse trainer, the affable Irishman Tommy Walsh, a New Yorker as complete a stranger to him as Baffert, and unlike the white-maned Californian, a man universally regarded as a lovely guy.

All Walsh had done was look at the mediocre winning time of the Florida Derby and suggest to the press that "Monarchos will have to step up a notch" to beat his talented but unproven colt Ommadon, whom he expected to start in the Wood. "My horse can run a mile and an eighth faster than that," Walsh said.

"Who the hell is Tommy Walsh? And who the hell is Ommadon?"

From downstairs the dominant female heard him yelling from his upstairs office, where he was alone.

"Anyway, how the hell do we know how fast Ommadon can run a mile and an eighth when he's never run a mile and an eighth before? Wait until Monarchos jerks a knot in Ommadon's ass and then let's see who needs to step it up a notch. Tommy Walsh, that's who."

What the hell he was talking about, the dominant female had no clue. Yes, who was Ommadon? She'd like to know. And who was Tommy Walsh? She had no idea. Nor did her husband, she suspected.

But no one could say her husband was all talk. The day before the Wood and the Bluegrass, there was a big $200,000 Grade 2 grass stakes race at Keeneland called The Maker's Mark Mile, named after a Kentucky bourbon whiskey. Though it was to be held on a Friday the 13th, even superstition could not deter him from entering Monarchos's sibling, Snake, who had been winning in tough allowance company. This step was taken over the objection of the trainer, an obstinate Swiss named Christopher Speckert, who had understudied the great Charlie Wittingham and had won a Breeders' Cup. Unlike the owner, Speckert was not infected with Monarchos fever. He did not believe simply being a relative of a Derby contender would make Snake competitive with the best grass horses in the world. In order that he might enter Snake in an allowance race later in the Keeneland meet, the trainer cautioned the rider, Mark Guidry, not to use the horse up in the stakes race unless he had a chance to finish in the money. As usual Snake ran his eyeballs out, but he was pushed six wide on the final turn and did not produce the patented family finish now made famous by his half-brother. Worse, Guidry followed Speckert's instructions. Instead of pushing Snake to finish strongly, which might have earned him third or fourth, the jockey eased him early, so he finished back in the pack like the 25 to 1 shot he'd been rated. The handicapper responsible for that, a nice guy named Mike Battaglia, had come in for a word lashing, too: "Idiot probably doesn't even know who Snake is. Handicaps on the basis of who the jock is. Maybe doesn't like Guidry or something."

Losing should not have been such a problem for a man who long ago had accepted it as an unavoidable part of life. But through the magnifying glass of someone so out of kilter, Snake's lackluster finish was seen as a needless embarrassment to Monarchos, his dam Regal Band—and Two Bucks. The farm had a pride of its own now that had been besmirched. A few days after the Florida Derby—and not coincidentally, he suspected—Keeneland had finally awarded him the privilege of purchasing half an interest in a permanent clubhouse reserved-seat box. Though its view was partially obscured by a support pole, the box meant he had become at least half a "swell" in Kentucky. Some old Nashville friends, partial owners in Snake, had been invited to sit in the evidence to view the race. They had been disappointed, too, but as the dominant female noted, they "at least had enough class not to say they wanted to run over the trainer and the jockey with their pickup truck."

Obviously she had not caused her husband's ego to atrophy, as he was always insisting. She regarded his bad loser behavior as far more humiliating than Snake's race. "Maybe you ought to stick to breeding these animals," she told him. "I don't think you have the temperament for racing."

His temperament would be tested and found lacking again the next day when he was secretly counting on a Monarchos victory to keep the rivalry with Point Given alive. That rivalry would be good for Kentucky breeders, good for the game and bad for evildoers, at least one of whom had already gotten what was coming to him—that "loudmouth" Tommy Walsh, the trainer with the gall to say that Monarchos would have to "step it up a notch" to beat his horse Ommadon.

News that Ommadon had suffered a bruised foot and would be unable to start in the Wood or the Derby had been greeted at Two Bucks like a winning lottery ticket. Gloating over a horse's injury was both uncharacteristic and unbecoming, or so he had been reminded by the dominant female, and unequivocal evidence that her husband now had no sense of rightness either, to go with his no sense of direction and bad racing temperament.

Through the modern miracle of satellite television transmission and the giant dish in their backyard, the races at Aqueduct and other tracks that broadcast simulcast signals on the new TVG Racing Network could be watched at Two Bucks, and both the Wood and Bluegrass had special coverage shown on network television. This scheduling was fortunate because their box at Keeneland was being used on Bluegrass day by the co-owners, the other half-swells.

During the preliminary races on TVG, the Two Bucks man began to speak harshly to the television set. The dominant female was not in the room and no one else was around. But from another part of the house, she could hear the voices of the TVG talking heads and then his own. He was railing against the track maintenance crew at Aqueduct.

The rumors had proven correct. On a track surface obviously geared to favor speed, front-running horses went wire to wire in all but one of the early races.

"The bastards have fixed it for Richly Blended," he told the TV. "No closer will win at Aqueduct today."

But he didn't believe that. Now he was posturing even for his own benefit. He still thought Monarchos invincible. That two of the talking heads on TVG had picked Richly Blended had infuriated him. "Idiots," he shouted. When analyst Gary Mandella, son of the great California trainer Richard Mandella, predicted that "Monarchos will have to make up a lot of ground this afternoon," the irate viewer was compelled to reply, "How the hell do you know? The race hasn't started."

When the dominant female came in to watch the race he told her they had no chance. The two network analysts had just picked Congaree.

When Richly Blended flew from the gate with Congaree right on his hip and the two went the first half mile of the Wood in 46 seconds, the pace looked fast enough to benefit a closer like Monarchos. And there he was sitting fifth, about eight to ten lengths behind, not as far back as he'd been in the Florida Derby. When they had gone three-quarters of a mile in 1:10, sure enough Richly Blended began to tire.

About the same time Chavez pulled the trigger on Monarchos, who shot up the rail and angled to the outside coming out of the final turn. The cheerleader jumped from his seat and drowned out the track announcer. "Here he comes, he's rolling."

And he was, too, mowing down the tired horses as he had at Gulfstream. Monarchos looked as if he was about to win again. Only Congaree was not tired and not about to be mowed down. Instead, he pushed a head in front and began his drive. Although Monarchos made up ground with every stride, he still hit the wire two and a half lengths behind Congaree.

"That's all right," was the final analysis in the Two Bucks living room. "The speed held. We didn't have to win that one anyway."

"We didn't?"

"No."

"That's good. Because we didn't."

Self-conscious about his behavior, he fell back on the sofa and the obvious.

"You can't win them all."

"Now, we don't have to worry about that. Do we?"

"No, now the pressure is off. Nobody will be expecting us to win. We won't be the favorite."

The yo-yo had wound himself back to up.

A few minutes later the best thing that could have happened to Monarchos that day did not happen. Saddled by Donna Ward at Keeneland and piloted by Jerry Bailey, America's most respected jockey, Hero's Tribute laid an Easter egg in the Bluegrass, finishing last in a field of seven. He had drawn post position number three, which put him in place to run just off the rail in lanes so "fast" that earlier in the week a couple of two-year-olds prepping for the training sale had been timed in 10-second-flat furlongs. But coming out of the gate, Hero got squeezed and took an awkward step, almost unseating Bailey. The slight hesitation was all that the fleet Millennium Wind needed to grab the fast-lane lead and run off with what was widely regarded as the toughest of the day's Derby preps. Left behind with Hero in the speedy Californian's exhaust were four other leading Derby prospects—the single-geared Dollar Bill, Invisible Ink, Songandaprayer, and the great Irish hope with the Italian connections—A P Valentine. The story was the same in the Arkansas Derby where another front-runner named Balto Star went immediately to the front and never looked back. All over the country speed had burned the last round of the Derby preps and with them Ward and Oxley's balanced two-horse strategy. They were now down to a single Derby entry, who had just been soundly beaten by what was generally regarded as Baffert's second-fastest horse.

At what was supposed to have been a dual victory celebration, Jack and Debby Oxley hosted the faithful at a private dinner in downtown Lexington, where they looked for a silver lining in the cloud. They found it in Ward's analysis of the day's races. Congaree's winning time of 1:47 4/5 in the Wood had been the fastest of all the preps that day, and Monarchos had been the only horse to close ground on the winner.

"Georgie Chavez rode a smart race," he said. "Monarchos finished good on a racetrack that was tough to finish on. Most important, he protected the horse, he didn't go over the top."

Monarchos was being trained to win the Kentucky Derby on May 5, Ward reminded the disappointed. Nobody will remember who won the Wood Memorial on April 14.

Well, almost nobody.

Three days later, Baffert, who was still sunning at Santa Anita, poured salt on their singed hide with a carefully orchestrated workout for Point Given. Calling on the resources of Prince Salman, the Californian arranged for another of the owner's many racehorses, a three-year-old colt named Saif, to be used as workmate, a "rabbit" to be given a six-length headstart so he could be run down from behind by Point Given, ostensibly to teach him what he is supposed to do in the race. Baffert, communicating with riders on both horses via walkie-talkie, has made this exercise a staple of his training program. The show begins with both horses traveling at a moderate pace six lengths apart. Both accelerate at the same time, and when the second horse begins to gain on the first, Baffert signals the rider on the "work horse" to "shut it down" while the star horse flies by at the wire at top speed. The routine produces both a fast work time and an excited press. "Point Given's Workout a Virtuoso," reported the *Daily Racing Form* the next day. "[He] served notice that he is deserving of favoritism in the Kentucky Derby. . . . The time, 46.80, was the fastest of 26 works at the distance Tuesday . . . finishing his final quarter mile in a brilliant 23-seconds flat."

Baffert announced that when Point Given left for Churchill Downs the following morning, Saif was going along on the plane, too. "He is the perfect work horse," the trainer said.

The show was on the road.

15

My horse has a hoof like a striped agate
His fetlock is like a fine eagle plume
His legs are like lightning
My horse has a tail like a thin black cloud
The Holy Wind blows through his mane.

NAVAJO SONG

The sweetness of beating villains is unfortunately matched by the bitterness of being conquered by them. Victories by California horses in the Wood and the Bluegrass, the two most important April prep races, again set the Kentucky Derby table up as a one-sided feast for West Coast trainers and big money.

Baffert's horses instantly became the first and second choices to take the roses, with Millennium Wind third.

"The West Coast team looks dominating," said the *Bloodstock Journal*. The English bookmaking firm William Hill dropped Point Given's odds to 3 to 1, and Mike Battaglia, who had made Churchill Downs' Derby morning line since 1975, said he had Point Given at 2 to 1 and Congaree second at 6 to 1. Monarchos, Battaglia said, would be "somewhere in the double digits."

This estimation elevated the smiling, good-natured and well-liked Battaglia high on the scale of the temporarily vilified.

"Hell, what else could you expect from Battaglia? He didn't like Snake the other day either and he hasn't been right since he picked Secretariat. So what?"

Even the *New York Times*, which had been a staunch Monarchos supporter, termed Baffert the "trainer most likely to succeed" at the Derby.

Nowhere was the Baffert euphoria greater than on the TVG racing network, which included Churchill Downs among its owners and sponsors. A sort of low-budget "ESPN of horse racing," the network featured a lineup of hip, young talking heads obviously selected to appeal to a hip young audience that racing did not have. Based in California, they were naturally in awe of Baffert, whom they recognized as the closest racing could come to a media star. He was "articulate," "accessible," "cute" and "the greatest trainer not yet in the Hall of Fame, but certain to get there."

The idolatrous attitude of TVG and the California-based correspondents who dominated *Daily Racing Form* coverage did not play well among the Monarchos faithful in Kentucky. It once even drove his irrepressibly buoyant and positive owner, Jack Oxley, to screw up his face and whisper to the breeder, "We aren't getting much respect in the media now, that's for sure."

To which the resident expert on press behavior responded as usual with his long-held and ever-ready explanation: "Don't mind them. The people in my old profession have become a herd of empty-headed sheep and whatever comes out of the mouth of one is immediately on the lips of them all. That's what's wrong with this country. It's full of very smart people without the confidence to use their independent intelligence. They're afraid of being instantly contradicted, which can happen in the information age."

The conviction and authority of his delivery coupled with the soundness of his reasoning validated the preconceived notions of his audience. It was a secret he had learned from covering some of the great demagogues of history. But beneath this measured, laid-back mellowness, he was fit to be tied and clandestinely locked in combat, his principal weapon being snide and abusive e-mails.

"How do idiots like you get on television?" asked one of his anonymous electronic missiles to TVG. "When are you and Battaglia going to remove your lips from Baffert's ass?"

At the time, the Monarchos man was so self-absorbed he had no idea that he had become the covert leader of a complaining Kentucky chorus. While the average racing fan may pick their Derby favorites for reasons as frivolous as a horse's name or the color of a jockey's silks, insiders sort theirs out on the basis of self-interest.

Although seven of the top ten horses in the *Daily Racing Form*'s "Derby Watch" in early April were Kentucky bred, traditional delineations had left Monarchos atop a very short list of Derby contenders who qualified as homebred heroes.

That is because the Derby is the public face of a $15 billion global industry that rests on a peculiar two-tiered economy, fueled at the top by the discretionary income of the foolhardy wealthy and at the bottom by the rent and grocery money risked at the betting windows by the most desperate and adventurous. From top to bottom it is more a game than a business, played by the rich and janitored by the poor, in which the disparity in quality of life can be graphically measured by the furlongs that separate the plush clubhouse box from the grimy backside toilets.

All the money in the game comes from a gamble of one kind or another and is taxed as the proceeds of sin by some level of government. A lot of people live off the exchange, but only a few veterinarians, trainers, jockeys and sales companies make a good living at it. Everybody else is in it for love and the periodic connection with a winner that will assure a break-even existence and some balance between the highs and lows.

In this sense the Derby each year becomes a great equalizer, with social and economic implications as complex and cockeyed as those connected with winning an Oscar. Who to root for and why depends on the row of seats from which you are watching the show.

Invariably, the horses and their cheering sections are segregated by lines of economic interests that flare like spokes, separating big from small, top from bottom, and Kentucky from everywhere else. But because most owners of Derby horses are generally wealthy relative to the rest of the racing community, the distinction between hero and villain often comes down to a single, historically significant characteristic—whether the horse's "connections" are hands-on professional horsemen, or are perceived as dilettantes from other walks of life who are simply trying to "buy the game." In Kentucky, even the wealthiest and most successful breeders traditionally have been true "horse people" who are there in the barns every day to form an attachment to the animals. It is a distinction as critical and emotional as the difference between the life and the death of a foal.

Late on Easter Sunday, the day after the disappointing loss by Monarchos in the Wood Memorial, a filly was born at Two Bucks. She was big and beautiful, deep liver chestnut in color with a wide white blaze and four white feet like her mother, Storm in Sight, who had delivered a dead foal the year before.

In light of that recent history, Storm in Sight's pregnancy had been closely monitored, and as in the case of Regal Band two months earlier, ultrasound scanning had detected a slight placental separation, which portends a premature, "red-bag" birth. But Storm foaled only ten days early, which is neither uncommon nor of particular concern, and the farm was prepared. Again the Two Bucks man was in the barn at precisely the right moment to assist in the delivery and administer oxygen to the filly, who came out alive and kicking. Sigita, the farm manager, was on the scene in five minutes, and the veterinarian, who lived nearby, arrived fifteen minutes later. Because "red-bag" babies often exhibit immune system deficiency, as a precaution they are administered antibiotics and colostrum that has been collected previously from a healthy mare and frozen.

Both the dominant female and Mr. Nonesuch, the barn cat, were on hand to perform their customary oversight and unanimously passed judgment on the new arrival, a daughter of 1997 Horse of the Year Favorite Trick, as the most striking filly in Two Bucks history.

Ninety minutes later, however, the picture changed. The filly, who was extraordinarily large for a premature baby, was still unable to stand and nurse. Although she appeared bright and anxious to get up for nutrition, her hindquarters lacked strength and coordination. Tube-feeding with her mother's milk appeared to improve the foal's attitude and invigorate her efforts, but daylight still found the filly helpless in the straw at her mother's feet.

When the rest of the farm help arrived for work, Storm in Sight and her foal were loaded into the farm van and driven to the Hagyard-Davidson-McGee Clinic maternity ward for intensive care designed primarily to keep the foal alive long enough to gain sufficient strength to stand.

The Monarchos man and the dominant female took turns at the Hagyard vigil, watching some of the world's best veterinarians try valiantly to save a baby that could not be saved. The tube-fed milk was not being digested, apparently the result of an underdeveloped digestive tract. Soon, the vets were battling infection and pneumonia. Forty-eight hours later, the decision was made to euthanize the foal.

Transporting the filly's disturbed and sedated dam back to Two Bucks, the breeder reflected on his failure, which was not an extraordinary event on a horse farm. Storm in Sight, the "bargain" mare at $55,000, had produced one live foal that brought $17,000—and two dead ones. Two years of production had been lost, and possibly $150,000 in farm revenue. The vet cost on the Favorite Trick filly—who lived less than three days—was $2,700. But it was only a pittance when compared to the amount of in-vain effort and emotional toll.

Lifting a gorgeous but dying foal, disposing of the carcass of an animal beloved for twenty years or twenty minutes, and calculating the connected financial and emotional loss are all integral to the horse business. Over twenty-five years, the Two Bucks man had done these deeds dozens of times, as most Kentucky horsemen have, no matter how big the farm or how wealthy its clientele. They see one another at the vet clinics where the critical decisions are often made and at the diagnostic and disposal center where the failures end up, and the hands-on horsemen know who is and who is not one of them. They know firsthand the difference between participating in a tragedy and being notified of it by telephone, and how such a loss impacts an owner of eight mares as opposed to one who owns a hundred.

So when one of the hands-on horsemen ends up with a horse in the Kentucky Derby instead of the diagnostic center dumpster, minor envy is quickly overridden by major celebration. A horse such as Monarchos, no matter the wealth of his owner, becomes a ray of hope for an entire way of life, a local hero. And where there is a hero, villains inevitably abound. Chief among them were A P Valentine and the Derby favorite himself, Point Given.

A P Valentine and Point Given were both foaled within ten miles of Two Bucks on big, famous farms far more important to the breeding industry. Point Given grew up on Mill Ridge, the master of which is Alice Chandler, daughter of one of the original Keeneland founders and generally regarded as the single most influential woman in the thoroughbred business. And Kentucky's leading horseman, Will Farish, was co-breeder of A P Valentine, who was raised on his showplace farm, Lane's End. Both are industry giants compared to the pygmy Two Bucks.

Why the mantle of hometown favorite did not fall on the neck of either of these two royally bred Kentucky horses was rooted in the beneath-the-surface industry intrigue that never makes the sports pages or the racing telecasts. While Chandler and Farish are admired in Kentucky as hands-on horse people, the owners who were bringing Point Given and A P Valentine back to contest the Kentucky Derby were not.

From a Kentucky viewpoint, if any horse had ever fallen into the hands of the Philistines, it was A P Valentine, the lovely colt so coveted by Jack Oxley at the Saratoga yearling sale that he missed seeing Monarchos entirely. A P Valentine had gone instead to a hobby horseman, Rick Pitino, the former University of Kentucky basketball coach. Although he had close friends among the industry insiders, Pitino was now known in the bluegrass as "Traitor Rick." Not only had he abandoned UK for the Boston Celtics, he had just left the Celtics and taken the head coaching job at the University of Louisville, the University of Kentucky's most hated basketball rival.

If this history alone wasn't enough to make A P Valentine a bad name, after a smashing victory in the Grade 1 Champagne stakes at Belmont as a two-year-old, he began to look like another Fusaichi Pegasus. Coolmore, which also had chosen not to buy the colt at Saratoga, took another look. Of all the horses a Kentucky Derby victory might validate as a sire, this particular Kentucky-bred colt fit most precisely John Magnier's "can't miss" stallion profile—at least on paper. The Coolmore Irishman purchased the colt's breeding rights from Pitino for an even more cool $15 million prior to the 2000 Breeders' Cup.

In reality both the price Magnier would ultimately shell out for the breeding rights to A P Valentine and his eventual value as a stallion depended on his performance in the big stakes races. If A P Valentine won the Derby, the Irish would have another $50 million stallion and another victory on their road to conquest of the American thoroughbred breeding industry.

A quarter of a century after rich American industrialists purchased the European thoroughbred breeding industry piece by piece, horse by horse, and moved it to Kentucky, the Irishman Magnier and a succession of partners had begun gradually reclaiming it, race by race, one stallion at a time, and dispersing it worldwide under the auspices of the global powerhouse Coolmore. Now no one, save possibly the ruling Maktoum brothers of oil-rich Dubai in the United Arab Emirates, could compete with Magnier when it came to buying promising yearlings or established racehorses with the potential of becoming sires.

Though largely unknown to the public outside his own country, this charismatic, driven Irish patriot had become the single most powerful force in a multibillion-dollar industry replete with charismatic, powerful and wealthy men. At age fifty-three, Magnier was now the Bill Gates of the horse business. No meaningful thoroughbred race, sale or trackside discussion could take place anywhere in the world anymore without the master of Coolmore playing a major role or having a major interest in its outcome. And although for the last half century Kentuckians had decided who owned stallions and at what fee they would stand at stud, it was now Magnier who set the rules.

Although Magnier is enigmatic and keeps Coolmore's financial dealings to himself, his conquest of the thoroughbred breeding business is an open book. Now and then in every business someone comes along who on the strength of an invention or idea changes the basic economic model or business paradigm.

Attaining this power took Magnier three decades and at least that many wealthy partners, all of whom shared his daring for high-stakes gambling on a seemingly impossible strategy, and all trusted his acumen for judging horseflesh. Since the mid–1970s he and his men have been trying to buy all the best-bred American stallion prospects before they become successful racehorses, the idea being that no matter how expensive they are as yearlings they will be more valuable as stallions. The tiny fraction that succeed as sires will more than pay for all those who do not.

However ridiculously ambitious and extravagant in theory, through precision targeting and careful selection Magnier and his men have proven the underlying principle to be sound. Not only did it work, it would have worked much more quickly and profitably had the cost not been driven up over the years by an equally determined buyer and eventual arch-rival, Sheikh Mohammed bin Rashid Al Maktoum of Dubai. But from time to time the indefatigable Irishman even found ways to use the Maktoums' seemingly endless supply of money for his own ends. Magnier's network of associates worldwide was so vast, and the fervor of Irish nationalism so strong, no one knows exactly which horses Coolmore and its partners already owned, which ones they were trying to buy, and which ones they wanted to sell at prices inflated by their own bidding. Auctions were so rife with rumor and Coolmore marketing was so efficient that the Maktoums were often thought to be bidding against the Irish on horses in which Coolmore already had a silent interest. Sheikh Mohammed's counterstrategy was simply to buy whatever he wanted at whatever price necessary to get it—to the delight of the rest of the industry. The Irish-Maktoum battle over prize yearlings and mares has kept horse values aloft and auctions exciting for two decades. In the 1980s their struggle once drove up to $13 million the price of a yearling who couldn't run. And the two sides were still at it in 2001, bidding up to nearly $7 million for the unproven offspring of certain sires. But no matter how high the yearling prices rise, Magnier appeared to have constructed an economic model that made them pay as stallions—at least on the grand scale at which he operated.

Simply by doubling the number of mares bred to a stallion—from an average of 70 or so on the traditional Kentucky model to more than 150—Magnier doubled the number of live foals and thus the revenue from stud fees. The simple mathematics of this automatically allowed him to pay twice as much for a racehorse as a traditional Kentucky stallion syndicator whose financial model was based on the supply-and-demand traditions of smaller, more select stallion books.

Over time Magnier added new wrinkles that increased profitability, lowered risks and shortened the payback—all of them acts of heresy to Kentucky traditionalists. Instead of watching his valuable possessions playing in their muddy paddocks during the fall and winter, he began sending them to the Southern Hemisphere to stand to a third more mares at reduced stud fees more affordable to Pacific Rim and South American countries. Then during their third or fourth year at stud—a time when demand for a new stallion's services drops dramatically in America while the industry waits to assess the performance of his offspring at the track—Magnier leased his best young sires to Japan or shipped them off to stand in Europe at one of his own farms, where they would be a rare new attraction.

Kentuckians considered all of these changes detrimental in the long term to both the health and value of the stallion. But the strength of Magnier's business model is not what happens in the long term. His updated approach fit perfectly the modern in-and-out investment strategy of today's speculators in every other global market—lower risk and faster payback.

Magnier's philosophy quickly caught on among some younger generation Kentucky horsemen, who appreciated the obvious short-term benefits of a numbers game. The larger stallion books increased the chances the stallion had of succeeding as a first-year sire: The more colts who went to the track, the more likely one of them could win a Breeders' Cup championship or a Triple Crown race; the more revenue a stallion produced in his first three years, the less the loss if and when he eventually failed as a sire, as most of them do.

In the past only a few popular stallions attracted 80 or more mares per year. But now the top stallions attract 170, and not surprisingly, a higher percentage of the better mares go to Coolmore stallions. Further flaunting proof of his conquest and dropping clues to its future direction, Magnier in 2001 cut deals that drew 36 top American-owned mares, who would normally have earned stud fees for Kentucky-based stallions, to Ireland to breed to Coolmore's most recent European racing sensation, Giant's Causeway.

Despite whispered animosity and isolated resistance, Coolmore had changed the game, probably forever, maybe for the better. Maybe not. For reasons as obvious as the prices at the next yearling auction, the prospects and implications of this shift in the balance of power never make the agenda of American breeders' meetings, the Jockey Club roundtable discussion or the feature stories in the industry press. But they rumble like tremors from hell beneath the surface of preparations for every big Grade 1 stakes race like the Kentucky Derby. It is the Grade 1 stakes winners that make the stallions, and to the chagrin of much of the breeding industry, Coolmore's traveling stallions had become what the game is all about.

A P Valentine was already destined for that role, and three weeks before the Kentucky Derby 2001, there were reasonable expectations that if Point Given won, he too would be in line for a Coolmore passport.

Even perfect Kentucky connections could not make Point Given a hometown boy for the simple reason that he fit such a threatening mold—a well-bred, foreign-owned, California-trained powerhouse whose future as a breeding stallion was then unsettled and unpredictable.

Unlike the Dubai sheikhs, Point Given's owner, Prince Salman, had no Kentucky farm of his own. Instead he had chosen to spread his Kentucky business around to a few well-connected breeding farms like Mill Ridge, where he boarded one of the world's premier mares, the great champion Sharp Cat.

No one will even say precisely how many horses the Prince owns—only "enough to accomplish his goals." But the number is in the neighborhood of 250 and from the outside his Thoroughbred Corporation appeared to be based on the same "buy-the-game" philosophy adopted by the Dubai sheikhs and the Irish. Throw enough cash at the Kentucky Derby and eventually you can own it, too.

Point Given winning the Derby would mean only more wealth and good fortune for a foreigner whose wealth derived from an accident of birth and inflated gasoline prices; another valued broodmare in the hands of foreigners; and even higher stud fees for his sire Thunder Gulch, already one of the Coolmore Irishman's "shuttle" sires—here today and gone tomorrow.

Thunder Gulch, winner of the 1995 Kentucky Derby, was raced by Magnier partner Michael Tabor, the Monte Carlo bookmaker rich from selling his 114 Arthur Prince betting shops. Introduced to stud in Kentucky at a $40,000 fee, Thunder Gulch had been leased to Japan for his third year, which meant a third of his stud fees and a third of his yearling revenue wouldn't even pass through Kentucky. The last thing Kentuckians wanted was for their famous race to produce another "traveling stallion" in the hands of the man most responsible for them.

Desert oil sheikhs, Irish patriots and dot.com billionaires from Silicon Valley are all cheered for heroism in the Lexington sales pavilions when in their quest for racing's Holy Grail they shell out millions for yearlings. But those who return to Louisville with a chance to claim the prize come automatically as pillagers to be repelled.

Even Sheikh Mohammed, whom Kentuckians credit with single-handedly holding up the thoroughbred industry during its darkest days and who has spent more money than anyone in history trying to win the Derby, is still regarded as a villain on the first Saturday of each May.

Flush with oil money, the fifty-three-year-old sheikh and his family have spent billions in the quest to dominate world horse racing, all of it, Sheikh Mohammed maintains, with the "commercial logic" of transforming his desert homeland into a tourist mecca and world horse-racing capital.

In the past fifteen years alone, the sheikh and his brothers have purchased more than 600 of the best-bred American yearlings from the top-scale Keeneland July sales and at least that many more from other American yearling auctions. In 1989, they bought 67 for $44,125,000, or 44 percent of all total sales, and it is still routine for them to spend $35 million at a single sale, most of it in head-to-head competition with the Irish.

Sheikh Mohammed fielded his first Derby horse in 1992 as part-owner of the American-bred two-year-old champion Arazi. Lightly trained and shipped directly from France to the Derby without racing preparation, Arazi finished a dull eighth. After that the sheikh got serious.

Each year since, his Godolphin racing stable has started with more than 100 carefully selected two-year-olds from the sales and the produce of Sheikh Mohammed's own vast breeding program. The Maktoums own more prime Kentucky farmland than any other single racing interest and populate them with only the best bloodstock collected over the past quarter of a century. But as is the prerogative of Bedouin rulers, Sheikh Mohammed insists on winning the Derby his way—which means by preparing his horses in Dubai and shipping them directly to Louisville, thereby skipping the grind of traditional American prep races.

At Al Quoz, his Dubai training facility—a man-made oasis—they live in shady, air-swept, screened-in barns, graze on manicured, irrigated paddocks, gallop on a private track and exercise in a 250-foot thoroughbred swimming lane.

The first crop of survivors from this new concerted effort in 1999 included his Arab-bred Aljabr, a lightly built son of the top Kentucky sire Storm Cat, and a horse named Worldly Manner, whom the sheikh had bought as a two-year-old out of Bob Baffert's California stable for $5 million. The return on the sheikh's investment was for Worldly Manner to finish seventh and Aljabr to be scratched shortly before the race with a health problem.

Sheikh Mohammed immediately began thinking ahead and that fall purchased privately another hot multimillion-dollar, two-year-old racehorse named Chief Seattle, a colt he'd earlier bypassed in the yearling sales. And over the winter he made an even more noticeable concession in style by hiring Bob Baffert's top assistant, Eoin Harty, to prepare his Derby horses in America. A string of thirty, including Chief Seattle, was assembled at Santa Anita for the fall two-year-old season. But in the winter and early spring those horses, too, had to be sent to Dubai, where Chief Seattle turned out to be just another Indian. Godolphin went to the 2000 Derby with China Visit and Curule, a joint entry that went off at 50 to 1 odds and ran like it.

"Failure" not being a word in Sheikh Mohammed's vocabulary, he had put his 2001 hopes on two top candidates, the Irish-bred Street Cry and the Florida-bred Express Tour. For Express Tour, who had attracted his attention with a series of Florida victories as a two-year-old, he paid $1.1 million.

When the two boarded their transport for Louisville in early April, the consensus among American handicappers and the racing press was that they need not bother. Wrote one *Daily Racing Form* expert, "Before I bet a horse from Dubai to win the Derby, I want to see one do it."

Having no ethnic bias whatsoever, Kentucky horsemen wished for all the Arab horses the same Derby luck they had for the Irish and the Californians—a safe trip and a late arrival at the finish line. This was not a matter of prejudice, but one of pocketbook and pride not unlike that which drove the Irish and the Arabs here in the first place.

16

Under his spurning feet, the road like an arrowly alpine river flowed. . . . And the landscape sped away behind like an ocean flying before the wind.

THOMAS BUCHANAN READ, American poet

Most of the year Churchill Downs lies slothful as a peacetime army post just south of downtown Louisville, the four dozen white barns lined up like barracks in a neighborhood defined by chainlink, its century-old twin spires the only clue it is really a temple. The hum from the interstate that snakes along its eastern edge toward Nashville and separates the track from the state fairgrounds and the city airport becomes a muffler to the jet noise, giving the place a dull undertone it would sound naked without. But each April, activity begins to add melody to the bass, the notes popping out like spring buds with the arrival of each new horse van and the increasing clatter of hooves on the asphalt, eventually merging in harmony here and there with the rising din of conversation at the track kitchen or the quickening pace of two- and four-footed traffic around the clocker's stand. It is a cacophony at first, like jazz musicians tuning up, but come the first of May the place is a full-blown, well-tuned orchestra that plays its heart out for a week.

The Kentucky Derby is the biggest, best-run equine sports event in the world—the centerpiece of a $34 billion thoroughbred industry that employs 500,000 people and pays half a billion dollars in state and local taxes. Its three-day impact on the Louisville economy alone is estimated at $218 million. Because the Derby kicks off the spring race meet at Churchill, virtually every major trainer, leading jockey and decent stakes horse in the country finds a reason to come. Derby Day itself will attract 150,000 or more, twice as many live spectators to the sport than on any other day of the year, and more people will watch it on worldwide television than all other horse races combined. It is therefore like the Super Bowl, a national political convention or natural disaster, "the place to be" for every race photographer, turf writer, handicapper, sports columnist with an expense account, a lot of freelancers without one and every local television news crew within driving distance.

The locals broadcast live all week from permanent backside headquarters around the hospitality tents, and camera crews station themselves along the regular traffic routes so they can grab interviews or photos with any horse, trainer, owner or celebrity that passes. And the parade is endless.

In recent years an important new wrinkle has appeared in the fabric. TVG dispatches its most popular and knowledgeable talking heads to the scene for a full week, its primary mission being a daily production called "The Works on TVG," which consists mainly of recording the early-morning exercises of the Derby entrants and playing them back several times during the day, interspersed with interviews and commentary.

As is the case with all media coverage, air time and news space is allotted according to prominence and entertainment value, which results in the movement of herds surrounding anything a television camera finds of interest.

Traditionally the barns of the top trainers or those bringing a leading contender have been regular stops on the press tour, where the conditioners are grilled like politicians. If horses had sock drawers, the press would want to sift through them. Most horse trainers appreciate this intrusion about as much as the old-timer Frank Whitely, who brought Damascus to the Derby in 1967. When asked how his horse had slept the night before, Whitely snapped, "Hell, how would I know? I didn't sleep with him." But then after the reporters left, he chuckled to his barn help because they knew that in fact he had, on a cot right outside Damascus's stall door.

For years the center of press attention was D. Wayne Lukas, the media-wise Hall of Famer who had started a horse in every Derby since 1981, won it four times and was always a threat to win it again. More recently he had come to share the limelight with Nick Zito and Bob Baffert, men fifteen years his junior who regarded him a career model when it came to the Kentucky Derby.

Individual horses are sometimes such natural stars that their trainers get by being silent straight men like Neil Drysdale was in 2000. His Fusaichi Pegasus was so impressive physically and unpredictable psychologically that reporters and cameras followed his every step in hopes of capturing him dumping a rider or bucking like a rodeo bronco. Every morning his behavior provided either excitement or suspense for TVG.

Besides knowing how to win big races, Baffert has an ability unique among trainers to make whatever horse he brings seem like the star of the show, even if it has no personality. Sometimes he does it with a name like Indian Charlie, taken from a satirical industry newsletter, or Captain Steve, who was named after a popular Louisville police detective. Sometimes he simply imbues a horse with human characteristics of his own manufacture. His 1997 winner Silver Charm, for instance, disliked one of his main rivals, Captain Bodgit, and therefore wanted to beat him more than he did the other, Free House, who "is his buddy from California." Silver Charm's owners, Bob and Beverly Lewis, and Mike Pegram, the owner of Captain Steve, were highly visible, friendly and well liked on their own, so turning their horses into Derby heroes was duck soup for Baffert.

Neither Point Given's name nor his aloof-appearing owner, Prince

Salman, being helpful in this regard, Baffert used the horse's unusual size, speed and penchant for rearing up when startled to give him the image of a playful but runaway locomotive.

The largest horse in the Derby was actually one of Sheikh Mohammed's entries, Express Tour, standing 17 and a half hands tall, who was in fact a grandson of Secretariat. He had displayed a trace of his great heart, too, in a gut-wrenching stretch drive to defeat his stablemate Street Cry in the UAE Derby. As for speed, he had plenty, and after being laid up with a sore foot, came back to dazzle onlookers in his only Churchill Downs workout, a steady three-quarters of a mile averaging 12 seconds a furlong.

In the hands of Baffert, Express Tour could have been turned into "the second coming" of his grandfather. But Sheikh Mohammed's trainers don't try to "market" his horses. So it was Point Given that got the press reputation for being "even bigger than Big Red."

Every move Point Given made prior to the Derby drew a press entourage akin to a head of state or central figure in a tabloid scandal, both being modern-day equals in the information world. Advance men actually went before Point Given, clearing his path of lurking photographers or anything else that might set him off. Whenever Point Given and Baffert moved, they went in a large crowd holding its breath.

In Point Given's first workout, he went by the grandstands with his head cocked up to the right like he was watching the watchers and was still clocked at the wire doing five furlongs in 59.3 seconds. He'd done the last quarter in 23 3/5 seconds, part of it while running sideways, and finished up by galloping out seven-eighths of a mile in 1:28, which Baffert termed "pretty good on a track [that] is deep as hell."

"That s.o.b. never gets tired," he said.

Although the racetrack crowd went abuzz over the sub-one-minute work on a track rated "good" but not "fast" by Churchill standards, Congaree followed it with a more impressive one. He hugged the rail all the way, rattling off steady equal-fraction furlongs and completed a half mile in just under 48 seconds. The rider never moved and the strapping chestnut kept arrow-straight in the stretch.

"He likes this track, doesn't he?" Baffert asked rhetorically. "This is an awesome horse."

The Blood-Horse's press accounts of the work also listed rival horses for whom Baffert had professed respect during the session. They included Express Tour, Millennium Wind and Balto Star—but not Monarchos.

The second act of the Baffert speed show took place the following Monday, the first day of "Derby Week," which features a weeklong racetrack promotion called "Dawn at the Downs." This daily event adds to what is already a circus atmosphere that turns the backside into a kind of trail drive gone sour, complete with chuckwagons and minstrels. Also it fills the grandstand with a breakfast crowd complete with commentators to explain the training taking place on the track and to identify the Derby horses.

Because most visitors can't tell one horse from another, all week the Derby horses are supposed to wear special saddlecloths bearing their name, as they would do on race day. The old trainers, like Seabiscuit's Tom Smith, used to try to hide their final prerace exercises from all watchers for one reason or another, usually to keep from affecting betting odds or giving away their race-day strategy. Some trainers are still like that, preferring to work their horses in the predawn hours before the crowds show up, when even the TVG cameras have trouble capturing their mood and movement.

To the delight of the press and racetrack marketers Baffert was never like that. He got to the racetrack later than most of his peers and always worked his most prominent horses for the biggest crowds possible. The cameras never had trouble keeping up with him. Baffert is now such a celebrity in Louisville that he has specially reserved parking spots at local restaurants. Everyone at the track knew that when he exited his barn carrying his walkie-talkie and got into his courtesy Jaguar, he was headed for the grandstand to watch his two Derby horses work. But for his final display of Point Given, he resorted to a subterfuge of sorts. To keep the grandstand breakfast crowd from startling Point Given with applause when he jogged by and was identified by the track announcer, the trainer sent the Big Red Train out without his special telltale saddlecloth.

With the press in tow high in the grandstand Baffert watched his horse trot by unnoticed and congratulated himself for shrewdness. Then, in the words of *The Blood-Horse*, "with his white hair glistening in the morning sun like a fresh mound of snow," Baffert took up his walkie-talkie to begin a final set of what were surely the most widely reported, impressive and ballyhooed prerace workouts in the entire 127-year history of the Kentucky Derby.

With his workmate Saif eight lengths in front, Point Given smoked him again for the television cameras and stunned the track clockers one more time, completing five furlongs in 58.1 seconds, the last eighth in 11.1.

Several minutes later Congaree came out without a saddletowel disguise and a workmate to whet his appetite. He did five-eighths of a mile as well, each faster than the other and the last one in 11 seconds flat, quicker even than the Big Red Train. Congaree continued to roll for another quarter mile, passing the seven-eighths pole in 1:11 and the final eighth in less than 13 seconds while being pulled up.

"Pretty close," Baffert concluded. "Hard to separate those two, huh?"

Baffert explained that Congaree could have gone even faster, but the exercise rider, Dana Barnes, was under instructions to slow him early. He didn't want Congaree to take on the speed horses early in the Derby, and she was able to rate him because "he's so handy. The other guy [Point Given] is a big goofball, who likes to look around. But they're both pretty impressive horses, and Point Given was all business today. They know something big is coming."

Back at his barn later that day and throughout the week Baffert repeated his assessment for the cameras, sometimes from the hood of the Jaguar where he liked to perch cross-legged beside an attractive blond companion, a former Louisville television news reporter.

Once more Baffert proved to be what the racing industry most badly needed, a celebrity that could not only perform on television himself but could cast and direct the show as well. By being accessible and by glibly humanizing his great beasts for the benefit of the press, he had virtually written and produced the Derby Week story for the handicappers and the press. And it was his own. As the influential *Blood-Horse* concluded, Baffert's "horses once again have left a long line of smoldering hoof prints in the Churchill Downs surface."

Even his rival, D. Wayne Lukas, without a Derby entry for the first time since 1981, gave no one but Baffert much of a chance to win the race.

"It's all in Baffert's barn," Lukas conceded. "He would be hard pressed not to win the Derby. I think he's holding all the cards."

Baffert's only other competitor for media attention, Nick Zito, who had two Derby victories, was still a favorite of the sizable New York press contingent, but his $15 million horse, A P Valentine, simply had not cooperated. His fifth place finish in the Bluegrass Stakes had ruined any chance of a favorite's role, and Zito had been pretty much relegated to the same position as Ward—answering the same questions over and over every morning while the press herd watched his horse take a bath. Cooling bath pictures are second only in popularity to sizzling workout clips. But Zito is a competitive guy. Zito had a blond companion too—his wife Kim—with whom to be photographed. And, departing from his usual training style, he had taken a page from Baffert's book by having A P Valentine run down a workmate from behind. Only this workmate, Lake Agawam, was more stubborn than Point Given's, or his jockey more poorly schooled, because each time A P Valentine had to work harder to get by. Yet twice Zito came close to matching Baffert's speed times for five-eighths—59.3 on the first occasion and 59 seconds flat on the Monday before the race.

No one appreciated the displays of speed more than the talking heads of TVG. They could use the stats the way political reporters use polls—as a basis for analysis. Covering a horse race is like covering an election. People want someone to be ahead before the contest has ever begun, but decisive issues and opinion polls are all there is to talk about.

So it was here at the first Kentucky Derby of the new millennium, at the very moment of its belated blossoming as a television sport, that the press had done its job. Six days before the contest, the critical election issue had been clearly identified and pinpointed. It was speed. And the final prerace polls had been taken. The clear leader and obvious winner was Bob Baffert and his two California horses, both big, red and uncommonly fast, and now linked together—a Big Red Train for sure. The race itself would just be a formality.

Meanwhile, moral dilemmas kept coming up at Two Bucks like daffodils, suddenly and in multiples. None was more obstinate than what to do about going to the Derby. By the time Monarchos attained stardom, the high-rolling gamblers at Two Bucks had already made their arrangements for the big day in May. They were going to stay home and watch the race on television like sensible people, which is really the best way to see it.

The alternative is to get in line early to buy decent seats at outrageous prices. From a box for six that costs $8,000 you might still end up peeking around a $400 hat just to see a cloud of dust. The first time they'd gone to the Derby was 1989, as guests of some Florida lawyers when he was still editor of the *Chicago Tribune*. Acting on the promise of "nice box seats" the dominant female had outfitted herself for the occasion in Michigan Avenue finery, at no insignificant cost. But the Floridians were obviously outsiders unfamiliar with the event. They had to park miles away and the box was ground level on the first turn, a spot from which it was impossible to see a horse the entire day. Sunday Silence won that year and the outing came to be known as "the Derby we heard Sunday Silence win" and an experience never to be repeated.

Good seats at the Derby are routinely preassigned to insiders, celebrities, corporate sponsors, politicians and VIPs such as the Kentucky Racing Commission, whose nine members each get to purchase a choice third-floor clubhouse box near the finish line for the ticket cover price of about $1,000. Having been spoiled by the privilege during his five years as a racing commissioner, the Two Bucks proprietor was now loath to spend eight times that for lesser accommodations.

Some friends and clients were not, however, and he had already used his old commission connections just to acquire modest restaurant table reservations for some out-of-towners who had requested tickets to the Derby. These were Snake's co-owners, two couples who were old friends, one of whom at the last minute had added his two daughters to the trip.

To acquire the tickets he had had to withdraw $10,000 from the farm bank account with which to satisfy the pound of cash demanded by the scalper for the luncheon table reservations in the Eclipse Room at Churchill, which would have been free on any other day. The cash had to be delivered like a bribe, all in small bills, divided into stacks of a hundred and wrapped in rubber bands, the better to report as income to the IRS no doubt. He had withdrawn an additional $1,500 to bet on the race, which meant that at least two-thirds of the money was at serious risk.

One of the couples, husband and wife lawyers from Nashville, had already reimbursed him for the tickets. This man was quick to his wallet, even with the arm slings and thumb casts he often sported, the rewards for short old guys who crash the boards in pickup basketball with athletes half their age. Fortunately his stunning, silver-haired wife was an evangelist as well as a lawyer, and therefore able to promote healing through prayer as well as filing to recover damages.

But the guy who needed four tickets was a notorious cheapskate who in the interest of salesmanship had been masquerading in the newspaper world for years as a gregarious, free-spending Irishman. In truth he was a sour, skinflint Scotsman, who knew nothing of horses and had never been to a race in his life. But he was a sport nonetheless, living proof that the lure of owning a racehorse could squeeze blood out of a turnip. Four years earlier he'd shelled out $25,000 for a one-third interest in a Two Bucks filly who broke her coffin bone on her second start and never earned a dime. Training and vet bills mounted to another $20,000 before she became a broodmare and aborted three consecutive foals. Yet he was still in the game—"big-time" in his view—now a one-third owner of Snake, half-sibling to a horse about to start in the most important race in the world. Even if he assumed the tickets to be gratis—which was highly likely in his case—and never paid for them, he had earned a spot closer to success than most owners ever get. Both horse racing and Two Bucks owed him a good time at his first Kentucky Derby.

Now all six available Derby seats were filled, and the fun-couple breeders of one of the Derby favorites were staying home—happily—a circumstance completely in keeping with their increasingly psychopathic condition. But the absurdity of their sending houseguests off to the Derby without a host escort troubled the dominant female, who surfaced the matter one day with her husband while they were out looking for a replacement farm should they decide to sell Two Bucks.

"The minute I go out and spend a fortune for a seat good enough that we could actually see Monarchos run in the Kentucky Derby, something terrible will happen," he told the dominant female in all seriousness. "Either he'll get hurt and won't run, the jockey will fall off or he'll run last. If any of those things are going to happen I'd just as soon watch it from home."

"You're right," she said.

This seldom-heard response alone should have been a tip-off that she, too, was losing it. But for once they were in agreement on an important issue. There, the decision had been made, the matter settled.

Then the cell phone rang. It was the famous Darby Dan Farm where Regal Band was born, whose owner, John Phillips, had already made inquiries about her possible repurchase. Darby Dan had one of those permanently assigned tables for twelve on the sixth floor of the Churchill Downs clubhouse known as "Millionaires' Row"—the kind that get resold sometimes for nearly $50,000—"and Mr. Phillips would like for you and your wife to be his guests for the Kentucky Derby."

The Kenturkeys on Millionaires' Row? In the best seats, high above the people jam, where the race actually can be seen rather than simply heard. A seat among the privileged where the dominant female's Chanel suits from Michigan Avenue would be right at home, but where her companion would not. For him, anyway, this invitation presented another daffodil dilemma.

Why, after all these years of privilege, was he still so uncomfortable with the idea of it? Not having been born to it didn't even become a realization until he was thirty years old. Being born free and healthy in America had been privilege enough, and still was. Privilege itself was not really so troublesome as his witnessed abuse of it by those who inherited it and believed it an entitlement. That, and the idea that some degree of privilege had always been for sale—like a seat on Millionaires' Row. Anybody with money can end up there. But even that particular herd has a pecking order, like the industry itself.

Racehorses having always been luxury items, privilege can be bought along with them in varying levels of quality. New money the likes of Coolmore and the Maktoums can always buy a table in "the club," but the best seats were purchased long ago at less inflated prices by the charter members, who pass them down to their heirs along with custody of the by-laws.

John Phillips's seats at the Kentucky Derby are a family heirloom, an entitlement like Darby Dan's box at Belmont, which goes back to "when Grandfather was on the building committee." Handsome, smart and as impeccably bred as Darby Dan's horses, Phillips was well-chosen as revivalist and conservator of the Galbreath tradition as industry pillar. He represented one of the best hopes for continued American leadership in both racing and breeding, and anyone should be flattered and honored by an invitation to sit at his Derby table.

But to the now tormented and conflicted cynic to whom the invitation had been extended, the kind gesture could not be separated from Phillips's earlier query about buying all or part of Regal Band at a rock-bottom price. He'd been introduced to Phillips several times at social gatherings, including the annual open-house receptions in the historic Darby Dan farmhouse that signaled the beginning of each breeding season. And each time the new farm boss had treated their meeting as if it were the first—a completely new experience. Obviously the man from Two Bucks had made no impression. John Phillips did not know him from a lump of coal. Now, finally, he had registered a distinct identity—the owner of a Derby dam who rightfully belonged back in the Darby Dan broodmare band. Now he was something to be cultivated, like a sunflower field.

He realized that this might be a grossly unfair evaluation of the invitation. His relationship with Darby Dan had preceded Phillips's takeover, and it was routine for big farms to entertain small clients like Two Bucks who bred mares to their stallions and for whom they consigned horses to auction. But now everything in his life somehow revolved around "the big mare" in his barn. If recovering a lost Darby Dan treasure was indeed the motivating factor in Phillips's generosity, why couldn't the prospect of eventually selling her to him be the motivation for acceptance?

Besides, Phillips did not seem the type to abuse privilege or regard it his entitlement. There was still the question about the propriety of his accepting a privileged seat on Millionaires' Row while his houseguests viewed the Derby from an inferior perspective. This matter he handled like the swell that Phillips's invitation suggested he was becoming. It's okay to have privilege, he reasoned, as long as you remember it's not okay not to have it.

There, the matter was settled all over again—with hardly a minute's hesitation and not a word of disagreement from the dominant female, who minus her laptop had slipped into contemplation of flowers and hats and $5,000 designer suits.

"Yes, thank you very much," he told Darby Dan. "We'd be delighted to accept Mr. Phillips's kind offer."

17

It's all right to live on a horse—if it's your own horse.

WALTER BRENNAN, suspecting Gary Cooper is a horse thief in *The Westerner,* 1940

Yes, there was a very good reason for getting up at 4:30 A.M. and driving the 70 miles to Louisville every morning, he assured the dominant female: so he could be at Churchill Downs by daylight to check on Monarchos.

It was, after all, only ten days until the Derby, which meant that Johnny Ward could no longer be trusted to tell the truth about his horse. Jack Oxley might, but who knew at this point if Ward was even giving him the whole story? A trainer might not tell the owner everything, particularly in the final days when he's trying to get the horse to the Kentucky Derby. At this late date Ward would be reluctant to tell Oxley that the last of his three "Derby darlings" was not going to make it. He would be trying to get him into the gate healthy enough to compete.

This new bout of paranoia over the physical condition of Monarchos had been incited by disturbing back-to-back reports from

Churchill Downs. First, Sheikh Mohammed's Street Cry, his hope for a European-bred Derby winner, had been declared out of the race with an ankle injury.

"That could have been Monarchos," the breeder had lamented to the dominant female. "It always happens. Horses can get hurt going to the post."

Two days later, Ward remained in Lexington to train his horses at Keeneland and Monarchos wasn't sent to the track at all, sparking speculation that he might have injured himself in a strong gallop the previous day. Rumors abounded there might be something wrong in Barn 42.

By this time the "spin" coming out of the trainers' mouths had reached Washington levels. One morning Bob Baffert had preceded his star, Point Given, out of the barn and issued a Secret Service–like order to the press: "No running when the big horse moves."

Ward's sincerity obviously had been no match for this kind of showmanship. Undoubtedly the Kentuckian had been the source of a *Daily Racing Form* report that Monarchos was suffering from sore hocks, which set a California talking head to speculating on TVG that there had been something suspect about the horse's stride as far back as the Florida Derby. This comment in turn provoked the breeder of Monarchos to actually consider spitting on his own television set.

Undoubtedly it was time to see the horse again for himself.

John Ward was obviously beleaguered, worn down by the press and pressure of the moment. He could not be glad to have anyone else at his barn gawking at Monarchos. If his horse had had a "double," as Seabiscuit did, he would have displayed him for the press instead. Frank Whitely once trotted out a gelding for visitors who'd come to see his great mare Ruffian and they never knew the difference. The press's second-guessing of Ward's training tactics had reduced him to offering as evidence of his own wisdom the similar training style of younger trainers Dallas Stewart and Todd Pletcher, both former

D. Wayne Lukas assistants. But even Pletcher's horses had worked faster, the press reminded him, and everybody else planned to work at least once the week of the Derby. Nothing he said in his own defense seemed to satisfy them.

Monarchos looked healthy and ready, leaner than he had been at the Florida Derby, and stronger, too. On the track in the early dawn of Monday the 23rd, Monarchos had galloped in the "shadow" of the rail, hugging the fence like some attached, motorized rabbit for greyhounds; slogging through the deep, hard going left by the harrows on the track edge. Then he had come off dancing sideways, still pulling on Beccia, his sides and nostrils showing no signs of having just run two miles. When he returned to the track on Thursday following his Wednesday off, it was the same, except that Beccia experienced even more trouble trying to pull him up. That day he'd only gone a mile and three-eighths.

The next morning Ward sent Monarchos out for his first timed exercise since the defeat in the Wood. It would be his only "work" prior to the Derby. Graciously, Jack Oxley invited the breeder to accompany him to the grandstand to watch. Oxley was his ebullient, ever-confident self. A gas exploration man with a well expected to come in any minute. If his horse was hurt and his trainer covering up, he either didn't know it or was a consummate Broadway actor.

Normally in the mornings Monarchos was asked to jog counterclockwise against the traffic all the way from the backside track entrance to the grandstand and then stand quietly for ten minutes or so alongside Mouse, the companion pony, before galloping his circles. But this morning in an effort to use the freshly harrowed track before it was spoiled by other horses, Azeff and Mouse led Monarchos and Beccia directly into a traffic lane and cut them loose.

When he reached the five-eighths pole on his second circle, where the timing was to begin, Monarchos was still being held so tightly by Beccia that he looked stiff, and he short-strided for the first furlong, taking nearly 13 seconds to complete it. He loosened up after that and accelerated smoothly through the next half mile. Ward timed the "move" in 1:01, but the Churchill clockers missed the first eighth altogether and caught him in an unspectacular 48.4 for the half mile, which did nothing to build excitement for "The Works" on TVG or the confidence of handicappers.

No matter how hard he tried, Ward could convince no one that the work had been just what he wanted and all that was necessary to ready his horse for the Derby. Surely, Monarchos would work again—"a little blowout or something" Derby week. No, said Ward, his horse is ready. The press couldn't believe it. The last Derby winner not to work the week before the race was Bold Forbes in 1976. Ward's horse had to be sore, or spent, or else he would be out on the track the final week sharpening up like the rest.

The track surface was getting faster day by day. The last Derby horse to work was the only one Sheikh Mohammed had left from the dozens with which he'd begun—the Florida-bred Express Tour. The assistant trainer, Tom Albertrani, sent Express Tour to the track Wednesday morning expecting him to go a half mile in 51 or 52 seconds. He was stunned when his horse was timed in 47.4.

Backside denizens at Churchill, especially the small stable trainers, had found it easy to root for the lunch-bucket horse and rider Oxley and Ward were sending out. If the Kentucky Derby wanted to make a positive statement to the world about horse racing and the people in it, this was it—the future they wanted to see.

Sam Ramer, publisher of *Backstretch*, who'd been around Churchill for twenty years and whose magazine spoke for his former profession as a trainer, sidled up to the man on reconnaissance outside a hospitality tent.

"Everybody likes your horse," he growled. "He's the best prepared, strongest galloping horse on the grounds. And they all want Johnny to win, too."

But as easy as it was for insiders to root for Monarchos, they found it just as hard to pick against Baffert. The odds against it were just too great.

Some of the "speed sheet" handicappers began to offer the explanation that Monarchos had "peaked"—run his best race—in the Florida Derby, then had "bounced"—regressed—in the Wood. If they were right, conventional wisdom dictated Monarchos would probably run a mediocre race next time out—in the Derby—before progressing again. Even a repeat of his Florida performance would not be good enough to beat either Point Given or Congaree, both of which were believed to be steadily moving forward and set to run their biggest race. In other words, Baffert had timed the training of his horses right on the money, but Ward had peaked his six weeks too early. The statement the Derby would make had already been scripted. The determining factor was speed, and outside the tight circle of Monarchos believers, there was little sentiment that anyone but Baffert could win.

There is an old equine expression that says "no secret is so close as that between a rider and his horse." The Two Bucks man became a firm believer in it after trying to talk to Jorge Chavez at Johnny Ward's barn during Derby week. His little lips were sealed, about the horse, the race, about everything.

It was all the doing of his agent, Richard DePass, who had refused to schedule an introduction, "if you're going to ask him about the race." Superstition was the religion of jock's agents, and DePass was a highly religious man.

"Oh, okay, I'll ask him about the weather, and about how he got so short," the breeder lied sarcastically. Of course he was going to ask him about the race. And he did, but Jorge just smiled and said nothing, to the delight of his agent.

But Chavez had been thinking about the Kentucky Derby for months. He had ridden it in his mind a thousand times. He dreamed of it at night, always waking up before he knew who had gotten to the wire first. Even before the Florida Derby, he had concluded that finally he had found the dream horse, one that could get him to the finish line first in the biggest race in the world.

Nothing that happened in the Wood had changed his mind. Once in gear Monarchos had steadily made up ground on the winner. At the end his horse was going faster, gaining with every stride even though Victor Espinoza was pounding away at Congaree with his whip. If the race had been another furlong longer—the Derby distance—Monarchos would have won. Chavez had some horse left and Espinoza did not. Of that he was confident.

But all the talk about Bob Baffert's horses was worrisome. Chavez tried to put it out of his mind, but that was all he read or heard. The weekend before the Derby the *Daily Racing Form* had carried an obligatory front-page story on Monarchos's only workout, mentioning that he'd been sore in the hocks and quoting Ward as saying "he'd been off, ever so slightly" in his back end. The story had been at the bottom of the page, dwarfed by a huge picture of Point Given entitled "The Great Chestnut Hope" that accompanied a story calling him "the most promising candidate to win the Triple Crown."

Chavez knew Johnny Ward had been lavishing praise on Congaree and calling Point Given a wonderful animal. He wondered if Ward was still confident about Monarchos. So when he dropped by Barn 42 to ride a horse for Donna Ward, he brought the matter up.

"Johnny, all you hear is about Congaree and this other horse; what are you thinking?"

"Georgie, I don't know," Ward replied. "They are both very good horses. They look pretty tough—hard to get around. What about you?"

Chavez saw Monarchos standing nearby. All he could think of was what it was like to be on his back when he was flying. He had never been on another horse like that. Chavez thought if any horse could win the Triple Crown, it would be his.

"Johnny," he said. "All you got to do is get him as good as he was at the Florida Derby. Then you got no problem. We win."

"We can do that, Georgie," Ward said. "I know we can have him that good."

The people around Monarchos every day had become a family now, from the Oxleys and Wards at the top all the way down through

Yvonne Azeff, Bryan Beccia, Tammy Holtz and the hotwalker, Terri Upton. There was never a minute in Monarchos's life that one of them was not nearby watching him. And what they were seeing they were keeping in the family.

Yet the secret to Ward's training was no secret at all. It was as old as the traditions he was trying to uphold. Satisfied with Monarchos's natural turn of foot, he had simply been building stamina into his horse with those steady but boring two-mile gallops. No matter what anybody else said, the Derby was an endurance contest. He and Oxley had been there before with two fast horses, both of whom were exhausted long before they ever saw the wire. Planning for the excitement of the Derby is usually inadequate. Horses and jockeys become wired by the magnitude of the moment, too anxious to conserve energy.

So what Ward had Beccia and Azeff do every day was to teach Monarchos to run hard and straight under a tight hold, steadily accelerating until he was loose and flying free at the end. They knew their horse had the long, low, daisy-cutting stride and the perfectly balanced physique that would allow him to cover ground as efficiently as any horse could. And every day he was building the fitness and discipline to hold it in reserve longer and longer and not go until he was asked. Each day that he dug in harder and harder at the gallop, he became stronger and stronger. The stiffness some keen eyes saw in his gait the first time around the track every day actually stemmed from the tightness of Beccia's hold. Monarchos didn't fight, bow his neck or toss his head like other horses fighting the bit, he just tried to pull his rider out of the saddle.

When Beccia finally pulled Monarchos up from his work that Friday, his own back was aching from a ferocious tug-of-war almost imperceptible to someone watching from the grandstand. Ward wanted five furlongs in "a minute and change" and the clock in Beccia's head had given him exactly that—even though it had almost pulled his back apart. Had Ward asked for 57 seconds, he could have gotten that, too. "He wanted more at all times," Beccia told Azeff when she and Mouse hooked up with them again. "Don't worry. He's ready. We don't want to change places with anyone."

In the final days before the race, while other trainers were doing speed burns for the press, Ward began sending Monarchos out to gallop in the dark morning hours before the noise and crowds took over. Sometimes Beccia galloped Monarchos counterclockwise in an effort to slow him down. Still he came off the track dancing sideways under a tight Beccia hold, the little jig known around the barn as "the Sparky shuffle." When they saw it, Azeff and Beccia would eyeball each other: "It's time." Their horse had just galloped two and a half miles and was still full of run. "If he is not fit by now," Azeff assured those doubting the wisdom of his having gotten a day off, "we ought to all go home."

Like everyone else at Churchill, Ward's team had gathered round the television monitors in the barn to watch the final "works" of Baffert's dynamic duo on TVG. Azeff was impressed but hardly intimidated.

She liked both of Baffert's horses, especially Congaree, who had flown back to Louisville from the Wood on the plane with Monarchos. He was big and confident, a formidable foe, and she regarded Baffert as a great trainer. But Azeff had worked for D. Wayne Lukas long enough that she never ran a horse thinking about finishing second. Among the assets she had brought to Ward's stable was the power of positive thinking and a keen understanding of how it played out with the animals to whom she had dedicated her life.

All the great trainers and all the great riders have had one thing in common—unabashed belief in themselves. It was what had made Lukas a Hall of Famer and it would eventually do the same for Baffert. They spread it through their barns as regularly as straw bedding, to the everlasting benefit of people and horses alike. Ward had shown that same kind of stuff by refusing to alter his training methods just to find safety in the herd. He believed in what he and his team were doing and so did Azeff, Beccia and the others.

So Monarchos had lucked up again. He was surrounded by people who had confidence in themselves and believed in him, none more than the celebrated rider who would climb aboard his back on Derby Day. Horses respond to people who have confidence and refuse those who don't. Horses have confidence in Jorge Chavez.

*

Most jockeys learn to ride as children and by the time they are teenagers are earning a living at it. Chavez spent his childhood looking for a meal and a warm place to sleep, mostly in the streets of Lima. Chavez got on a horse early, too, when he was four or five and living temporarily with his grandfather in the Peruvian countryside. But the horse was not for pleasure or racing; it was how his family got from place to place. Chavez fell off and landed on his face.

Chavez remembered being homeless at age ten, rummaging for food in garbage cans and sleeping in abandoned cars. One of his sisters killed herself when he was fifteen. And he remembered that "nobody ever found me and asked me if I had enough to eat or clothes to wear."

By the time he was twenty, Chavez was earning a living doing any job offered to a grown man, who at 4 feet 10 inches tall was still smaller and looking up to everyone else. He had washed cars, plucked chickens, butchered cattle, repaired stoves and was taking up bus tickets. His dream was to become an electrical technician that worked on automobiles. But all his life he had been the smallest, the last to eat, the kid with the least, the most unlikely to see his dream fulfilled. When someone took him to the racetrack in Lima one day, what he first noticed were the jockeys. Far away behind their security fences, they looked like children costumed for some kind of entertainment. But the friend took him back to the track again, and this time they were admitted inside the jockey quarters. For Chavez it was an epiphany.

"For the first time I realized they were regular older guys like me . . . that I was not the only one who was so small," he said, "and I knew that I had found my place."

Chavez was put to work as a groom, walking horses and mucking stalls. He learned to love horses and care for them from the ground up, which is the best way. And once he got up on one, they could not get him down.

"The first time my horse went fast I did not feel my feet," he said. "It was something magic."

Soon he was watching videotapes of great jockeys like Willie Shoemaker and Laffit Pincay, Jr., and learning to imitate their styles. And less than two years after he started riding, Jorge Chavez became Peru's leading jockey, making the equivalent of $1,000 a week, enough to afford a vacation. In 1988 he went to Miami, where he visited the Calder Race Course, and he quickly realized he could make five times as much money riding in America.

"Miami was so clean and pretty, not like my country where it is dirty and you see a lot of stuff on the ground," he recalled. "And then one day it rained. Oh, my God. I thought it was the end of the world . . . because it only sprinkles in Peru . . . but this thunder and lightning I had never seen before. To me it was a wonderful place. It was unbelievable."

On his second day at Calder, Chavez won two races, and he soon earned a reputation as a "rough rider." Despite eighty-five days of suspension, he won the leading rider title at Calder during his first year. Before long he was headed for the tough New York circuit where the purses were better. There the railbirds named him "Chop-Chop" for his rapid stick work and learned to bet him because "he don't get beat no noses." For six years he won more stakes and more races than anyone, virtually without recognition until he hooked up with the Wards at Gulfstream.

Now Chavez appears a man newly honed by money and success, from his gleaming, perfectly capped teeth that sit like short soldiers behind a permanent smile to his little tailored blue jeans and shiny boots. The year he won the Breeders' Cup on Beautiful Pleasure—1999—Chavez earned $17 million and the Eclipse Award as America's leading jockey.

Whatever is said of his style, Chavez's reputation for honesty, hard work and effort is unsurpassed. But what has endeared Chavez to trainers and his fellow jockeys is what distinguishes him most among them—his humility.

Ward has referred to his jockey as "one of the finest human beings" he has ever known. And when Jack Oxley read somewhere that the

Greek ruler whose surname he had chosen for his horse had the first name "Georgios," he took it as an omen. He'd always called Chavez "Georgie." He knew he had his Derby team.

Unable to forget his start in life and ever grateful for the "miracle" that changed it, Chavez lavishes everyone with the kindness he missed as a child. An unabashed patriot, he credits America for his good fortune. He has established a foundation that collects and distributes money for homeless children in Peru. And he goes there himself, often hiring taxis and riding through the streets. When he sees children whose lives remind him of his own, he stops and hands out cash on the spot.

"Maybe it is not so much but it is the difference between them eating that day or not," he said. "I will never be able to forget what that feeling is like. When I see them I see myself and I cannot go past them in my car. If nothing else they know there is someone who cares and they will keep trying. So I must keep trying to make sure they know."

The Chavez commitment to keep trying is contagious. His effort to win a race makes jockeys who don't try look conspicuous. Trainers are ashamed to give him a mount that won't try. And horses that always try seem to run even harder when he is on their back. Horses or people, Chavez can "move them up."

Ward believed that Monarchos had gained confidence every time Chavez had ridden him. On Friday before the Derby, Chavez stopped by to see Ward again for another confidence check of his own.

"How good is our horse today, Johnny?" the jockey wanted to know.

After the day of rest on Wednesday, Monarchos had galloped in the morning Thursday and had been schooled in the paddock behind the grandstand to get him accustomed to the crowd and noise. He had behaved perfectly. On Friday morning he had galloped again and had come back doing the Sparky shuffle. His coat was shiny, his appetite ferocious. Azeff and Beccia swore he was ready. Ward looked down into the beaming brown face of the little guy before him.

"Monarchos is as good as he was for Florida, Georgie," Ward said, "maybe better."

Chavez flashed Ward his biggest smile. That was what he wanted to hear. At the post position draw, Ward had used his thirteenth choice to draw the remaining slot closest to the one Chavez had wanted, an outside post—number 16 in the 17-horse field. Chavez preferred number 14, but anywhere on the outside where he could avoid the traffic would be okay. The race was already planned in his mind, how he would break, which lane he would go for, where his horse would be at all times during the race. He knew he had the chance he had been waiting for, the chance to finish the dream.

"We win then, Johnny," the little guy said. "Don't worry. We got the Mercedes, they got the Yugo."

Chavez knew the difference in the foreign-made automobiles. He now drove the biggest, best and fastest Mercedes made. And he had slept in a Yugo.

All week long TVG kept rerunning the tape of Point Given's final workout, along with analysis by one of its talking heads, a California-based Irish trainer named Frank Lyons, who concluded by saying, "Nobody would be surprised if he wins by 10."

At Two Bucks Farm in Versailles, a location where at least one television was always tuned to TVG, the commentator's pronouncement came to be invariably punctuated by a vulgar, three-word invective suggesting that Lyons go some place and attempt the anatomically impossible.

Out of habit, Lyons was cursed again when he appeared on TVG to discuss the post position draw and morning line odds. Just as track oddsmaker Mike Battaglia had predicted three weeks earlier, Baffert's horses were his favorites, Point Given at 9 to 5 and Congaree at 5 to 1. That Point Given was less than 2 to 1 against one of the deepest, most talented Derby fields in years was an extraordinary expression of confidence. While he had never run a bad race, Point Given had also never beaten any horses of the quality he was about to face. It was the image built for him that was intimidating. Only Ward—perhaps returning the favor of Baffert's slight of Monarchos prior to the Wood—had expressed any doubts about the favorite. Congaree was the Baffert horse he feared most, Ward said again, when interviewed after the post position draw.

Before his recent reconnaissance mission, the breeder of Monarchos might well have reeled into religious fanaticism or even sorcery when the news came that the horse had drawn the thirteenth choice of gate positions for the Derby.

But despite his outbursts at television talking heads, his trips to Churchill Downs had left the spy agent from Versailles as sanguine of spirit as he had always been of complexion. Finally he had seen enough. And it was a picture in perfect symmetry. Of all the Derby horse owners, Oxley had paid dues the longest, a man with a master's degree in racehorses earned with patience and effort as well as his money. If bookmakers made odds on owners, the Oxleys would have been favored to be the most deserving of victory and the most understanding and gracious in defeat.

The Ward barn and its hard-working gray horse and humble jockey were truly carrying Oxley's colors. Like the owner himself, his trainer, horse and rider spoke more of endurance than show, more of sincerity than pretense, less of money than of hard work. And barring some bizarre last-minute disaster, they had gotten Regal Band's baby to the Kentucky Derby, which her owner had believed in his heart would never really happen.

Not only was Monarchos going to the Derby, his performance—win or lose—was going to be a credit to his mother and the farm he came from. The breeder was certain of it. Expert predictions do not register in addled brains.

For him, the post position draw had been a harbinger of good fortune. Monarchos and Point Given had ended up side by side at the end of the line—gates 16 and 17—hero and villain out there together where they could measure each other and look each other in the eye.

And in his dreams that Wednesday night before the Derby, the issue had been settled.

That night as sleep ran him down at Two Bucks he was thinking about how Chavez had jumped off Monarchos at the Florida Derby and bowed before his daughters, honoring them with the orchids from the winner's wreath.

Sometime during the night the devil nightmare that had been tormenting him for years returned, the one in which he is lost and keeps searching endlessly for a place he cannot find. In it, he is again a newspaperman—back in an important job with an office and big salary. Yet he is a man with nothing to do. No duties, no responsibilities. Unable to write or edit, or even find the place where he is expected to deliver a speech. A nightmare for sure, though more sad than scary.

But toward morning he dreamed again, this time of Chavez. And in this dream he was a jockey himself. A white-haired, six-foot-tall, 210-pound, fifty-eight-year-old jockey, ridiculous in knee-high boots, tight white pants, love handles bulging beneath bright red and gold silks. Under one arm was a red crash helmet much too small for his head and in one age-spotted hand a riding crop. Even in the dream he knew he wasn't going to ride in the big race, but he'd dressed for it anyway, like a third-string scrub destined to suit up for the championship game, if only to warm the bench. And there he was, behind the security fence of the jockey quarters with grown men the size of children, all dressing before mirrors in colorful costumes. And in the mirror he saw the absurdity of himself, a ruddy old giant amidst a sea of dark, elf-like athletes, and found it remarkably easy to reconcile. Monarchos could not win the Kentucky Derby without him. Though he no longer owned him, barely knew his new owners or his trainer and could in no way influence the outcome of the race, the horse needed him there dressed for action. For he—and no one else—had endowed this horse with the one asset that had gotten him this far and would prove most valuable in the fierce battle to come—luck. Luck, he knew, was as contagious as confidence and Derby Fever.

18

The grandstand became an undulating, endless sea of earthtone fedoras and ladies' spring hats. Fans lay on, stood over and clung to every support structure. . . . They ran out of programs before the first race, . . . the supply of hot dog buns was exhausted by early afternoon.

LAURA HILLENBRAND,

describing the 1938 Bay Meadows Handicap, in *Seabiscuit*

Tarmacs were jammed all over the Bluegrass. Planes swooped in from Europe, Dubai, Ireland, Japan and Saudi Arabia, disgorging owners, celebrities and houseguests laden with hat boxes and garment bags. SUVs and limousines were being gassed up and anxious hosts were juggling social itineraries and arguing with restaurant maitre d's over dinner reservations.

At Two Bucks Farm, as doubts about Monarchos actually starting in the Kentucky Derby had declined, so had the level of cerebral dysfunction. The obscene responses to the talking heads on TVG, still shouted routinely, were no longer the harbinger of imminent total nervous breakdown on the part of the owner.

For their six houseguests, the dominant female had arranged three days of free meals—various complimentary breakfasts, lunches and dinners, among them a gracious invitation to a post-Derby dinner hosted by the Oxleys, who had made reservations for thirty at a

Louisville restaurant. This prospect raised one final moral dilemma for her husband, whose raw nerves she observed were clearly on the mend.

"An extra testicle can't take up a third of Oxley's seats," he complained. By now she knew what he meant by the term and was not offended to be included in it.

"If our guests don't go, we can't go," the dominant female reasoned. "We're already being rude enough by not sitting with them at the Derby."

His years of experience in both politics and conflict resolution had not been wasted. "How about this?" he suggested. "If Monarchos loses, we have to go to a consolation party—and there will be plenty of seats. But if Monarchos wins, we don't go to the victory party. It will be jammed, so many people the Oxleys won't even miss us. Then our excess guests won't create a problem. How about that?"

The dominant female fixed him with her most threatening glare.

"If Monarchos wins," she declared, "I'm going."

That was that. But so heavy were the odds in the breeder's favor that he deemed further conflict unnecessary, especially in front of houseguests.

The lawyers had driven up from Nashville, but the skinflint, surprisingly, had sprung for a charter flight for his family from Kansas City, raising hopes that he might pay for his own tickets. These hopes were dashed quickly, however, by one look at the aircraft in which he had traveled to Lexington. It looked like the plane Amelia Earhart was flying when she disappeared.

However, the women who alighted with him—his wife and two daughters—were a different story. They were dressed as if they'd had long experience spending someone else's money, and made it clear they planned to bet big-time on the Derby the following day. As preparation, the Two Bucks party went to the posh Thoroughbred Club at nearby Keeneland for lunch and an afternoon of practice betting on the Churchill races, which were being simulcast on the dining room monitors.

The women took to wagering the way they obviously had to haberdashery and—tutored by the Nashville lawyers—were soon placing complicated exotic bets as if they'd grown up at the track. Their bankrolling sugar daddy, however, kept misspeaking Keeneland as "Kneeland," which was the surname of a newspaper guy he knew—and trying to bet a "tribeca"—the name of Robert De Niro's film company, instead of a "trifecta," the correct term for the routine three-horse parlay.

From all indications, the Derby Weekend was shaping up to be long and grueling. For starters, the mother of Monarchos decided to ovulate on Derby Day.

Genius horse breeders know such things because they pay veterinarians vast sums of money to ultrasound and manually palpate the ovaries of mares during estrus, to learn the texture of the follicles and determine precisely when ovulation will occur.

Long before Monarchos won the Florida Derby, Regal Band had been booked back to Maria's Mon, a decision requiring no genius whatsoever. Serious racehorses being so hard to produce, trying an obviously successful cross a second time was a no-brainer.

However, to the now omen-conscious breeder, the timing of Regal Band's date with Maria's Mon could only mean one thing: Monarchos was going to win the Derby later that afternoon, while the conception of a full sibling was under way.

Obviously of the same opinion, the people at the Pin Oak Stud breeding shed treated Regal Band's arrival with the pomp and ceremony due a mare who had done so much for the farm, including the initiation of her "teasing process" with a kiss between the eyes from the farm manager, Clifford Barry, followed by cheers and polite applause.

For her part, Regal Band kicked at the teaser but took right up with Maria's Mon—another omen to all concerned.

Every year before the Kentucky Derby, one dream animates the entire horse racing industry—the chance to have a Superhorse—a horse faster than a speeding bullet, able to melt strong steel with the heat from flashing hooves, a horse capable of accomplishing the industry equivalent of leaping over a tall building in a single bound—winning the Triple Crown. More than two decades had passed since American racing had had a Triple Crown winner. The track records at the Derby and the Belmont Stakes were both as old as the memory of Secretariat, who probably set the Preakness record as well that year (1973) but was deprived of it by a clock malfunction. Only Secretariat had ever run the Derby in less than two minutes—a Superhorse feat.

For years, the credit-card company Visa had offered a $5 million bonus to any horse that could win the Triple Crown. But in the preceding five years, three horses had won the Derby and the Preakness, only to lose the Belmont Stakes. Two of those horses—Silver Charm and Real Quiet—were trained by Baffert and are commemorated in plaques on Barn 33, where Point Given and Congaree were being housed. On the day before the Derby, Visa chairman Carl Pascarella sought Baffert out at his barns, hugged him for the television cameras and wished him well. The story made the cable channels and the big newspapers.

Everyone knew that a horse that won Visa's money could be exalted and promoted like never before. And they all believed Baffert's California horse had the best chance of making it. Even the trainer of Derby contender Millennium Wind, the respected David Hofmans, had said, "If Point Given doesn't win the Triple Crown, something is wrong."

On Derby Day, Point Given stood in esteem head and shoulders above the rest of the field, just as he did in physical stature. That morning on the way back from stretching his legs on the track, Point Given had put on another show for the cameras, rearing, pawing the air—doing "the Watusi," in the words of Bob Baffert—and dumping his exercise rider Pepe Aragon.

It was great television. And what would happen on television was the overriding concern of everyone connected with Churchill Downs, including the track superintendent, Butch Lehr.

*

The man in charge of the track surface at Churchill Downs had long been considered a genius in his field. That's because until recently the oval on which Butch Lehr had spent most of his life working was generally regarded one of the two or three best dirt surfaces in America. There were no track lanes at Churchill demonstrably different from the others, as is the case at many other top tracks. And usually Lehr's track dictated a uniform pace that favored no particular running style. Horses could win running fast on the front or sprinting from behind in the final stretch drive.

Because trainers believed that unlike some other track superintendents Lehr knew what he was doing, they cheered when Churchill Downs purchased hard-bottomed Hollywood Park a couple of years ago. They believed Lehr would loosen it up and lessen the wear and tear on their horses. But since Churchill had taken over, the Hollywood Park track had not changed. Instead the Churchill Downs track appeared to have become faster and less predictable.

From the day the Derby horses began arriving, Lehr had personally assured the trainers that the track they trained on would be the one they had to race over on Derby Day and that it would be as safe as he could make it. And he had kept his promise. The track had gotten faster day by day and was growing faster as the Derby approached.

Many of the eastern trainers began to complain, including New Yorker Joe Orseno, who trained for Frank Stronach, the Austrian-Canadian automobile-parts magnate who was not only America's leading breeder and owner but also Churchill's biggest competitor in racetrack ownership. After winning the Breeders' Cup Juvenile at Churchill Downs the previous October, Stronach's two-year-old champion Macho Uno had to be rested all winter and would miss the Derby. In his place Orseno had brought a Stronach "backup" named Thunder Blitz. "Some of these horses are going to have a hard time coming back in two weeks (for the Preakness) after running on a paved road," Orseno griped.

Johnny Ward led the chorus. "If you're going to run the Kentucky Derby on a track like this, you ought to move it to Hollywood Park."

But some other trainers had been telling Lehr the track was too deep and cuppy, which he knew to be the main cause of sudden, dramatic breakdowns. Two years earlier a horse belonging to Churchill Downs board chairman Will Farish had been injured training on a track that Lehr had watered sparsely and the world had come down on him. Lehr knew he couldn't please them all, that he was caught in the middle. A hard fast track had fewer risks because consistency could be better assured. A dry, cuppy one might produce the kind of tragedy that no one wanted to see on television.

The weather during Derby week was dry, with the temperature in the low 80s. Perfect for fans, tough on Lehr. The lack of rain suggested the track would be dry. But humidity can jump up like a rabbit along the Ohio River virtually without warning. Humidity would put moisture in the track, causing it to stick together here and there, creating the inconsistency and the cuppiness dangerous to horses, infuriating to trainers and feared most by Lehr.

With no rain in sight, the Monday before the Derby Lehr had flooded his track and packed it down—which sealed the water underneath—and then he continued to water it throughout the week.

On the day of the Derby, it was 84 degrees and the humidity low. Lehr pronounced the track "fast" and "conditions perfect." And for what Churchill Downs and the racing business needed, they were.

After a twenty-five-year affiliation with ABC Sports, Churchill Downs had negotiated a new television contract with NBC, which had previously competed with the Derby by showing NBA basketball playoffs in the same time slot. For NBC's inaugural Derby, the starting time had been pushed a half hour later, to 6:11 P.M., so the racing show could precede an NBA playoff game, virtually guaranteeing the biggest audience ever. Thirty-eight different cameras, including one in a blimp, were being used. This was going to be a good show, and the impact of such a fast track was soon felt.

In the first race on Derby Day, a three-year-old filly named Love at Noon and trained by Bob Baffert set a new track record for six and a half furlongs—1:14.34. In the third race, a Grade 3 stakes called the

Lane's End Handicap, a five-year-old colt broke the seven-furlong record in 1:20.50. In the next race, a couple of two-year-old fillies named City Street and Open Story finished in a dead heat and set yet another track record of 57.28 for five furlongs, two-tenths of a second faster than the previous record. Of the three new records, this one was the most extraordinary. From a standing gate start both fillies had run five-eighths of a mile faster than Point Given or Congaree had ever done, even when timed from a running start in one of Baffert's media shows in California.

A guy who knew something about racetracks had left a blueprint for situations like this that neither Churchill Downs nor any public corporation could afford to ignore: The race is not always to the swift nor the battle to the strong, Damon Runyon wrote, but that's the way to bet it.

On Millionaires' Row, how track conditions would play out in the Derby was being explained to the swells by an expert on the subject, the only woman ever to ride the winner of a Triple Crown race—the recently retired jockey Julie Krone.

Krone was intimately familiar with the racetrack and believed she knew how the Derby would unfold. A tiny athlete, with the face and voice of a kewpie doll, she knelt in a chair and outlined the race with her fingers on a tablecloth, a crowd of enraptured swells around her, quiet so they could interpret her squeaking.

"On a really fast track everything sets up perfectly for the off-the-pace horses," she explained. "That's this second flight that will be sitting right behind the leaders coming out of the final turn. The speed horses—Songandaprayer, Balto Star, Keats and Millennium Wind—those guys should be cooked by then and will drift apart in the stretch.

"The horses right behind them—Point Given, Congaree, Express Tour and maybe A P Valentine . . . "—she moved them along on the table with her hand—"they will inherit the lead and one of them—Point Given or Congaree probably—will win."

There it was. Right from the horse's mouth. Almost. The dominant female hardly ever hears the pronouncement of another about which she cannot raise a doubt.

"What about the closers like Monarchos? Won't the second flight be tired, too?"

Krone, unaware of any connection between the horse and her questioner, squeaked back honestly.

"They won't have a chance. Closers like Monarchos, Invisible Ink, and Thunder Blitz won't be able to gain ground because the second flight—Point Given and Congaree—won't be tired. They'll rest sitting off the pace and will be impossible to catch."

"Well, that's it, honey," the breeder of Monarchos said to the dominant female when Krone had concluded. Though still sanguine, he was worn out from all the talk about Baffert's horses. "We might as well go on home now."

The crowd of swells broke up in hoots and squeals of laughter. Krone looked bemused but confused. The joke was lost on her.

"They bred Monarchos," someone told her, nodding at the Kenturkeys.

"Oh, I'm sorry," said Krone, now a child chastened.

"Don't be," replied the dominant female, curtly.

Although the ex-jockey was twenty-five years younger and in better shape, the dominant female was twice her size, just as athletic and probably more ornery. And the only question in her husband's mind was whether she could throw Julie Krone off the sixth-floor balcony of Millionaires' Row without losing her black straw Michigan Avenue hat with yellow roses on it.

Rather than wait to find out, he decided to go share Krone's encouraging analysis with his houseguests, three floors below in the considerably cooler Eclipse Room.

The backside of Churchill on Derby Day looks like a tent city picnic. The trainers and barn help entertain their friends and families at the barns. At Barn 42 the X-chromosomes around "Sparky" whiled away the long afternoon wait with anything that worked—from the *Daily Racing Form* Derby preview to novels by Joyce Carol Oates.

Yvonne Azeff and her mother were visiting with a friend from Florida who had an hour earlier been married by the racetrack chaplain on the backside near the six-and-a-half-furlong pole, so the Kentucky Derby would always be their anniversary. She brought Azeff a good-luck garter to wear under her lucky Florida Derby suit when she walked over to the paddock later with Monarchos. The new suit Azeff had bought for the Wood Memorial had been sidelined by superstition.

Tammy Holtz was trying to decide whether to put on the bright blue cap and shirt that the marketing folks from Visa had delivered to the barn and requested that grooms wear to the paddock. She might. She might not.

By four o'clock the barn's lawn chairs were occupied by the Wards and the Oxleys, who would lead the Monarchos parade over to the saddling paddock. Donna Ward was lovely in Derby rose red, and her husband's hair lay properly trained across his head. Debby Oxley's designer had done her up in the stable colors of pale blue and maize, and Jack's "lucky" underwear had again been cleverly hidden under a gray "high-flowing well" business suit. All sported big blue-and-yellow "Monarchos Rules" buttons on their chests.

Five minutes after the call went out in the barns summoning the Derby horses for the eighth race, Azeff and Holtz took Monarchos out of his stall. They always called the Derby horses early and Ward didn't want him standing in line any longer than necessary before the walk over to the grandstand. His hind ankles were wrapped in the red rundown bandages that signify the Ward stable, and the signature bridle, with the white Australian nose strip and cheek pieces that made him look like a gladiator horse, was in place. Terri Upton slipped a lead shank on his halter for the walk to the saddling paddock, which included an emotional trip through the "gauntlet"—a track opening lined with people that can prove unnerving for already-wired thoroughbreds. As reward for their work, Beccia and Holtz would go, too. For the people around a horse en route to the gate of the Kentucky Derby, it is the minute when time begins to stand still and they begin to pray that their horses will, too.

A half hour before the Kentucky Derby, the saddling paddock at Churchill resembled a joint outing of oil princes of one kind or another and the United States Senate, with everyone overdressed, overprotected and overcovered by the press. It was also flecked here and there with sponsors, track executives and assorted interlopers with unexplained access. With rare exception, all were in the final throes of Derby Fever.

Among the stricken who had no business there was the breeder of Monarchos, who somehow had obtained two precious paddock passes and was now waiting outside saddling stall 16 for Monarchos to arrive. Three stalls away, he saw the managing owner of Invisible Ink, tall John Fort, whose snub of Monarchos had irritated him at the Florida Derby. Fort was choking up again the way they had both done at Saratoga when the Unbridled colt died. This time Fort had been overcome with emotion while trying to talk to NBC about Invisible Ink's remarkable recovery from the bout of colitis that had almost killed him.

That his horse had not only recovered but made it to the starting gate of the most important race in the world was a testament to Fort's personal effort and commitment. For the past twenty years nobody had tried harder to succeed in the racing business than John Fort. He had raised and spent millions of dollars. He had bought some mediocre horses, maxed out his credit cards, and watched potential superstars die or get injured before they could get to the track. Finaliy he was there, Invisible Ink the proof of his success, the validation of a life's work. The light had come on in that dark room where he had been working all these years. That his courageous "Inky" was going off at odds of 50 to 1 did not matter. The oddsmakers were wrong and Fort knew it. His horse had a chance to win the Kentucky Derby and he was unashamedly crying tears of joy.

The sight of a six-and-a-half-foot-tall grown man tearing up in the paddock at Churchill is only slightly more rare than the sight of the track president, Tom Meeker, strolling through it with a smile on his face. But Derby Day is a progenitor of unusual juxtaposition. Meeker, a tough, no-nonsense former Marine credited with building Churchill into a major public corporation, moved like a man on a mission. His destination turned out to be the last saddling stall, that of horse number 17, where the press was huddled en masse. The favorite, Point Given; his owner, Prince Salman; trainer Bob Baffert and a sizable entourage were still a few minutes away, so Meeker decided to wait, assuming a ramrod rigid welcoming position inside the enclosure.

One stall over, the decision by the track's chief executive to favor only one horse with his presence for the benefit of the television network was taken as a personal offense by the breeder of Monarchos. This display smacked of a conspiracy. Television coverage had been geared to Point Given, the track surface had been prepared for Point Given and now the head of Churchill Downs was signaling the world before the race began that he was for Point Given, too.

Meeker's arrival was the icing on the nut cake. Why run the race? Why not just bring the trophy down and present it to the prince now and be done with it? A few seconds ago the Two Bucks man had been as ecstatic as John Fort, a man perfectly content just to have bred a horse that made it to the Kentucky Derby. And he knew full well that once the gate opened, any one of six or seven horses had a chance to win. But now he'd just as soon not run the race at all. Cancel the Derby. Cancel the whole goddam Triple Crown.

Obviously, signs of his recovery to mental health had been premature. Behind the placid, laid-back front he'd been putting up all day, his windmill was still tilted. Outside the paddock fence in the front row of gawkers were two guys wearing helmets carved out of watermelon rinds, which they claimed kept them cool. The Monarchos man wanted to borrow one and wear it up to Meeker and ask him in front of the television cameras what the hell he was doing in Point Given's saddling enclosure. Why not move over one stall and welcome Johnny Ward, the only Kentucky-born trainer in the race, and his American owner, Jack Oxley, who owned a Kentucky farm and whose wife, Debby, was a Louisville native? Isn't this the *Kentucky* Derby?

But even a man so off his rocker could see that someone was already in the stall where Monarchos was to be saddled. And she looked very familiar in her yellow suit from the Milan designer and the black straw hat that covered up her new spike hairdo that looked as if it had been cut in a temper tantrum. What was Meeker doing in Point Given's stall? And what was the dominant female doing in Monarchos's stall?

Meeker was facing outward toward the crowd, obviously so the cameras could see his face. But the dominant female had her back to the opening, her face to the wall, the black straw lid tilted forward. Her elbows were bent in perfect unison. He'd seen that posture a million times. It was now obvious to the Monarchos man what the dominant female was up to.

Of the sixteen horses led over together in order through the gauntlet, Monarchos was the last to arrive, his entry as quiet as his training had been. Because of Point Given's previous histrionics, Baffert had requested exemption from the gauntlet and had brought his horse to the track via a more direct route from his barn. So his escort contingent—twice the size of any other—arrived last and separately, a two-section train no less with the Superhorse bringing up the rear like a beast of royalty.

The welcome for Baffert and his horse by the second-largest crowd in Derby history—154,000-plus—was deafening. A woman scurrying to make room for Baffert's accompanying press horde rolled her eyes and said, "Nothing like a grand entrance."

And from his spot a few stalls away, John Fort eyed the size of Baffert's traveling party and reached an important conclusion. "Their confidence comes from strength in numbers," he told the group around Invisible Ink. "Remember that. When Baffert's horse and jockey get out on that track, they're on their own."

Once the main attraction had reached the center ring and the cameras were rolling, the jockeys, who had been lined up for a group picture, spilled out of their nearby quarters like a dozen and a half brightly colored toys and spread like paint through the paddock to get final instructions from their trainers.

The big tote board now had Monarchos at 10 to 1. It might as well have been 50. Millennium Wind, Balto Star, Congaree and Dollar Bill were all now at more favorable single-digit odds, but none close to Point Given at 2 to 1.

Forget the odds, the press hype, the rhetoric, the television worship of a Superhorse. The month-long war of words and tactics between Ward and Baffert and the burning rivalry between Monarchos and Point Given was still smoldering in the whispered conversations between trainers and jockeys.

Both Baffert and Ward knew that only four or five of the seventeen starters would still be running when the race got to its final eighth of a mile—and that these two horses would be among them.

Ward had always known what only a few of the most respected speed analysts had finally realized: that Monarchos had run the last five-eighths of a mile in the Wood at Aqueduct even faster than he had at Gulfstream—in 1 minute and four-fifths of a second. He was moving up, not regressing.

Ward believed Point Given's jockey, Gary Stevens, to be the best tactical rider in the game, but he cautioned Chavez against following his lead or being influenced by what did.

"There's plenty of speed in the race. It will dictate what the others do. Ride your race. If you are patient, you will win."

Baffert, for his part, believed that Point Given's size and power was intimidating to other horses, and he wanted Stevens to ride him that way to take full advantage. The possibility that Monarchos could repeat the move he'd made in the Florida Derby was the only thing

Baffert saw standing between him and the Derby winner's circle that had defined his career.

Whatever Stevens did, Baffert warned, when the pack turns for home "don't let Monarchos get the first run on you."

Whatever the whispered conversations between trainers and jockeys, they were of less importance than the one going on outside stall 16. Yes, the dominant female had been doing exactly as her husband had suspected. And now she admitted it. She had been praying.

"God, I know I don't deserve this," she had prayed. "But please, let Monarchos win the Kentucky Derby."

Hearing the confession, her husband teared up like John Fort. Earlier in the day, his friend Father Mike, a Jesuit, had blessed Monarchos long distance from an altar in San Francisco. And Chavez's mother-in-law, a devout Catholic, had already lit a votive candle and prayed that St. Martin de Porres, who'd worked miracles of flight, would be riding with Jorge. Perhaps even the persuasive evangelist-lawyer upstairs in the Eclipse Room could be talked into arguing Monarchos's case to a higher court as well.

On second thought, Tom Meeker, don't cancel this Derby after all. Hold on to that trophy for a couple of more minutes because for all their strength in numbers Point Given and Bob Baffert and NBC have no idea what all they're up against.

19

When I am bestride him, I soar. I am a hawk; He trots the air: The earth sings when he touches it. . . . He is pure air and fire.

WILLIAM SHAKESPEARE, *Henry V*

When the horses come on the track for the Kentucky Derby, something magical happens to those who are there watching. They catch up with and are admitted to the time capsule in which the people around the horses have already been traveling for hours. It is a static place where all bodies and forces are at rest in equilibrium. There is no past, there is no future. Only a present—real time—a "now" that lasts two minutes. The novelist John Steinbeck called it "an emotion, a turbulence, an explosion, one of the most beautiful and satisfying things I have experienced."

What words might he have found had one of the horses been one he raised, owned or trained, lived in a barn with for months—or rode into the winner's circle? Consider the level of internal turbulence that can drive a person with a swell seat at the Derby to say, as the dominant female did to her husband minutes before the starter's bell:

"I can't watch. I am going to sit in a corner by myself somewhere because I can't bear to watch it."

"You're kidding."

"No, I can't watch. I'm already sick to my stomach."

The horses were heading for the gate. She did not look seriously ill. Proper husbandly compassion was promptly put on hold.

"I'll find you when it's over then," the Monarchos man said. "I'm taking the binoculars up on the roof so I can see it all—every single step."

He had always found the view from the press seats more unobstructed than that from among the swells. The swell seats were more comfortable, he realized, but never to him. Had he watched the race at home on television as originally planned, however, he might have slit his wrists before it ever started. The story lines of NBC's telecast had been carefully written, and everybody followed the script. This Kentucky Derby was about California. Baffert got the lion's share of the attention, boasting about the prowess of his horses and reclining on the hood of his Jaguar with his blond. NBC liked the Millennium Wind angle, too: a horse with constantly bleeding heels being ridden by fifty-four-year-old Laffit Pincay, Jr., California's leading rider and the winningest jockey ever. John Fort's emotional journey with Invisible Ink had been too good to ignore, but Johnny Ward, the only Kentucky trainer, was worth only about thirty seconds.

The network's analysts were unanimous in their support of the favorite, Point Given. And when its expert race caller Tom Durkin talked the final few horses into the gate, horse number 16 slipped into the next-to-last gate spot unmentioned while Durkin gushed about number 17: "And there is Point Given, . . . a magnificent-looking thoroughbred, standing 17 hands tall. . . . "

When the bell sounded, Gary Stevens gunned his locomotive out of the gate in precisely the intimidating fashion his trainer had instructed him. In an obvious rush toward a spot in "the second flight" in order not to be hung wide down the straightaway, Stevens aimed Point Given left out of the gate and ran right over Monarchos and Chavez, sideswiping them as he passed and slamming them into number 15, Jamaican Rum.

"Sonofabitch," yelled the man with the binoculars from the roof atop Millionaires' Row. It was the last sound he remembered hearing. His "now" had begun and would last for hours, maybe even days.

Down on Butch Lehr's hard-packed clay, the just-slammed Jorge Chavez remained undaunted. He had ridden in this rambunctious posse before, atop undistinguished long shots—Ulises in 1994, Adonis in 1999 and Trippi in 2000—horses unheard of since and on which he knew he had no chance. The one under him now had given him a chance. "I've got to do it now," he told himself. "I can't let this chance pass."

Jockeys meditate before a race, like pro football linebackers trying to psyche themselves up to destroy a quarterback. But NFL headhunters get the chance every week. The Derby only comes once a year, and even then a jockey may not get a ride, or not on a good horse, and even on the best horse there is no assurance of winning. The Derby is the hardest race to win, the one that sets them apart, puts them down in history and elevates them to the highest rank among their peers. All his life Jorge Chavez had been waiting for the chance, and now Johnny Ward had given it to him. He was on a horse with a chance to win the Kentucky Derby, one that hadn't lost a stride even after being run over by the big s.o.b. coming out of the gate.

Chavez steered Monarchos confidently in behind the rush and found himself a ground-saving spot on the rail at the head of a five-horse pack of confirmed closers. What he saw ahead of him looked a lot like the Florida Derby. Songandaprayer had been shot from a gun out of the number one spot and was hauling ass. Two other inside speedsters were breathing down his neck and so was Chavez's idol Laffit Pincay, Jr., aboard Millennium Wind, bloody heels and all. His old nemesis, Congaree, was tucked in behind, just like the experts said he would be. Point Given and the Arab hope Express Tour headed up the second flight with the nutcake Talk Is Money struggling between them.

Chavez realized the front was flying, but his horse had settled into a Beccia-pace gallop next to the rail and was beginning to take hold of the track. He urged him forward, moving his hands a little. Monarchos lengthened his stride, but was still on his left lead, struggling around the first turn in thirteenth place, fourteen lengths behind the leaders.

No wonder he was having trouble keeping up. Songandaprayer had just scorched the first quarter mile in 22 1/5 seconds. The Derby won by Secretariat had started in 23.2.

In Oxley's box, Ward had caught the quarter-mile fraction and called it out to the owner. Exactly the kind of pace he had hoped for. And Songandaprayer kept it up, with Balto Star right on his hip. They were hooked. The half mile went in 44.86 seconds—the fastest in Kentucky Derby history, nearly 3 full seconds faster than ever. Ward called that fraction out for Oxley, too, and felt even better about what he was watching.

Everyone thought jockey Aaron Gryder was pushing Bobby Hurley's horse on the lead, but he wasn't. What happened to Songandaprayer is what happens to speed horses at the Derby. The adrenaline shoots one to the front, and the others try to keep up. Balto Star and Millennium Wind had been beaten out of the gate by Songandaprayer and they were after him. It is their nature, jockeys be damned. All they can do is hang on.

It was only after Monarchos switched to his right lead going down the backstretch that Chavez felt his horse relax and begin to dig in. He started moving his arms a little faster now and angled Monarchos off the rail to the outside of Invisible Ink, who was two lengths ahead of him.

Tall John Fort, who had his binoculars fixed on Invisible Ink, could now see clearly. He watched the two horses go by the track kitchen. His 50-to-1 shot was having what every owner and trainer prays for—a perfect trip. Fort knew that he had one of the four or five horses that would last the distance. He had one of the best jockeys in the world in John Velazquez and together they were in the perfect spot to make a run.

On the roof of Millionaires' Row the guy who had no business there had not taken his binoculars off Monarchos and Chavez and so he had not seen the fractions. He had not heard them screamed out excitedly by the track announcer because he could no longer hear anything. But he could see that the pack was flying and that Regal Band's baby was gaining on them anyway. Monarchos was cruising now, each stride longer than the last, each stretch of his neck tugging Chavez's hands farther from his body.

Still in front after three-quarters of a mile, Songandaprayer had burned himself a spot in history with another record time of 1:09.2. Ward called that one out to Oxley and began to think what he should not dare. He knew that Monarchos liked the second turn on a racetrack best of all. Everybody connected with him knew it. And anyone who saw the Florida Derby should have known it. He was tenth now, and Chavez gave him the signal. And before anyone, including Gary Stevens aboard Point Given, realized it, they had done what Bob Baffert told them not to do. They had let Monarchos get "first run."

In Oxley's box, Donna Ward was standing in her chair. "Oh, Johnny, he's coming," she said, grabbing her husband's shoulder.

The guy on the roof saw the burst of speed and knew the race was over as far as he was concerned. Monarchos was going to finish as he had in Florida. He might not win. But he didn't have to. A horse from Two Bucks from a $14,000 mare and a $7,500 stud fee was about to beat most of the other horses in the Kentucky Derby. Win or lose, he was going to finish like a hero.

Johnny Ward saw the time of the mile—1:35 flat—and knew he was about to be a hero, too. The first two flights of the rushing pack should be cooked and his horse was just getting to the part of the racetrack he liked the best. He knew there were two gears left to shift.

Entering the final turn, Julie Krone's prediction came true. The speed horses started to fade and the second bunch inherited the lead. Aboard Congaree, Victor Espinoza found himself in the driver's seat. Songandaprayer was giving up on his inside, but Congaree had been relaxed down the backstretch and still had some run. There was no one in front of him. Espinoza thought "maybe" this was it. But like everyone else, he was expecting what track announcer Tom Durkin told the world was happening right at that moment on Congaree's outside hip—"the pent-up power of Point Given" being unleashed by Gary Stevens.

But when Stevens pulled down the throttle on the Big Red Train, it was already out of steam. The train pulled up beside Congaree but not for long. This was no workmate Saif being shut down by walkie-talkie. Congaree refused to be passed.

Behind them Monarchos was rolling five wide in the track, one chop by Chavez having set off an explosion that sent tremors all the way to the owners' boxes.

"Honey, we're going to win it!" shouted Donna Ward. She was pounding on her husband's shoulders and clutching his neck. The Oxleys were transfixed in front of them. Debby Oxley thought she had stopped breathing.

With a quarter of a mile to go, Chavez cruised up alongside Invisible Ink, as jockey John Velazquez realized he was about to be blocked behind Point Given. For an instant Velazquez saw a hole and went for it, but the hole was moving faster than he was. Chavez and Monarchos had shut him off, blowing past Point Given in the process. Chavez touched no one and never saw either horse. All he saw was the sixteenth pole and the leader Congaree.

It was at that moment—at the sixteenth pole—that Chavez knew the ending. He knew who was going to hit the wire first in the Kentucky Derby of his dreams.

Monarchos had passed eight horses on the turn and was still on his left lead—the wrong lead. He had a gear to go and Congaree was doing what the riders of closers love to see happening to horses in front of them. Despite being whipped furiously by Espinoza, Congaree was "backing up." He was done. Chavez knew it.

So did the Monarchos man on the roof, whose binoculars had already dropped to his chest. He was slipping into a coma of ecstasy—a "now" that he hoped would never end. He had one last conscious thought that betrayed profanely the glory of the moment: "My God, the sonofabitch is going to win the damn Kentucky Derby."

In the owners' boxes Jack Oxley realized that he was watching his highest-flowing well coming in, hurtling toward the finish line. That morning he had told Debby, "I think we're going to win the Kentucky Derby today." And behind him Johnny Ward swallowed the welling in his throat long enough to shout the obvious—that they were about to. "We're going to win the Kentucky Derby!" Then the awareness of his accomplishment clogged his throat and wet his eyes. He was trying not to sob about it in public. Debby Oxley was hugging her husband and trying to get her breath.

Chavez folded his stick, loosened his hold on Monarchos and urged him on to his right lead. His Mercedes slipped into overdrive and sped him on to glory.

The race was over. Monarchos had crushed the strongest Kentucky Derby field in years. He won by four and a half lengths, the second biggest margin in thirty years. And he had given Churchill Downs, the horse racing industry and NBC exactly what they all had wanted—speed. His Derby time of 1:59 4/5, or to be more specific, 1:59.97, made him the second horse in history to run the Derby in under 2 minutes. Only Secretariat—at 1:59 2/5—had run faster. Johnny Ward's horse had worked his bullet when it mattered the most. And everyone had a Triple Crown horse—just not the one they expected.

A short staircase separates the rooftop between the Twin Spires of Churchill Downs from Millionaires' Row, but it did not exist inside the soundproof tomb of astonishment where the genius breeder now lived. In *Star Trek*–style he had somehow been beamed down to the sixth floor into a mob scene. Animated people, some teary-eyed, some smiling, waved their arms and hands in his direction. Some were gathered in a corner around an unfamiliar figure, a woman in disarray. Her hat was askew, her glasses cockeyed beneath her nose. Tears were streaming down her face. Her mouth was opening and closing like a fish breathing behind an aquarium glass. And then for the first time, he heard sound. A familiar voice—"He won! He won!"

It was coming from the center of attention—from the frenzied woman who he could now see had locked arms with John Phillips's wife, Beth. They were doing some kind of whirlaway jig, jumping up and down and around and around at the same time, squealing all the while. Seeing him, the frenzied woman broke free and ran to him, locking her arms around his neck and drenching him in wetness of kisses and tears. The dominant female had watched Regal Band's baby cross the finish line after all, and the sight of it had driven her to behavior so out of character as to make her virtually unrecognizable. From some deep well of shyness or reserve had gushed the first public show of happiness he'd ever seen, the first display of affection in front of others he'd ever experienced. If their own wedding day had been among her happiest moments, her feminist independence had kept from him the acknowledgment. But there was no secret to her joy now. From the tight parameters of dignity that rigidly suppressed her emotions had sprung a Jack-in-the-Box he'd never expected to see. She was hugging and kissing him now—in public—and among the cheering swells they spun together in a cocoon of disbelief. In the ridiculous, they had found the sublime.

Not surprisingly, the Kenturkeys got lost on the way to the winner's circle, blocked by chain-link fences first and delayed further by surly security guards. It is hard to find your way in a fog, especially for someone with no sense of direction. The celebration was delayed anyway by a specious claim of foul by Invisible Ink's jockey, John Velazquez, who said Monarchos had impeded his progress when he moved over and "almost touched my horse." The claim momentarily threw cold water on the happy face of Jorge Chavez and forced a steward's inquiry, but it proved only melodrama for TV. They don't take down a Kentucky Derby winner for flying by horses that have no hope of winning.

Velazquez, who rode Invisible Ink by a wobbly Congaree at the wire, acknowledged he probably would not have claimed foul in any other race. But he had finished second, and "I figured that in the Derby, I should take a shot." For history, if for nothing else.

For Jack Oxley, who owned 24 percent of Invisible Ink, the "shot" taken by Velazquez meant only an endless moment of bemused irony. (He had claimed foul against himself.) And Inky's trainer, Todd Pletcher, never gave credence to the claim. But for tall John Fort, it was more gold in the pot at the end of his rainbow, already glittering from the runner-up finish of a 50-to-1 shot. No matter what his jockey and trainer believed, to Fort his hard-luck horse had come back from the dead all the way to the Kentucky Derby and only lost it on a foul. No longer was he the blind man in the dark room looking for the black hat that wasn't there. He had the hat in his hand, only it was white, and he was wearing it to a victory party of his own.

In Kentucky at least, the steward's inquiry that delayed NBC's award presentation ceremony was worth waiting for. Jack Oxley was a proud but gracious winner whose name was easily pronounced by the governor, a winner who wore an acceptable suit and did not need an interpreter to credit his trainer's methods and deliver a message that horse racing needed delivered:

"Nothing could be more exciting, more incredible, more thrilling, more astonishing, more unbelievable than today. There's nothing like winning the Kentucky Derby. If you've already taken off the planet somehow, it takes you to a higher orbit, for sure."

The statement Kentucky hoped the sport's signature event would make about thoroughbred horse racing had been made. The art of breeding racehorses had once again triumphed over the business of mass-producing them. A humble Kentuckian with a small stable and reverence for tradition had beaten the "factory" trainers at their own game—speed—with a horse from a castoff mare and a bargain-basement stallion that had come off a small farm to become the grand beast of the Koran, a creature like no other with the treasures of earth between his eyes. A horse who would fly without wings and who like so many others before him would prove once more that this game is one that cannot be bought.

AFTERWORD

The sun shines bright on my old Kentucky home
'Tis summer, the people are gay
The corn top's ripe and the meadow's in bloom
While the birds make music all the day.

STEPHEN FOSTER, *My Old Kentucky Home*

What Stephen Foster forgot to include in his ode was a prescription for psychic disorders that strike any old Kentucky home connected with a winner of the Kentucky Derby.

The newly minted breeding genius and the nearly bubbly dominant female returned at midnight to a place as unrecognizable as they had become to themselves.

Sixteen balloons festooned the front gates. Ribbons and signs handmade by frolicking well-wishers delirious over the home-team victory by "#16" were posted along the fences at Two Bucks. On one a kid had scrawled a stick-horse figure of Monarchos and designated him as "Joseph's horse"—thereby claiming ownership along with the rest of the state.

Unlike the professional handicappers a lot of Kentuckians had bet their hearts rather than their heads, wagering heavily on Monarchos, and had been handsomely rewarded at 10 to 1. "A lot of people won a lot of money on your horse," reported a sign left on the windshield of a farm vehicle.

The maintenance chief at Two Bucks, Gary Powell, a native Kentuckian who was so irked by the sight of Baffert reclining on a Jaguar hood that he bet Monarchos across the board, reaped double satisfaction. "Old Baffert got himself a good Kentucky ass-whupping yesterday," he announced to his fellow workers. "And my family got itself a new entertainment center."

Alas, the houseguest lawyers from Nashville and the big spenders from Kansas City were not among the big winners. Though they had bet Monarchos out of loyalty to their host, they had like many others been steered by the pundits to include the "invincible" Point Given in the "exotic" bets toward which they were inclined and not the improbable long shot Invisible Ink. So as usual, the numbers game was won by Churchill Downs.

But before boarding his ancient biplane "charter" back to Kansas City, the big spender unexpectedly settled up for his Derby tickets, no doubt in gratitude for the most exciting horse racing outing of his life. As might have been anticipated, the Oxleys' Derby celebration party spread over the entire restaurant, and the Two Bucks houseguests ended up celebrating with the winning owner, trainer and jockey—an experience not likely to ever be repeated.

The morning after the Derby, the e-mail, voice mail boxes and answering machines at Two Bucks were clogged with congratulatory calls. When the message "voice" announces, "You have twenty-seven new messages and six saved messages," something extraordinary has occurred in your life. Some of the calls were from strangers, others from people not heard from in twenty-five years. One caller's message to the dominant female began, "You might not remember me but I'm the woman you met on the floor of exercise class several years ago." The cost of new popularity was promptly reflected in the farm cell phone bills. Normally around $300 per month, they totaled $811.32 for the month of May.

However, some of the calls held the promise of fame—interviews with the *New York Times* and *U.S. News & World Report*—and perhaps even wealth. Some relayed offers to breed Regal Band to expensive thoroughbred stallions whose managers previously would have turned their noses up at such an idea. They were purveyors of the notion that if Regal Band could produce a Derby winner from a breeding to a $7,500 stallion, as the breeder's friend Jane Smiley observed, "you could breed her to an expensive stallion and the resulting foal would sprout wings and fly."

One bloodstock agent, undeterred by knowledge that on Derby day the dam of the subsequent winner had been re-bred to the sire who produced him, left the promise of a $1 million offer from a British client "if she gets in foal okay." People were lining up to visit the farm and inspect her 2001 foal, the new filly born the day after the Florida Derby.

In the national press, old friends repaid past favors and kindnesses with glowing accounts of the "miracle" that had occurred that Saturday on a Kentucky racetrack, and they were in concert as to its nature—the resurrection of a human relic from their profession, the rising of a phoenix who had once set himself afire and now had sprung from the ashes on a gray horse. Winning the Derby was compared to Pulitzer Prizes won decades earlier by newspapers under his stewardship. They labeled the one-time editor a role model and hero for every ink-stained wretch who'd ever thumbed his nose at management and longed for a new life after newspapers. None labeled him in print "the lucky bastard" they knew him to be, though they said so in their telephone calls. They were merely helping him settle old scores—and some of their own, maybe.

In Kentucky, the attention newly aimed at Two Bucks was that normally reserved for lottery winners. Brokers called with stock investment opportunities, inventors with their patents and service clubs with their luncheon speech invitations. Development officers from universities where he'd left no marks suddenly wanted to take him to dinner. And a neighbor who'd never spoken to him in ten years waylaid him outside the agriculture agent's office to offer him additional and adjacent land. "You can certainly afford it now," the farmer was certain.

Some congratulatory messages were rich with delectable irony. One particularly class-conscious stud farm that had once found Regal Band an "unacceptable" mate for a $25,000 stud now sought her as a "foal share" mate to one with an $80,000 fee. Fat chance.

Others were merely infuriating. The sales company Fasig-Tipton had decided to feature Monarchos on the cover of its 2001 August Saratoga yearling sale, precisely the auction in which he had not been wanted because "he didn't belong" and in which he had in fact failed to sell in 1999. And, "Oh, by the way," Fasig-Tipton informed Two Bucks, the Derby winner's yearling half-sister—whose admission to the 2001 Saratoga sale had been "on hold and under consideration until we see what happens with the Derby"—"well, of course, she's welcome in any of our sales now."

Of course she is.

Ultimately, the filly's future would be blurred by a lack of resolution typical of her owner's relationship with the dominant female: "You can't sell her. What's wrong with you? She's Regal Band's baby."

"So all our reward is supposed to be emotional, huh?"

Into this state of confused exaltation came a congratulatory flower arrangement from Pin Oak Stud, complete with carrots for momma Regal Band from proud papa Maria's Mon. The thank you note in return from the dominant female left no doubt as to the condition in which it had found the recipients. "My husband is still so excited that he ate the carrots himself and fed the flowers to the mare," she wrote to Josephine Abercrombie.

A week after the Derby, there on the cover of the *Daily Racing Form* was a loving family portrait to cherish forever. In it was the famous Derby dam herself, whose insurance coverage had just been upped to cover her increased value. At her side was the dominant female, captured in a moment apparently so gloriously happy no one would believe she could possibly have ever dreamed of moving to New Mexico. Alongside them was the hulking two-month-old sibling, also newly insured at ridiculous cost, being exhibited by the breeding genius himself. Unlike the contented faces of his three female companions, his face screwed up painfully like a man squinting directly into the sun or suffering a gas attack. Could this be instead a stressful frown, the reflection of still another wave of subconscious paranoid torment?

Absolutely. Always in search of something to make him uneasy, fresh out of live villains and bad luck but still suspended in disbelief, the breeding genius had resorted to fear of the supernatural.

"You know what this all means," he'd told the dominant female. "We cannot possibly have this kind of luck. Something terrible is about to happen to us. Maybe I'm going to die soon and this is the last mortal act before my final reward."

Never one for instinctive agreement with her husband and with him now occupying her usual negative ground, the dominant female was forced into a more positive but convoluted and equally insane analysis of events.

"No, I don't think you're going to die. I don't think this is about us at all. I think God is paying back someone else for something bad they've done. Either God didn't want Baffert and the prince to win the Derby, or He's letting us win to punish someone bad who didn't want us to win."

"Somebody in Chicago maybe."

Ah, yes, that's it. Our winning the Derby was someone else's punishment—the conclusion of an expert on vengeance.

For all the chatter about training methods, there may be truth in the railbird's observation: "Training horses is easy: You just get yourself a fast one and send him out there and tell the jockey to stay to the left and hurry back."

Still, winning Triple Crown races imbues the winner with permanent glory and the losers with an inferiority complex. Alydar lost the Derby, the Preakness and the Belmont to Affirmed by a total of less than two lengths, and when his trainer, John Veitch, was leaving the barn after the final defeat, he was spotted by a New York track habitué. "Hey, Veitch," the heckler yelled, "You know the difference between Alydar and Affirmed?"

"What's that?" replied Veitch.

"Laz Barrera," said the heckler, which was the name of Affirmed's trainer.

When Monarchos crossed the wire at the 2001 Kentucky Derby, he put indelible marks in the lives of the people around him—mileposts that separate everything "before" from everything "afterward."

Johnny Ward, for instance, a "good" trainer before the Derby, instantly became a "great" one—an industry leader newly revered among his peers nationally and celebrated at home in Kentucky. On the day of the Derby, Ward had been forced to park in an alley at Churchill Downs because he lacked the proper credentials to get in the trainer's lot, and when he tried to go from the owners' boxes to the winner's circle, the security personnel blocked his way. "But I just won the Kentucky Derby," he protested, and was not allowed through until witnesses attested to both his identity and achievement.

That is not likely to happen again. Ward's face has been on the front of every sports page and racing publication in the country, from the *Daily Racing Form* to the *New York Times*, which extolled him as a paragon of patience and horsemanship and an upholder of tradition. His Kentucky friends have launched a campaign for his appointment to the State Racing Commission, a badge of prestige in his business even though it is a political football kicked around by each new governor.

If Ward ran for public office himself now, he could get elected. Any horse he enters in a race is considered a threat to win. And he is on every owner's list of "trainers who could get me to the Derby." But any Derby aspirant will have to contest for a spot in Ward's barn with Jack Oxley, now more intent than ever on keeping them all filled. Doing the impossible once only makes achievers like Oxley want to do it again. Next time, he hopes, it will be with a horse bred on his own Midway farm, which is now teeming with wonderfully pedigreed race mares capable of raising champions. But a burgeoning breeding operation of his own did not stop their owner from stocking up on expensive, well-bred colts with Derby pedigrees at every possible opportunity during the 2001 sales, including a $1.3 million son of Seattle Slew, a $750,000 grandson of A. P. Indy and the second highest priced Maria's Mon offspring ever at $525,000.

During the year the Oxleys spend time at their homes in Colorado, Florida, and Saratoga and at their Kentucky farm, Fawn's Leap, where the night after the Derby the gate was decorated by well-wishers with dozens of empty "nacho" bags, in tribute to their champion "More-nachos." And no matter where they are living at the moment, a huge dining room adornment moves with them—the Kentucky Derby winner's trophy—displayed if possible in front of a large mirror that makes it appear as two. Moving two trophies around to appear as four is no problem at all, Oxley says, at least until they have won four. Every home should have one.

Winning the Derby brought Jorge Chavez his just deserts—celebrity to match his prowess as a jockey. Chavez had achieved the ultimate counterbalance to his childhood despair—a monumental reward for never giving up, which is what had saved him in the streets.

While handing out the long-stemmed roses from the Derby garland to his family, recollections of that unhappy childhood were not far from his mind. But his greatest joy in winning was the knowledge that "this is what children, my grandchildren . . . everybody . . . will remember."

A week later, after the haze of exhilaration had cleared, a feeling of uneasiness came over him, a kind of uncertainty that he had felt long ago. The feeling surprised him and he confided it to his wife, Margarita.

"Margarita, I did it. I finally did it," he said. "All my dreams have come true, but something is wrong. I should be happy, but I'm not."

"Yes, you have dreamed and all your dreams have come true," she replied. "What is there to be unhappy about?"

"Because I don't know, what am I supposed to do now? When all your dreams have come true, what are you supposed to do?"

Margarita smiled at her husband. "The same thing you have always done. Dream some more. You must go out and win the next race. Win all the races. Win the Kentucky Derby again."

Jorge Chavez smiles now at the simplicity of the wisdom of her words.

"Margarita was right. I went out and won a race. As soon as I won, I was happy again."

It was a stakes race for Johnny Ward, on a good filly.

"He gave me the filly in '99 [Beautiful Pleasure]. And now he gives me this horse [Monarchos] and he told me exactly how it all was going to happen. After this, I told Johnny, I've got to call you 'Dad.'"

The night after the Derby, Bob Baffert hid from the press, bitterly disappointed at the performance of his horses after figuring he "had 'em over a barrel."

The next week Baffert trained his horses at Churchill without cameras, entourage or the persistent track habitués who hang around wanting favors from a celebrity.

"That's the one beauty about losing," he quipped. "Everybody drops you like a burnt match."

Though he retained the loaned Jaguar and the parking spots with his name on them, Baffert's role as racing's golden boy was assumed—overnight and only temporarily—by Ward, whose horse was now the only one with a chance to win the Triple Crown. Naturally, Ward credited his more traditional training methods and said they assured he'd have a fresh horse for the Preakness two weeks later.

This prediction did not come true. Although cofavored with Point Given and in virtually every expert's top three picks, Monarchos looked and ran like a horse either tired or hurt. In retrospect, it may have been both. Although apparently training well before the race, he seemed unhappy in the saddling paddock, his coat dull, its pewter color washed out. On the track his stride looked restricted and his footing tenuous as he struggled through the loose sandy surface of Pimlico to finish sixth. For the twenty-third year in a row, there would be no Triple Crown winner.

Point Given redeemed himself in the Preakness with a two-and-a-quarter-length victory and Congaree ran third, once again being passed at the wire, this time by A P Valentine. And the Big Red Train improved the performance impressively three weeks later by annihilating the field in the Belmont Stakes by twelve and a half lengths. The superhorse Baffert had been promising everyone had finally shown up. Point Given had peaked at the Belmont, as Monarchos had done at the Derby. A P Valentine was again a distant runner-up.

Monarchos ran considerably better at Belmont but still finished third. There was obviously something wrong. And the following week they found it when Monarchos went gimpy for a few strides while exercising and two days later refused to extend his right front leg for a farrier, who was trying to replace his shoes. A subsequent radiograph disclosed a hairline crack in his right knee, already partially healed. When the injury—a likely result of stress—actually began to affect his performance is a matter of conjecture. But clearly he had never been the same horse after the Derby, and Ward said later he believed that's where the injury occurred. Although the injury was not career ending, Monarchos was done for the year, depriving racing of what could have been a stirring battle with Point Given for Horse of the Year honors.

Any hope that the rivalry might resume and stir public interest for the following year was dashed when Point Given was abruptly retired in late August: He had strained a tendon and would no longer compete.

Like his sire, Maria's Mon, Monarchos attempted a comeback, but was never the same horse again. After running an unimpressive third in an allowance race at Gulfstream in January 2002, he injured a tendon in his left foreleg and was retired to stud. As expected it was done in the most revered Kentucky tradition—syndicated by Claiborne Farm in the manner of Secretariat. He was expected to stand for a reasonable first year fee of $25,000, affordable even for his breeder.

If indeed Point Given was "another Secretariat" with the marketing appeal of Seabiscuit to draw people to horse racing, the sport would never benefit. He had become another racehorse "too valuable as a sire" to rehabilitate and risk on the racetrack, even for an extraordinarily wealthy oil prince of Saudi Arabia.

News of Point Given's retirement prompted an instant rewriting of the Kentucky Derby story of the previous May—and of history. The name of the 2001 winner—Monarchos—quickly became the same as that of the 1915 winner: Regret.

To the racing press, the tragedy of Point Given's career was not that he wouldn't be around to prove his greatness, but that he had somehow managed to freakishly lose the Kentucky Derby and with it the precious Triple Crown. Because Point Given had moved unimpeded and at will throughout the race some explanation had to be found. So the press blamed the track for being too hard for such a heavy horse, and blamed the best tactical rider in the game, Gary Stevens, for faulty tactics. Only Steve Haskin of *The Blood-Horse* and Rick Bozich of the *Louisville Courier-Journal* could see clearly through the tears to write the truth. The Derby track had been prepared for California speed, which it produced. Gary Stevens had been told by Baffert to take his horse up close to the front and wait for the leaders to tire, which is exactly what he did and what they did. All that went wrong was that a faster, better prepared horse came from thirteenth place and blew the Big Red Train's doors off going by. It was not as if Point Given had been nipped by a nose at the wire. He was beaten by eleven and a half lengths and finished fifth, well behind a 50 to 1 shot.

Baffert and Point Given didn't lose the Derby. Ward and a horse running faster than any but Secretariat won it. But if there was a culprit to blame for Point Given not winning the Derby and for the industry not having a Triple Crown winner, it might well be the combination of industry obsession with "speed" and neglect over the nature and inconsistent condition of track surfaces.

While Ward and Baffert continued to snipe verbally at each other over tactics throughout the summer, the rigors of their Triple Crown battle left them both afoot in the fall for the second most important race of the year, when the three-year-olds take on older horses for Horse of the Year honors in the $2 million Breeders' Cup Classic. For the second consecutive year no horse that contested all three legs of the American Triple Crown was left standing to take on the three-year-olds from Europe and Asia and older horses from around the world.

Not only were Point Given and Monarchos sidelined, so were all the other serious Derby contenders. Invisible Ink needed chips removed from three ankles. Millennium Wind had been given the rest of the year off for his feet to heal. Congaree twisted his knee in a race at Saratoga and had to go home for the year, and the $15 million A P Valentine never won again and was retired in early October.

Whether firing off Bob Baffert bullet works or galloping two and half miles more slowly for Johnny Ward, the three-year-old horses once again found Derby training too physically or psychologically demanding. Even the best conformed, soundest and best cared-for animals do not often survive the grueling training necessary to get a young horse ready to contest a mile and a quarter race on the first Saturday in May.

That is why the Derby is so difficult to win, and why Baffert so candidly acknowledged last year that unless you win all three Triple Crown races, the Derby is really the only one that matters.

"Nobody ever asks you," he said. "if you won the Preakness."

With America's best young racehorses on the shelf the most important and impressive potential sires showcased in the World Thoroughbred Championships were those airmailed from Sheikh Mohammed's oasis in Dubai and the emerald paddocks of John Magnier's homeland, further proof of the success of their continuing assault on the Kentucky bastion of thoroughbred breeding in America.

Of the eight "world championship" races on Breeders' Cup Day, the Europeans won five, including both male and female two-year-old championships. American pride was barely saved when the 2000 Horse of the Year, Tiznow, a four-year-old who never ran in the Kentucky Derby, became the first in history to win two Classics in a row. Like Monarchos, Tiznow is a blue-collar horse and because of an even more modest heritage has perhaps even less attraction as a commercial sire.

The most significant stallion prospect with a Kentucky connection to win on Breeders' Cup Day was the two-year-old champion, a horse named Johannesburg that had been bred in Kentucky. But when he returned to the winner's circle it was the Irish flags that were unfurled: Johannesburg (who had already wrapped up the European two-year-old crown), his sire Hennessey and his dam Myth all were owned by John Magnier's Coolmore.

With so much stallion power already in his stable, Magnier did not find Point Given compelling enough to add to Coolmore's roster of "traveling stallions," where he would have stood alongside his sire Thunder Gulch.

Prince Salman did shop his horse to Coolmore, however, at a $50 million asking price, and with a debilitating caveat that he not be shuttled to Southern Hemisphere service in the off-season. Without year-round cash flow, sharp-penciled Coolmore could not make the deal work on paper—even if Point Given's stud fee was set at $150,000, twice that of his Derby-winning sire. So Prince Salman retained a substantial interest in Point Given and sent him to stud at Three Chimneys in Woodford County, a lovely stallion boutique where he was syndicated in the traditional Kentucky manner and will stand in 2002 for an introductory fee of $125,000.

Stallion boutiques such as Three Chimneys have long been an important option for owners who want to sell shares in their horse to other breeders, in fact their only alternative to selling America's best racehorses to global breeding empires like Darley and Coolmore.

Just as Monarchos's victory increased the potential of the humbly bred Maria's Mon to become a successful sire, it also enhanced the viability of Josephine Abercrombie's Pin Oak Stud as a breeding farm. Monarchos elevated Maria's Mon on the leading sire lists and tripled his stud fee to $35,000. Many of the major breeding farms in Kentucky owe their existence to a single stallion capable of producing a Derby winner. This phenomenon is what has preserved the Kentucky thoroughbred industry's path to survival in a global economy dominated by the advantages of size, scale and international marketing. And it remains the only hope of preserving one of America's great traditions—a thoroughbred horse industry centered in Kentucky.

As nature dictates, the stallions stay where the mares are. But as the Irish and Arabs have recently demonstrated, where the most profitable, desirable and elite stallions travel, the most profitable, desirable and elite mares often follow. It is a trend of "traveling mares" that Kentucky's breeding industry likely could not survive.

Sudden and painful returns to reality are emblematic of the horse business. The day after the Derby, Two Bucks was snapped out of its stupor of incoherent elation by the same jolt that shook the rest of the industry. Veterinarians discovered that a mysterious uterine epidemic—believed to be cyanide poisoning—was killing late-term foals and early-term fetuses in Kentucky mares.

Eventually designated as Mare Reproductive Loss Syndrome and still unexplained to this day, it killed 20 percent of the 2001–2002 foal crop, through early abortions or stillbirths, and cost the industry an estimated $336 million. Possible causes ranged from a prolific crop of tent caterpillars spreading cyanide from the leaves of wild cherry trees prevalent in Kentucky pastures to mycotoxins formed on the famous grass by unusual weather patterns. Few farms were spared and cherry-tree laden Two Bucks was not among them. A combination of early-term abortions in the fall of 2000 and stillbirths in the spring of 2001 reduced Two Bucks' 2001 foal crop from eleven to three.

In the subsequent public clamor, the newly prominent proprietor of Two Bucks found himself on a two-member television panel with industry titan John R. Gaines, truly a Renaissance man of vast wealth and knowledge, whose genius in the thoroughbred business had been certified by years of success. Heir to a dog-food and real-estate fortune, Gaines had pioneered development of the stallion syndication system, built a magnificent stud farm and bred the great stallion Halo, sire of Kentucky Derby winner Sunday Silence. The Breeders' Cup had been his idea, too, and he had been the impetus behind the new NTRA marketing thrust.

And now here was the industry's leading visionary in the forefront again, trying to mobilize public response to help the horse-breeding industry deal with this new epidemic. What he wanted was what Kentucky horse breeders had sought unsuccessfully since the days when

Daniel Boone was a state legislator—simple recognition by the Kentucky state government of horse breeding as an industry important to the state's economy. And on the panel with him was this industry pygmy, someone Gaines himself had once characterized accurately as "insignificant in the business."

But in the minds of the audience at least, the playing field leveled substantially when the television host asked the two panelists to recount their most thrilling, proudest and most rewarding moment in the horse business. With all he had done, the eminently accomplished Gaines instantly pointed to a day twenty years earlier when he saw his homebred Bold Bidder win something called the Strub Stakes, a Grade 2 race held at Santa Anita. And naturally for the industry pygmy there was no choice at all. As thrills go, watching an animal that you raised win the greatest race in the world has few equals. No matter what else he had or would accomplish, his answer to such a question would most likely never change.

It was at this point that the gentle fog into which he had slipped when Monarchos made his "Derby move" finally lifted. He thought of the message on the front of a card he had received congratulating him on his "great triomphe": "One fine morning I'm gonna reach up and grab a handfulla stars and look over at God and say, 'How 'bout that!'" Surprisingly, the card had come from Gaines.

The realization was electrifying. Not only was he out of the coma, he was out of the fog. Monarchos had done for his life exactly what Invisible Ink had done for John Fort's. The same validation of life's work that had brought light and vision to the dark and blind had also brought direction to a man who'd lost all sense of it. No longer would he be forced to wander painfully lost in yesterday's dreams.

For him another "one fine morning" had dawned—as was his luck. He had made a place for himself in the exciting "business" of breeding racehorses where, while overseen by the dominant female and Al the Jack Russell, he could happily ascend one beanstalk after another in hopes that the two inevitables in his future—death and bankruptcy—might somehow miraculously coincide.

ACKNOWLEDGMENTS

I owe a debt of gratitude to many who helped make this book possible, none of whom bear any responsibility for its shortcomings. Chief among them are the owners of Monarchos—Debby and Jack Oxley—his trainers Donna and Johnny Ward, and jockey Jorge Chavez, for their cooperation and support; and to John Kotas for his research, publisher Peter Osnos for his encouragement, editor Paul Golob for excellent guidance, and my friends Jane Smiley and Dan Thomasson for advice and inspiration.

Many others contributed time, patience, information, and expertise, including: Tom Amoss, Yvonne Azeff, Clifford Barry, James E. (Ted) Bassett, Bryan Beccia, Dr. Michael J. Beyer, Edward Bowen, Dr. Doug Byars, Michael Cartee, Richard DePass, Suzanne C. Depp, Michael Dickinson, Dr. Daryl G. Easley, John Fort, Richard Galpin, Arthur B. Hancock III, Bernard Hettel, C. Bruce Hundley, Brereton C. Jones, John T. L. Jones, Jr., Arnold Kirkpatrick, Wayne G. Lyster III, Cheryl Manista,

William Mauk, Terry Meyocks, Bobby Miller, Frank Mitchell, Nick Nicholson, Frank Penn, John W. Phillips, Susie Picou-Oldham, Mitchell C. Preger, Jr., Sam Ramer, Walt Robertson, David Santen, Tim Smith, Christopher Speckert, T. Wayne Sweezey, Dr. Paul Thorpe, and Hash Weinstein. Thanks also to several authors whose books or articles were a rich source of lore and background information, principally Andy Beyer, Carole Case, Steven Crist, Joe Drape, Steve Haskin, David L. Heckerman, Laura Hillenbrand, Frank Jennings, Andy Plattner, William L. Quirin, Nick Robinson, Patrick Robinson, and Mary Jean Wall.

Thanks, too, to my friends Stone Roberts, Judy and Smoot Fahlgren, Jane Ann and Frank Woods and Susan and John McMeel, without whom this adventure would have been less fun; and deepest gratitude to my wife Mary Anne, without whom it would have been likely impossible and definitely less exciting.

ABOUT THE AUTHOR

Jim Squires began his writing career in newspapers as a reporter for the Nashville *Tennessean* in 1962. He later served as Washington bureau chief for the *Chicago Tribune*, covering Watergate and the resignation of President Richard Nixon. From 1977 until 1981, he served as editor of the *Orlando Sentinel*, and from 1981 until 1990 as editor of the *Chicago Tribune*, which won seven Pulitzer Prizes during his tenure. A Nieman Fellow at Harvard University in 1970–1971, he lectured at Harvard on democracy and the press in 1991 and served as media adviser to Ross Perot when he ran for president in 1992. His previous books include a press critique, *Read All About It! The Corporate Takeover of America's Newspapers*, and a tale of Southern politics, *The Secrets of the Hopewell Box*. Since 1992, he has been raising horses in Versailles, Kentucky, where he lives with his wife, Mary Anne.

PublicAffairs is a publishing house founded in 1997. It is a tribute to the standards, values, and flair of three persons who have served as mentors to countless reporters, writers, editors, and book people of all kinds, including me.

I. F. STONE, proprietor of *I. F. Stone's Weekly,* combined a commitment to the First Amendment with entrepreneurial zeal and reporting skill and became one of the great independent journalists in American history. At the age of eighty, Izzy published *The Trial of Socrates,* which was a national bestseller. He wrote the book after he taught himself ancient Greek.

BENJAMIN C. BRADLEE was for nearly thirty years the charismatic editorial leader of *The Washington Post.* It was Ben who gave the *Post* the range and courage to pursue such historic issues as Watergate. He supported his reporters with a tenacity that made them fearless and it is no accident that so many became authors of influential, best-selling books.

ROBERT L. BERNSTEIN, the chief executive of Random House for more than a quarter century, guided one of the nation's premier publishing houses. Bob was personally responsible for many books of political dissent and argument that challenged tyranny around the globe. He is also the founder and longtime chair of Human Rights Watch, one of the most respected human rights organizations in the world.

For fifty years, the banner of Public Affairs Press was carried by its owner, Morris B. Schnapper, who published Gandhi, Nasser, Toynbee, Truman, and about 1,500 other authors. In 1983, Schnapper was described by *The Washington Post* as "a redoubtable gadfly." His legacy will endure in the books to come.

Peter Osnos, *Publisher*